Morning Everyone

Morning Everyone

A Sportswriter's Life

Simon Hughes

ORION

First published in hardback in Great Britain in 2005 by
Orion Books
an imprint of the Orion Publishing Group Ltd
Orion House, 5 Upper St Martin's Lane,
London WC2H 9EA

1 2 3 4 5 6 7 8 9 10

A CIP catalogue record for this book is available
from the British Library.

ISBN: 0 75286 931 0

Printed in Great Britain by Mackays of Chatham plc

Every effort has been made to fulfil requirements with regard
to reproducing copyright material. The author and publisher
will be glad to rectify any omissions at the earliest opportunity.

The Orion publishing group's policy is to use papers that
are natural, renewable and recyclable products and made
from wood grown in sustainable forests. The logging and
manufacturing processes are expected to conform to the
environmental regulations of the country of origin.

www.orionbooks.co.uk

To Tanya
with massive love

Thanks to:

Gwen for the direction
Damian for the dedication
Tony for the wit
Gary for the opportunity
Keith for the encouragement
Athers for the lifts
Richie for the inspiration

Contents

PART I – Careering About: 1987–99

PART II – Mission Control: 2000–05

PART I

CAREERING ABOUT
1987–99

CHAPTER 1 – Life of Riley

My name has never sold newspapers, but I've rubbed shoulders with the sportsmen who have. This book gives you the inside track on those people, as I loiter among them gauging what makes them tick.

There are the colossi – Botham, Warne, Woods and Jordan – men whose exploits have redefined their sports. There are the great duos – Redgrave and Pinsent, Johnson and Wilkinson, Flintoff and Pietersen – whose ability and willpower have piloted their attempts at global domination. There are the England cricket captains – from Gower and Gooch to Atherton and Hussain – whose teams stumbled from one débâcle to the next (with the odd triumph) until the national team eventually flowered under Michael Vaughan. There are the nearly men of English sport – Gough, Henman and Coulthard – who almost scaled the heights but tended to fall at the final hurdle. And there are the footballers. Well, they rarely give me the time of day, so we'll forget about them.

As a former professional cricketer, I shared the field with some illustrious names. I found it revealed their true nature, unearthing what lay beneath. I discovered a hint of insecurity behind Botham's fearlessness, a waspish humour behind Atherton's straight bat. As a sportswriter, I've maintained this interaction with the modern stars. I've watched them and listened to them. Quite apart from that, I've bowled at them, batted against them, trained with them, played golf (badly) with them, travelled with them, worked with them, relaxed with them, cooked for them and poked fun at them.

Their focus and fragility – their soul – are laid bare. Warne, for all his evil cunning, just wants to be loved. Flintoff, a rampaging bull on the field, is one big softie off it.

And as English cricket has grappled for a toehold in the world these past eighteen years, one person has surveyed the scene with a scrupulous eye and a studious mind: Richie Benaud, the cream-jacketed master of understatement. He has dispensed observation and magnanimity here for forty-two years. We know the face and we know the voice. Now, after fourteen years sharing commentary boxes, production offices and dinner tables with Benaud, I can show you the man.

As England finally exorcise their Ashes demons in 2005, Benaud's work is done. How did they do that, having been the worst team in the world six years before? Having watched virtually every ball, often in slow motion several times over from Channel 4's videotape truck – alternately referred to as the caravan or the dungeon – I'm in an ideal position to judge.

Sports journalism is at the heart of this journey. Sportswriting is up there with restaurant reviewing and film censorship as the best excuse for a job on earth. You're waited on hand and foot, you get the best seat in the house for free, you're indulging your hobby and you get paid to do it. It shouldn't be called work at all. It should be called professional loafing. And when you get a grandstand view of the epic 2005 Ashes series, you really have had your loaf and eaten it.

OK, sportswriters don't get into their privileged positions by chance. They're usually sports enthusiasts who've worked their way up from being a gofer on the Kent *Messenger* or the press officer for Stenhousemuir. They've laboured long and hard at the sporting coalface, chipping away at the sports editor's indifference until they finally got noticed. They've had to conjure back-page leads out of mere rumours and large features out of five minutes of platitudes from Alan Shearer.

My story's no different. From the age of ten, when I constructed a home-made snooker table out of a Subbuteo pitch bordered by volumes of *Encyclopaedia Britannica*, I was destined for a life of sport and words. Fifteen years playing county cricket gave me a slight head start in sports journalism, but I still had to knock, knock, knock at doors before finally being let in (and conjure a large feature out of thirty seconds with Robbie Fowler). Once I was through I was certain it was the place I wanted to be. Having inveigled myself into television commentary – requiring a unique mix of journalism and bravado – I found my *métier*.

The incredible Ashes series of 2005 was manna from heaven for all those who wrote or talked about it. The drama, the intrigue, the intensity, the duels, the sheer physical effort of one hero, Flintoff, against the sleight of hand of the other, Warne, made it irresistible viewing from start to finish. That compelling struggle and the scenes of national euphoria when England finally regained the little urn are what, as sportswriters, you live for.

CHAPTER 2

PRE-SEASON TRAINING

'... And Lillee comes in again, shirt tails flapping, he's past Umpire Spencer and he bowls to Boycott, a delivery on the leg stump, and with a little flourish Boycott whips it away off his hip, up and over square leg and one bounce into the fence. Quite a stroke for a quarter to twelve on the first morning of the Test! It takes England along to 36 for no wicket in the seventh over ...'

You won't remember that little incident from the Ashes Test at Old Trafford in 1972, because it didn't happen. (If you didn't get the hint from the first sentence you obviously never saw Geoff Boycott bat.) The batsman (and bowler) was twelve-year-old me in ripped jeans and a check Ben Sherman, throwing a tennis ball against the garden wall and hitting the rebound into a flower bed. The commentator was me as well, of course, followed rapidly by my father's voice from the back door:

'Simon! How many times have I told you to *mind the nasturtiums*!?'

'I *am* minding the nasturtiums!'

'You're not, I saw that last shot go straight into them.'

'I couldn't help ih. Lillee goh thah one to bounce up a bih.'

'Lillee? ... Well just *be more careful*! And it's got, and that and bit.'

I did this for several hours a day, throwing at different speeds and trajectories using a variety of different tennis balls – soft and hairy to replicate a slow pitch at Nottingham, hard

6

and bald to replicate a fast one at Perth. In my games, England always won the Ashes, of course. As for me, I was rarely bowled and *never* LBW, and I soon believed I'd be the next Graham Gooch. But, restricted by the sitting-room windows on one side and the bloody nasturtiums on the other, my batting remained retarded. In my first season in county cricket – as a fast bowler with Middlesex – my batting average was 0.00. More Graham Norton than Graham Gooch. Well, if in doubt, blame the parents.

At twenty-one, my dream – to score the winning runs for England in an Ashes series – was already fading. An alternative – to take the winning wicket for England in an Ashes series – was scuppered by my regular habit of bowling rubbish to moderate county batsmen. The England selectors decided to ignore my claims of 3 for 6 in fourteen balls against Northants. I was picked in the 1986–87 England tour party to Australia, but only by a *Times* journalist whom I'd plied with lager two nights earlier. So I converted my sole ambition into one day being there *reporting* the day England won the Ashes. Even if it meant keeping my life-support machine on to do so.

I'd been grooming my writing skills for years. Once I'd gleaned as much as I could about syntax from the *Beano* and *Dandy* annuals, I studied the cricket reports of E. W. Swanton in the *Daily Telegraph*: 'Thereupon, Cowdrey pushed and persuaded the ball about with the air of a jovial uncle enjoying himself with the youngsters …' For balance and enjoyment I read the columns of Arthur Marshall. 'I would have thought that the knowledge that you are going to be leapt upon by half a dozen congratulatory but sweaty team-mates would be inducement not to score a goal,' he wrote one winter Sunday.

At thirteen, I burst into print, writing a report of the first school Under 14 football match of the season, in a red cashier's book normally used when my sister and I played post offices.

16/1/73 (away)   Latymer U/14s 2 Slough GS 4
                      Hughes
                      Corry

A very scrappy match, Latymer's tackling wasn't hard
enough, especially after Fowler had lost his boot over the
fence, and Bensley, the centre-back, kept wandering onto the
touchline to whisper stuff to his girlfriend. Hughes was
the exception, providing many clever through passes which
the forwards couldn't quite latch on to. After one of several
strange decisions by the referee (theirs), Hunt shouted at
him and his father came on the pitch swearing that he was a
cross-eyed poof but he took no notice. Hughes's goal, a deft
left-foot curler, was disallowed because there were no nets
and the goalkeeper said it missed.

Saturday reporting became a tradition in my house after that.
I'd wait until the evening when the events of that morning
had fully formed in my mind. Then at a time when most
fourteen-year-old boys were at youth clubs playing mixed
table tennis – a euphemism for snogging – I'd be in my
father's study, assembling my prose: 'Bensley, put off by the
distraction of Hunt's big-chested mother leaning forwards to
pick up her cigarette lighter, missed his tackle and Quinton
scored.'

This went on for several years (until Hunt was dropped
and his mother stopped coming), culminating in the occasional entry in the school magazine. I did the same for school
cricket, and practised at home in the holidays. Instead of
experimenting with cigarette lighters, I was trying out my
father's war-issue typewriter. I'd be watching the Test match
on the BBC assiduously, monitoring Richie Benaud's efficient
use of words – 'super shot!', 'marvellus deliveree' – or switching to the radio commentary to sample John Arlott's irreverent observations: 'Ah, there's the New Zealand coach Bob
Cunis on the balcony ... Interesting name Cunis, neither one
thing nor the other ...'

I made notes and typed in the details when a wicket fell on a home-made scorecard. During the lunch interval I'd tap out a quick résumé of the morning's play.

After winning the toss, Ian Chappell asked England to bat first. A frightening-looking Dennis Lillee found early movement and soon darted one back into Boycott's pads. He survived that and nudged his way into double figures, often stealing the strike from his partner John Edrich with a single off the last ball of the over. England reached 42 for 0 by lunch. I turned to ask my dad what he thought of the morning's play, but he was asleep.

MOONLIGHTING

I got my first media job the summer I left school. Admittedly it mainly involved cleaning out the chip fryer at the *Radio Times* print works (occasionally being let loose at the stove to reheat the employees' beans on toast) but at employment bureaux they always recommend infiltrating the corridors of power in any way you can. I didn't further my media career, but at least I got a free copy of the magazine to take home whenever I wanted.

Within a year of becoming a professional cricketer, my unique journalistic gifts had been recognised. A man from the press approached me at a club dinner. I could tell he was from the press as his tie was at half mast and he had a slightly false smile. Oh, and it said 'Press' on his lapel. He persuaded me to write a weekly column for the *Ealing Gazette*, cheesily called 'Simon Says'. I scribbled down pieces mainly about Mike Gatting's calorific intake into a foolscap book and dictated them over the phone. The copytakers were abysmal and it was a painful business.

'Gatting devoured ...'
'De vowed?'

'Devour ... ed.'

'De ... vow ... head? Is that a cricket term, luv?'

'Devoured ... D.E.V.O.U.R.E.D. ... the boeuf bourguignon
... er ... the beef stew at lunch.'

I was paid five pounds a column but by the time the faulty
Lord's dressing-room payphone had gobbled my money and
I'd bought Gatting a placatory drink, I wasn't left with much.
After two years, the pay did rise to ten pounds, but my offer
to cover England's 1982–83 tour to Australia for them was
rejected out of hand. England were comprehensively beaten
anyway.

The *Ealing Gazette* had a circulation of about thirty-two,
but already I was treated with slight suspicion by some players, aware that I was divulging the innermost secrets of their
cricket cases (jars of pickle, athlete's foot powder, *Penthouse*,
maps showing the whereabouts of every Little Chef in
Britain). The county's administrative staff, concerned that I
might betray the reality of their working day, which included halting everything – meetings, stock-taking, disciplinary
hearings – for tea and scones at 4 p.m., attempted to pull me
into line, insisting I had everything vetted.

Although this proved harder than initially imagined
because they couldn't read my writing, there was no alternative: I had to go undercover. I contributed a monthly column
to the *Cricketer* magazine (circulation about forty-seven)
entitled 'From the Inside' with the cryptic byline 'A County
Cricketer'. I thought it was perfect camouflage, although
Gatting did once say, 'Can't you find something better to
write about than my diet?'

This was in the midst of the Thatcher years of work, work,
work and spend, spend, spend, and my output was a prolific
five columns a month, revealing vital details like Ian Botham's
pre-match routine (10.15 a.m.: arrive at ground; 10.20: get in
hot bath; 10.40: fill water pistol; 10.50: fill not out batsmen's
gloves with shaving foam). I was earning a reputation and
enough money through writing to buy myself a Papermate

with refills. It was time for some proper journalism.

Initially this manifested itself in a 'job' at the *West Australian* in Perth. I'd spent the winter there playing unpaid club cricket, and, low on funds, befriended the paper's main sports reporter. When the managing director was on holiday, I was installed as their first 'world news editor'. As Perth was a highly parochial town, this position was only redeemable if there was a devastating earthquake or the outbreak of World War Three. When the managing director came back from holiday I was relieved of the post.

Remaining in England for the autumn of 1986, I ventured into EC4 armed with a newly purchased A4 notebook and Michael Frayn's *Towards the End of the Morning*, the definitive novel about Fleet Street. I emerged onto the distinguished pavement trod by Dr Samuel Johnson (who famously wrote for the *Gentleman's Magazine*) and later a young Boris Johnson (unaware that the *Spectator* had been relocated). I sniffed the air for the combined essence of inky metal, carbon paper and journalistic skulduggery which Frayn had evoked so well. Alas, I could smell only petrol fumes.

I had come for an interview with Reg Hayter, the corpulent proprietor of Hayter's Sports Agency, an assemblage of fledgling sports reporters who supplied copy to news agencies and various regional, national and overseas newspapers that couldn't afford – or were too tight to pay for – sports correspondents of their own.

I started with an advantage. Reg, a sort of sportswriters' godfather, was also a cricketers' agent who was regularly encountered at Lord's and favourably inclined towards Middlesex players. I had just won Middlesex's player of the year award (a pair of cufflinks from Austin Reed). He had read a few of my columns. I fully expected him to rave about my exceptional sporting insights and elegant prose and dispatch me forthwith to Liverpool v. Arsenal for Reuters news agency. My report would be read all over Europe, America and the Far East. He proceeded to send me to London Transport Tube Drivers v. Bus Conductors at the Acton works ground. I was to type up my report and hand it in to him for assessment. If it was any good, an abbreviated version might make it into *LT Weekly*, their in-house newsletter.

I laboured all weekend over my write-up of a skill-less 3–3 draw, sent it in and received it back two days later covered in red marker pen. 'Not a bad effort!' he'd scrawled at the bottom. 'Are you OK for Guinness v. Allied Domecq on Saturday for the Licensed Victuallers' newsletter?' I phoned him to say I was.

'Ah, young Hughes, there's been a change of plan,' Reg replied. 'We're rather understaffed this weekend. I'd like you to do Spurs v. Everton for the Belfast *Sunday Telegraph*.'

This was a huge moment. It was a clash of heavyweights – Hoddle and Waddle against Trevor Steven and Peter Reid – over which I was assigned to cast my shrewd journalistic eye. More importantly, it would be the first time I could get in to watch my own team at White Hart Lane with a proper ticket rather than a box of cauliflowers and a fake caterer's pass (a foolproof method also useful for rugby internationals at Twickenham).

In fact, when the time came I didn't get a seat, and was obliged to perch on the end of the press bench next to a man wearing prehistoric headphones shouting into a battered radio microphone. But I did get an unimpeded view of the match and complimentary tea in a polystyrene cup at half time. There was a catch, though. The match was scheduled to finish at 4.45. The Belfast *Sunday Telegraph* deadline was 4.30. Everton had obviously come seeking a draw and cramped Spurs' style. Shortly after half time the score was 0–0 and I structured my 250 words around the Merseysiders' resolute defence. I also criticised Spurs' lack of invention in attack.

I borrowed the radio man's phone and rang my copy through on time. There were ten minutes to go but it was obviously going to be a goalless draw and I'd seen enough. I made a beeline for the exit to beat the crush and was just boarding a number 259 bus when the roar went up for Clive

Allen's and Spurs' second in injury time. I could use the excuse that I was prevented from alerting the desk because there was a lengthy queue outside the one nearby phone box (which probably didn't work anyway). The truth is it didn't occur to me.

Most sports journalists have a similar tale of embarrassment due to an early getaway. None is better than the experience of a man we all know and love, Henry Blofeld. In May 1983 Bloers was covering a county match at Chelmsford for the *Guardian*. The first day had been washed out. On the second, a Monday, Essex managed 280 thanks to a typically ebullient hundred from Keith Fletcher. Bloers's 280 words were constructed round this innings. As soon as the Essex innings ended around 5.15, he phoned in his report, finishing it by saying '... and in reply, Surrey were blank for blank'. He left a message asking the subs to fill in the appropriate numbers.

With a pressing social engagement in London, he made for his car and headed off onto the A12. Two hours later he phoned the *Guardian* sports desk from a restaurant pay-phone to check if everything was OK, as all responsible sports journalists should.

'Well, er, yes, everything's fine,' was the sub's slightly hesitant reply, 'but you know where you put "and in reply Surrey were blank for blank"?'

'Yes?' said Bloers.

'Well ... the missing figures were fourteen and ten.'

'Fourteen and ten? ... *Well, my dear old thing!*'

He had missed Surrey being bowled out in under an hour for 14, exceeding by only 2 the lowest first-class score in cricket history. There but for the grace of God ...

INDEPENDENTLY MINDED

After my 'Turgid Spurs Held at Bay' story, I wasn't expecting to hear much from Hayter's Sports Agency for a while. Fortunately, a new newspaper came along to fill the void. In

October 1986 the *Independent* was launched with a fanfare of stylish publicity and an intensive 'It is, are you?' campaign. With no winter job, but no bills and no dependants, I certainly was.

Having heard of its creation through the cricket press grapevine, I'd been to see the editorial team in the summer to sound them out. The new paper was located in an unprepossessing office block on City Road. The sports editor, Charlie Burgess, sat in a small glass cubicle within a large open-plan room full of blinking VDUs. It all looked very smart and professional, and nothing like the *West Australian*'s chaotic offices I'd sampled the previous winter, full of spewing telex machines and reeking of BO. Formerly at the *Guardian*, as many of the first batch of *Independent* journalists were, Burgess was a large man with a thick mop of hair and a soothing voice who kindly commissioned virtually any idea that was proposed to him. If you had come in and said there was a great story to be done about naked volleyball on Copacabana Beach, he would have considered sending you. His rather gruff Mancunian deputy, Simon Kelner, then went about separating the wheat from the chaff.

After that first mid-summer introduction, I'd written a couple of cricket columns for their dummy editions, which they seemed pleased with, and as the official launch of the newspaper drew near, I was called in for another meeting.

'We like your stuff on cricket, dear,' Burgess said. 'Can you write on anything else … rugby, for instance?'

'Yes, no problem,' I lied.

I was sent off to cover Harlequins v. Rosslyn Park for the paper proper in its first week of circulation. The *Independent* was selling itself as a fresh, new, impartial eye on the world, and in this case the marriage between me and it was perfect. I had never been to a first-class rugby match in my life. The task was further complicated by an unexpected call from Hayter's booking me to cover the semi-final of the Hockey World Cup between England and West Germany. The hockey was at midday in Willesden; the rugby at 3 p.m.

at Twickenham. I thought I'd be able to do both. I sat in the press area at Willesden congratulating myself on having lined up two separate sporting assignments on the same day, and enthusiastically jotted observations in my new notebook, while noticing the long-haired correspondent to my right, Simon Barnes, noting down nothing at all. Perhaps Barnes visualised the match going into extra time and didn't want to end up with reams of superfluous notes. In the event it did, and I was obliged to stay to the bitter end (and a stunning England victory) which then gave me only twenty minutes for the dash across west London. The traffic was terrible and it took forty-five. I missed most of the first half of the rugby. I had at least made contingency plans. My uncle Tony, a rugby aficionado, was going to the game anyway, and kept a note of the main incidents on the back of a couple of bank giros he had in his wallet. 'That's what you call chequebook journalism,' he said, handing them to me when I arrived. His observations formed the bulk of my report, which my mother later helped polish.

The piece sat proudly in the middle of page 31 of the first Monday edition of the *Independent* (it had been launched the previous Tuesday). Charlie Burgess rang me mid-morning.

'Lovely piece, dear,' he said, 'such a mature tone. It reads almost as if it's been written by someone else.'

'Thanks,' I said, expecting immediate upgrading to a prime First Division football match the following Saturday.

'Hope you can do Maidstone against Blackheath for us next weekend,' he went on.

I said I could.

Sport had nothing like the same prominence in the papers then as it does now. The *Daily Telegraph*, for instance, had five pages of sport sandwiched between the business section and the TV guide. The back page was given over to general news, the weather and the crossword. On winter Saturdays rugby and overseas tennis commanded at least equal space with football – a quarter of a page. The swathes of profiles, gossip, ghosted columns and rehashed press releases, which we now take for granted, hadn't yet been conceived.

The *Independent* was creating quite a stir with its sports coverage, and not only through stylish reports and arresting black-and-white images on the back page. There was also the advent of Martin Johnson (the scribe, not the England second row). Christened 'Scoop' like just about everyone else who'd come through the ranks of local papers, he had originally been hired as the paper's rugby correspondent, but was currently covering England's cricket tour of Australia. An irreverent writer and compulsive mickey-taker, as it seems are most Johnsons (q.v. Samuel and Boris), he had quickly bucked the traditions of stiff, colourless cricket reporting. On 10 November he filed from Perth his immortal commentary on England's prospects of retaining the Ashes. Mike Gatting's team were struggling in the match against Western Australia, having already lost to Queensland, and Johnson wrote: 'Don't despair is the message from this observer. It seems to me England have only three major problems – they can't bat, they can't bowl and they can't field.'

To go with his idiosyncratic humour and wry observation, Johnson has never allied much accurate prediction, however. Eight days later England hammered Australia by seven wickets in the first Test. To be fair, it was a development not many had expected, least of all the England team themselves, and it was Gatting's first win in six Tests as captain.

What nobody realised at the time was that the 1986–87 Australian side was a rabble. Poorly selected and tamely captained, it featured too many moderate players. A number of these were allegedly inducted into the team in a secret dressing-room ceremony performed by a Sydney woman known immodestly as the Town Chewer.

I occasionally received one of Johnson's reports on my computer screen in the *Independent* offices, where I was training to be a sub-editor. I found the work fascinating at first – particularly when Johnson's entertaining stuff landed. I relished sampling different writers' language (if the sub-primary-school stuff from news agencies could be classed as language), rejigging paragraphs here and there, cutting the story to fit the desired space – known in the trade as Hyphenate and Justifying (H & J for short) – and thinking up a catchy headline. One was 'Shepton Mallet hammers Richards and Garner'.

Around that time, Somerset County Cricket Club were in turmoil. The committee's decision to sack the great West Indians Viv Richards and Joel Garner and replace them with the New Zealander Martin Crowe had aroused a public outcry. Ian Botham was at the centre of it, having declared he would storm off in protest. But, in an impressive display of solidarity at the Shepton Mallet farmers' hall, the members heavily outvoted the dissenters, and Richards, Garner and Botham were gone.

I filed a story for the *Indy* from the meeting, trying to capture the emotive atmosphere in a place that normally staged cattle auctions. Back in the newspaper's offices the following day for a late subbing shift, I was told the paper's editor and founder, Andreas Whittam Smith, had been impressed by the piece. I was glowing with pride. He nodded in my direction late that afternoon as he went into his office. I saw him sit down and pick up the phone. One immediately rang on my desk and I was fully imagining it would be Andreas complimenting my work and perhaps suggesting a regular Saturday column.

'Hello?' I said expectantly.

'Two chicken tikka masalas, one pilau rice, some Bombay aloo and two peshwari nan,' said a voice.

'Sorry?'

'Hello … is this the Taj Tandoori?'

'No it's not the Taj Tandoori,' I said indignantly, and slammed down the phone. It turned out that my number was only one digit different from a local curry house.

SUB-PLOTS

It was a slightly tricky transition going from cricketer in summer to sub-editor in winter. The great thing about cricket is
you're one individual within a team of eleven, so there's plenty of scope for stardom. Working on a newspaper, you're one
in several thousand. Sifting through stories, you're more like
human termites, picking up morsels, tasting them, rejecting
or accepting them, transporting them into the mound, for the
chief ant's approval. I was conscious of my lack of experience
in this field, and rather aware that I had wheedled my way in
while others had spent twelve years doing local weddings or
death knocks on the Workington *Advertiser*. There was certainly an array of backgrounds. One sub had previously been
a photographer's assistant for *Knave*, which mainly involved
dribbling ice on models' breasts. He was always the one trying to get pictures of a bikini-clad Cindy Crawford or Sam
Fox to go with a sports story, no matter how spurious the
link.

The subbing of the sports pages was broken up into shifts,
each with its pros and cons. The morning subs had the light-
est workload, and the agenda setting was interesting, but you
often had to field calls from disgruntled reporters who
phoned up to complain about their precious pieces being cut,
abandoned or altered. I told the hacks they were lucky. I had
recently been sent to cover a football match at Tranmere and
my patiently compiled 250 words had been cut to just two:
'Attendance 8750.' It didn't wash, and I quickly learned that
relations between reporters and subs were often strained.
The sports reporters, who liked being referred to as writers,
thought the sub-editors were imbeciles. Subs thought
reporters had egos the size of the Albert Hall. Writers rarely
deigned to cross the threshold of the office. The explanation
from within the office was that this was because they couldn't
squeeze their heads through the office door.

The afternoon work was better, as stories began emerging.

There was a buzz in the department as each was evaluated and dealt out among the subs. By evening, things had really hotted up and scandals were flying in. Ron Atkinson was sacked by Manchester United one night, and someone called Alex Ferguson was appointed in his place. 'He won't last long,' I said. 'What would he know, coming from Aberdeen?'

A succession of late shifts did for me. I simply didn't have the requisite encyclopedic knowledge of sport or quick-cutting mind or love of arriving back home at one in the morning, pissed yet able to recite all the previous night's speedway results.

Actually, I'm bending the truth. What really did for me was this news item which I pulled off the wires and rewrote:

Bob Johnston, the 28-year-old centre-forward of West Bromwich Albion's blind football team, controversially defeated in the semi-finals of the Paralympics B1 (totally blind) Cup four years ago, says the team have set their sights on winning the title this time.

Set their sights! I didn't spot it at the time, of course. I only realised the next day when I came into the office. Everyone I encountered lurched about with imaginary white sticks and kept bumping into desks. I volunteered for hardly any sub-bing shifts after that.

LATE ARRIVAL

It was a blessing in disguise, as I became aware of what I really wanted to do: write (or talk) about cricket. However, the *Independent* obviously wasn't going to send me to cover the end of the 1986/7 Ashes series in Australia. So I sent myself. It was December and England were one up after three Tests. I booked myself a flight to Sydney on New Year's Eve 1986 to see the climax.

There was one snag. The climax occurred on 29 December,

thirty-six hours before I left. The Australians had capitulated in less than three days in the fourth Test, routed by the neckless wonder Gladstone Small. Chris Broad had set up victory with his third century of the series, and England had retained the Ashes with one Test remaining. At home the papers led with pictures of Mike Gatting being drenched in champagne and wondered what had happened to Australia's renowned will to win. Gobbled up by the Town Chewer, perhaps?

So England had won the Ashes, beer was 78p a pint, Jackie Wilson's 1957 hit 'Reet Petite' was no.1 in the charts, and US President Ronald Reagan was apologising for the Iran arms deal. Just to give a bit of perspective to the BW (Before Warne).

Down Under, the recriminations had already begun by the time I arrived. One headline was 'Can Pat Cash Bat or Bowl?' A group of traditionalists launched a campaign called SONG (Save Our National Game). In his column, the legendary Australian leg-spinner Bill O'Reilly thundered, 'No one threatens our position in the mullock heap: we flounder supreme.' He called for the resignation of the selectors, but far from resigning they produced another wild card. They selected a completely unknown spinner for the final Test, Peter Taylor, who was so surprised he thought they had meant to contact his namesake Mark. The local headline 'Peter Who?' said it all.

The England players were experiencing waves of euphoria when I landed in Sydney on New Year's Day 1987. They'd binned their swish hotel – frequented by the likes of Elton John, currently on tour in Australia but with no voice after a throat operation – and reclined in an array of plush penthouses on the top floor of an apartment block in the eastern suburbs. They strode around town as if they owned it and threw extravagant parties. Their elevated status rubbed off on all of us. The words 'England cricket team' were like open sesame at the gates of the Sydney Cricket Ground for the fifth Test (I was lying, but I didn't have a ticket). They gained me automatic entry to the members' enclosure and, of course, the England dressing room, but more importantly my association with Gatting's men also immediately landed me a job with the *Australian* newspaper.

The *Australian* was something of a throwback after my recent experiences at the cool, slick *Independent*. The offices were in a dingy back street near the main rail terminal at Redfern, and leaving after dark always ran the risk of being accosted by some sad wino who was either a journalist or possibly an Australian cricketer, looking for work. Inside, the paper was still stuck in the hot-metal age. The sports department resounded to the din of typewriters, teleprinter machines spewing out copy and men shouting, 'Forty-seven goes in ten minutes!' Each article was printed out, then had to be typeset by hand into metal galleys to be loaded into the printing press downstairs. It was there that I learned about the old ways of newspapers, and that the colon (the punctuation mark, not the internal organ) was the origin of the term 'dog's bollocks'.

Amazingly, I was also allowed to do more or less what I pleased (the sports editor was English), so I worked in the office as a sub twice a week and went out and compiled features on the other days. They even let me write about Rugby League and Aussie Rules. I sat in the crowd at one such match and experienced at first hand real, dinkum Aussie humour. When a goal is scored and one of the umpires behind the posts does that funny, robotic signalling and is about to stick his hands out horizontally in front of himself, about eighteen inches apart, some wag inevitably shouts out, 'Oi, how big's yer dick?' It's funny the first time, and the second, and maybe even the third. Not the twenty-third.

England were on a roll. They went on to win the Benson and Hedges Challenge in Perth and, after the inconsequential loss of the fifth Test (due in the main to a prolonged hangover), the Benson and Hedges World Series Cup, clinched famously when Allan Lamb clattered 18 off the last over in Sydney. Loitering in the press box that evening with nothing to do, I was handed a microphone and tape-recorder by *Test*

Match Special's Peter Baxter, and sent to grab a quick radio interview. Lamb, already supping beer in the Australian dressing room – in the very place where the Town Chewer allegedly performed her rites – was more or less unintelligible, but it was a first as far as I was concerned.

Simultaneously, Dennis Conner's *Stars and Stripes* defeated Alan Bond's *Australia IV* to regain the America's Cup in Perth. The Aussies *did* give a Castlemaine XXXX about what was going on in the sporting world. They blamed everyone from Kerry Packer's Channel 9, for a damaging, one-day cricket overload, to Bob Hawke, the prime minister, for the lack of favourable wind off the coast of Western Australia.

A lot of the credit for England's success should have gone to Mickey Stewart, universally referred to as 'Manager', even by his own son, Alec. Stewart Senior brought several years of experience at Surrey to bear on England, principally discipline (he even got Botham in the nets), common sense and continuity. His employers, the Test and County Cricket Board (TCCB), in an uncharacteristic bout of rationale, immediately made him England's first full-time cricket manager. Unfortunately, though, their ambitious proactivity began and ended there. Stewart's stated intention on getting the job was 'to have in mind who our leading twenty-four players are so they could meet and practise together at the end of the season and in April'. It sowed the seed for a move to have the England players under the jurisdiction more of the Board than their counties; effectively, it was a first proposal for central contracts. That was in March 1987. The England and Wales Cricket Board (ECB), with typical alacrity, finally introduced them in April 2000.

CHAPTER 3 – 1987–89

DOUBLE TROUBLE

In May 1987 I made my debut as a national newspaper columnist with the weekly 'Cricketer's Diary' in the *Independent*. The other important event of the year, apart from the October hurricane and the Stock Exchange crash, was the first sighting of the word 'cunt' in the sports pages of a national newspaper. It was that man 'Scoop' again (Martin Johnson), this time spelling out in full the precise words uttered between Mike Gatting and the Pakistani umpire Shakoor Rana in Faisalabad. 'You fucking cheating cunt' was the extent of it – printed without asterisks in the *Independent* (and, not to be outdone on street cred, the *Guardian*). It was quite a development, and it got Mary Whitehouse, the lady who only days earlier had complained about the alarming number of blasphemies on TV (one every ninety minutes, apparently), into a right old lather. Gatting survived this cricketing taboo, but was then sacked six months later for a far more spurious, non-cricket-related incident.

Still playing for Gatting's Middlesex, I had landed myself into a bit of bother off the field too, through my *Independent* diaries. These weekly ruminations from the county circuit had a pay-off line at the bottom: 'Simon Hughes composed his column while practising horizontal ducking techniques in preparation for facing Malcolm Marshall' or some other such attempted witticism. The column's format was successful (in stark contrast to the ducking techniques, as I was out, bowled Marshall, first ball) and soon it was popular with readers. It was unpopular with some players, though, who felt I was betraying state secrets. One, Sussex's captain Ian 'Gunner' Gould, had justifiable cause for complaint. Gunner was a sociable chap who liked a pint. I featured him in an 'Endangered Species' section, revealing that his 'usual habitat' was 'the Robin Hood Arms' and his 'favourite song' was 'Andy Fairweather Low's "Wide Eyed and Legless"'. The article was published the same week that Sussex had, unbeknown to me, suspended a player, Tony Pigott, for being drunk and causing an affray. So the timing wasn't ideal.

While many of my playing colleagues stuffed *Penthouse* or Sam Fox calendars down the sides of their cricket cases for a rainy day, I had my notebook and a *Roget's Thesaurus* down the side of mine. Flicking through the fat tome earned me intrigued looks at first, as if they suspected it was an alternative *Kama Sutra* or something. When they realised it was just a list of boring old words, they lost interest. Occasionally they took to defacing it when I was batting (they had to be damn quick). Alongside the synonyms for 'Obese' was scrawled 'Gatting'; below 'Parsimony' someone had written 'Philip Tufnell'; and under 'Odour' was 'Sykes = dog breath' – a reference to Tufnell's slightly unkempt spin-twin. Next to 'Disorder' was written 'Hughes'. I suspected the hand of that premier stirrer Angus Fraser.

A sopping wet summer impeded England's progress after their Ashes heroics. There were five Tests, all against Pakistan, and only one ended in a result, a win for the visitors. It was the first time Pakistan had won a series in England and it made Imran Khan, the captain, a legend in his own country as well as in Tramp nightclub.

The fifth and final Test at The Oval began on 7 August (about the date the first Test ends these days). The emerging Fraser had edged me out of the Middlesex team so I was temporarily unemployed. I commentated on the Test for Cricketcall, a new telephone service from BT, supplying ball-by-ball feeds of county and Test cricket to people who were supposed to be working. I sat in a poky box at The Oval to describe the game alongside the legendary former England batsman Colin Milburn. Relaying the play was not always a straightforward assignment, since we were located low down at deep third man behind a pillar. Only half the pitch was visible, an added problem for Milburn, my summariser, since he had only one eye. Still, a restricted view was an advantage on the last day as England blocked out for a draw and Botham, in an uncharacteristic metamorphosis as Boycott, took four and a half hours for his 51.

My last column of the season, written inevitably from the wastes of shelterless Derby, where the dressing rooms badly needed fumigating, reflected on the stark reality facing professional cricketers in mid-September. Most were obliged to surrender their sponsored Peugeots, collect their P45s and turn their hands to less palatable occupations, like catching chickens with a hoop on the end of a stick in the case of one Gloucestershire player.

I, on the other hand, was all right, Jack. I would be broadcasting to the 'world'. I was hired, for the princely sum of thirty pounds a day, to produce sports features for British Forces Broadcasting Services (BFBS). From our carpeted studios beside the Great Western mainline station at Paddington, we would be reporting all the big sports stories, like 'Gurkhas Cadet Wins Archery Tourny', to British forces stationed in Gibraltar, Cyprus, Papua New Guinea and various other global hot spots.

It was hugely demanding work. Once you'd sat around for a few hours discussing football and popped out to the pub for lunch (paid for by HM Government), then come back and settled on your subject matter for the week, you were presented with a leather case the size of a small picnic hamper. This contained a reel-to-reel tape-recorder called a Uher. You were also presented with a tape-recorder 'operator' – that is, a posh girl to carry the device and push 'Record' at the right moment – and dispatched off in a taxi (paid for by HM Government). You were asked to return ... well, soonish. If that's OK. Having returned with the promised ten-minute interview with the Cambridge Boat Club president, recorded over lunch at the Hurlingham Club (paid for by HM Government), you were supplied with someone else to fiddle about editing the tape. Finally, after scribbling out a short script (typed up by Tape-Recorder Girl), you were ready to record your 'package' in a studio about the size of Mission Control, but better equipped. You could take as long as you liked to lay down your links (Studio 2 was used only once a day – for the Kid Jensen show) and then hang around at the end of the day to listen to your item about university rowing flatteringly introduced by a polished presenter such as Barry Davies or Ralph Dellor. It was radio from a feather bed.

This was the life. As well as BFBS and my *Independent* work, I'd been kept on by Cricketcall to do county features during the winter. Most excitingly, I also got a call from *Test Match Special*'s legendary producer Peter Baxter to come in to Broadcasting House for an interview. There might be some opportunities for me at the BBC, he said.

The Beeb. The most trusted voice in the world, the Holy Grail of broadcasting, from a wannabe's point of view. *TMS* was the nation's favourite, exuding soothing familiarity, like Terry Wogan or Mr Kipling's cakes. It was warm, sentimental, jovial, sometimes irreverent but always coherent (unless Fred Trueman was speaking). It offered everything I had always wanted: the best view of the game, a proper lunch hour rather than the twenty-minute feeding frenzy we had as players, and the chance to woo five million listeners in company with Johnners, CMJ, Bloers and the like. I was envisaging a life of commentary, cakes and guest appearances on *Call My Bluff*, and it was becoming difficult to see how I was going to be able to fit in any actual cricket the following summer.

I'd flattened the creases out of my Middlesex blazer with an *Encyclopaedia Britannica* like I used to do at school. I'd gargled before I left. But the interview with Baxter didn't begin well. It almost didn't begin at all. I became disorientated in Broadcasting House's maze of NHS-type corridors, then, trying the back stairs, I managed to lock myself on the wrong side of an emergency exit, and had to summon security. It's easily done, and several visits later I still didn't know my way around. It's the kind of bewildering rabbit warren where first-timers could go missing, presumed dead, before being found three weeks later trapped in a store cupboard. Twenty minutes late and panting, I arrived in Baxter's office, a small room overflowing with tape-recorders and books. He couldn't have been nicer, ignoring my tardiness and my over-familiarity – calling him 'Bartex' (his pet name among Test players, after its misspelling on an Indian hotel message board) even though we'd scarcely met. He talked about looking to the future, finding the next generation of commentators. I was already thinking ahead to the Ashes series eighteen months hence, wondering if I'd be the ball-by-ball man or the between-overs summariser.

After a few minutes Baxter presented me with a briefcase. This could have contained a four-year contract, next summer's schedule and some personalised *TMS* headphones. Instead I found inside a rectangular box with various terminals and coloured lights. It looked like bomb-making equipment. Baxter told me it was a 'COOBE', a device for sending radio-quality speech down the line from various provincial grounds. Thus, Lancashire's Graeme Fowler, Nick Cook of Northants and I would link up a few times a summer and chat about the county game in an item to be transmitted during Test match tea intervals.

Although it dashed my hopes of a perch next to Johnners and Bloers in the *TMS* box, I was quite excited by the prospect. It would be useful experience and put me in pole position should one of the commentators suddenly develop a speech impediment. It was also a good incentive to remain in the Middlesex team, loitering at the sharp end, picking up titbits from the county circuit. Finally, there was the possibility that if I ripped through the Surrey batting order with an inspired spell, I could then gallop upstairs to the press box with my COOBE, plug in and breathlessly report my deeds on the Radio 2 evening sports bulletin.

The reality was a little different. In the summer of 1988 I did stay in the Middlesex team, but the only ripping I did was of the sheets with my bowling figures on them. I *was* breathless on radio. This was largely due to some precarious locations from which I was obliged to record the 'County Talk' item in the evenings after play. At the Bournemouth ground, for instance, the special socket into which I plugged the COOBE was halfway up a telegraph pole behind the sightscreen. I was balancing on the top rung of the grounds-man's ladder in semi-dusk, COOBE in one hand, mike in the other, wires draped round my neck, trying to contribute to a debate about uncovered pitches while endeavouring to avoid being hung by BBC radio equipment. 'Mmm, we heard your broadcast,' my dad said later on the phone. 'Pretty good.' I sensed a 'but' coming. 'But your vowels when you pronounce "bowler" aren't quite right. And don't forget there are two "t"s in "twenty".'

UNGENTLEMANLY CONDUCT

'Twennie'-three was the sum total of my wickets for Middlesex that summer. It was also the number of players England tried in a vain attempt to compete with Viv Richards's West Indies. They wouldn't have managed it even if they'd fielded all twenty-three in the same match. England were an absolute shambles from top to bottom. The press, of which I was now a part-time member, certainly contributed to their downfall.

A Midlands news agency located a barmaid with slack knicker elastic who worked in an establishment near the England team's hotel and paid her to loosen her tongue. It was a perfect honey trap and Mike Gatting seemed to stumble right into it (so perhaps it would have been more appropriate to call it a Branston Pickle trap). Being the highest bidder, the *Sun* (along with *Today*) got the story, first alleging that there had been a 'sex orgy' at the team hotel one evening after play, then the next day naming Gatting as one of the players involved. He protested his innocence, but was sacked as captain a few hours later.

Conspiracy theorists suggest this was all a Machiavellian plot to destabilise English cricket, orchestrated by the machinations of Rupert Murdoch, who is, of course, Australian (or at least was then, before he became an American). What is undisputed is that Gatting was condemned to having an oddly unbalanced captaincy record: played 23, won 2 (the Tests in Australia), lost 5, drawn 16. Despite being the last English captain to win the Ashes, his Test win ratio of 9 per cent is about the lowest there is.

So began a sequence of four England captains in five matches, in the midst of a spell of three years (1987–90) when England managed one solitary Test victory, against Sri Lanka. Too many chiefs and not enough Indians? Well, no 'Indians' at all, in fact. Journalists and politicians who posed that perennial question 'What is wrong with English cricket?' were, as usual, off the pace. The question should have been what was *right* with it?

The men of the Fourth Estate were a small part of the problem. 'Gatting-gate' wasn't the first time tabloid guttersnipes had scavenged on England cricketers. They'd been drawn in by the spicy world of Ian Botham several years before; by his conviction for possessing cannabis in 1985, for instance, as well as his general boisterousness on tour. Ruthless opportunists spied on his home, rummaged through his dustbins and quizzed his young children. 'Are those your handcuffs, Liam, or did you get them out of your dad's washbag?'

Cricketers have always shagged and got drunk. They spend so much time away, it's almost compulsory. One of Gatting's first team talks as Middlesex captain included the perfectly reasonable advice: 'If you're going to bonk a bird or get pissed, do it before midnight.' Prior to Botham, what happened on tour stayed on tour. The travelling cricket reporters knew everything but said (and wrote) nothing. Botham's presence in the team drew in a breed of merciless newsmongers to dangle their bait at the players (usually moderately paid, amply endowed hospitality girls) and wait for their catch. His leapfrogging between the *Daily Mirror* and the *Sun* as a columnist only incited general tabloid rivalry.

It wasn't always female bait, of course. Gatting was giving me a lift into the Worcester ground in September 1988 when we were confronted at the entrance by, of all people, the umpire Shakoor Rana. Spying two photographers near by, Gatting muttered, 'Oh God,' put his head down and drove on to the car park. Above a picture of Gatting turning away in the *Sun* the next day was the headline: 'Gatting Treated Me Like Dirt'. The accompanying piece portrayed Rana as having stumped up his own fare from Pakistan in the spirit of détente. We soon ascertained it was a stunt dreamed up and paid for by the *Sun*.

Such antics enlarged the gulf between the players and the media which, I suppose, has always existed. Professional cricketers say they don't read the papers, but of course they do: they read the bits about themselves (or at least hear about them). They might have made a duck or taken none for 100, but anything less than total flattery in the press and they fling the rag away in contempt, exclaiming, 'What game was *he* watching?' or 'How many times has *he* bowled to Gooch in a force-nine gale?'

All sportsmen are born with fragile egos. They know when they've erred and can't handle it being emphasised. This is why, irrespective of the howler he's just made, a returning batsman is received back into the dressing room with only one of two utterances: 'Well played' or 'Bad luck'. The team-mate who mutters to a dismissed colleague as he's disconsolately unbuckling his pads, 'That was a shit shot!' doesn't usually remain a team-mate for very long.

Reality shatters the uneasy truce between sportsmen and

journalists. I, cricketer and weekly columnist, was already caught in the crossfire. If I escaped the riot of spotty arses and sweaty jockstraps in the dressing room and entered the press box to write my column, I got funny looks from some reporters. When I walked into the bar after a game, certain county players exclaimed in an audible whisper, 'Oi, here comes the press, watch your backs!' I wouldn't have minded, but they were team-mates, not opponents.

Overall, I'd had a lousy summer on the field, but done quite well, I thought, on the journalistic front. I'd given the low-down on Gatting's fall from grace. I'd expressed the real flaw in English cricket – there was too much of it. I'd dug up some pithy detail from the county circuit, like the Yorkshire supporter who, after his side had reached 5 for 0 in reply to Lancashire's 150, was heard to exclaim, 'Grand, at least we've saved t'follow-on.' I was thinking of applying for a pay rise at the paper. At Hove, I thought again. After a Sussex batsman had shouldered arms to one of my deliveries, a wag shouted, 'Oi, Hughes, that was about as accurate as most of your stuff in the *Independent*.' The ball was signalled a wide.

HIDDEN TALENT

Forget the disruptive influence of the press. The 1989 England team's real handicaps were lack of ability and lack of time. The two were linked. Rushing between Test and county matches left no scope for preparation or recuperation. The players were overwrought, undernourished and sex-starved. On Tuesday night the chosen players would be haring from a three-day match at Bristol or Chelmsford to the venue for the next Test. After ritual humiliation at the hands of the West Indies, they'd be limping back down the motorway to begin a county match the very next day. They were dazed and confused, like rabbits in headlights, and about as much use.

A rethink was needed. Four-day county cricket was

introduced and the number of matches reduced, to offer players more quality time to work, rest and play. Like many columnists, I heralded this brave move, championing it as a victory for the liberals and a defeat for the Luddites. It would fortify the English game in advance of the arrival of the 1989 Australians. The batsmen would be more attuned to building long innings, the bowlers better acquainted with extended perseverance. Australia, still rebuilding, wouldn't know what had hit them. Four-day cricket – way to go! The result: Australia won 4–0.

Various things conspired against England. No talent was one, though that hardly justified the selectors picking twenty-nine different players during the series. The weather – more Australian than Australia – was another. The alliance of the testy Australian captain Allan Border with the pragmatic, straight-talking coach Bobby Simpson, aping the successful Gatting–Stewart England partnership of 1986–87, was another. Border, essentially a nice bloke, had turned nasty. 'What d'you think this is, a fucking tea party? No, you can't have a fucking glass of water!' he told a startled Robin Smith, one afternoon. Oh, and Sydney's Town Chewer had had her jaw wired up.

England had injuries. But, in spite of the domestic changes, the batsmen were unable to build long innings, and the bowlers were incapable of extended perseverance. Steve Waugh wasn't dismissed until the third Test: that was more than fourteen hours of batting. 'Bring back three-day cricket!' was the deafening clamour from the press. 'Uncovered pitches, Second World War rationing, the feudal system. Anything but this!'

England had also shot themselves in the head. Stewart (the manager) and Ted Dexter (the chairman of selectors) had wanted Gatting reinstated as captain, but they were over-ruled by cricket committee chairman Ossie Wheatley, who preferred David Gower. The latter, while he was smooth and articulate, was a bit too debonair for the hard grind of trying to lead a team against a bunch of determined Aussies. He walked out of one press conference during the Lord's Test because he had tickets for the show *Anything Goes*. He was promptly vilified.

You had to sympathise. He was seeking an escape from the almost daily media briefings which had somehow become mandatory for the England captain since Gower's previous stint in charge. Like several future captains, he was mystified as to why cricket writers couldn't just report the game as they saw it, rather than rely on post-match quotes. He had a point: it was as if he were doing their job for them. But the stakes in the tabloid agenda were rising: they had to sensationalise to sell. The divide between captain and correspondents widened, and by the fourth Test his resignation looked a foregone conclusion. But during that match the news emerged that a thoroughly disillusioned Gatting was leading a rebel team to South Africa, including half the current side. Gower carried on and England were annihilated. It left a sour taste in the mouth of Michael Atherton, who'd been twelfth man for that game and was yet to make his Test debut. He and others were entitled to wonder why England couldn't work together. The Three Musketeers were of course to blame. It was they who coined the phrase 'all for one and one for all'. But they were French.

Around the counties there was much hand-wringing. Mainly by me. I'd read somewhere that repetitive squeezing of a tennis ball in your right hand stimulated the left side of your brain, the part that processes words. I did it whenever I had a spare moment in the dressing room. It had a negative effect on my writing. (I offended various people, notably the Middlesex coach for saying that all county coaches did was carry around a bag of balls and open the sandwiches at teatime.) It definitely enhanced my bowling, though, particularly the spin on my slower ball. I took loads of wickets with it and it had become a minor talking point. That is until Neil Smith hit it into the Nursery End seats to win the 1989 NatWest final for Warwickshire. Then it was a major talking point. 'Don't ever bowl that piece of fucking shite again,' the

Middlesex players ordered when they'd eventually got over the loss of £25,000. The West Indian Desmond Haynes, our overseas player that summer, is still smarting from it nearly two decades later.

UP AND AT 'EM

Seam bowlers generally had a prosperous summer. The authorities (by whom I mean the TCCB) ignored the bleedin' obvious – that English batting technique was hopeless – and instead penalised the bowlers. After the briefest of experiments in a dodgy net, attended by the secretary A. C. Smith and his would-be successor T. M. Lamb, they announced the balls for the 1990 season would be largely devoid of our chief tool in trade – a seam (the new ones resembled snooker balls) – and that pitches should be flatter than English ale.

At national level there was a change of regime during the winter. Gower was finally dismissed, and Graham Gooch became England's twelfth captain in ten years for the 1990 tour of the West Indies. He immediately instigated a long-overdue, harsh training regime, employing ex-army drill sergeant and confirmed sadist Colin Tomlins to put the lads through their paces. I went to watch them at the Lilleshall National Sports Centre one afternoon. There were Lamb, Smith and Hemmings doing orienteering, scrambling through muddy fields, vaulting fences, with Tomlins at their heels, barking, 'Check the map reference!' There were circuits, sprints, body-fat analyses. Later, there were serious practice sessions in superb facilities under the supervision of a host of distinguished experts – Boycott, Knott and Arnold. There was proper attention to detail for the first time.

Gatting's rebels didn't undertake any such sophisticated preparation. Despite five of them (Gatting himself, Emburey, Athey, Dilley and Broad) being Ashes winners only three years before, they were regarded as pariahs and no one would accommodate them. They had to make do with a perfunctory net, in secret, to dodge the media flak. Gatting had bullet-proof windows and security cameras installed around his home. It wasn't much better when they arrived in South Africa. There were protests and demonstrations and vicious threats. Left-wing columnists had a field day.

Desperate to build a better rapport with the press after a spate of misquotes and general savaging, David Graveney, the rebels' manager, requested all questions be put in writing in future; they would then be answered in similar fashion. Later that day at training, Graveney was cautiously approached by a posse of reporters brandishing an envelope. In it was a sheet of A4 on which had been scribbled, 'Please can we borrow your football?'

Meanwhile, I was doing training of a rather different kind. Cricketcall, which had provided me with useful income, had died. The cause? Office managers blocking employees' access to all 0898 numbers, believing them to be a work deterrent. It would be gratifying to think all these brokers and accountants were tuned in to Middlesex Cricketcall, hanging on my every word, but the most well-patronised 0898 numbers were sex lines.

To augment my cricket earnings of £11,000 and in a bid ultimately to wheedle my way into the *Test Match Special* commentary box, I enrolled as a sports producer at Greater London Radio. Under the auspices of the BBC, this was a total contrast to my previous experience at Forces Broadcasting. There were no leisurely jaunts, gentle interviews or plummily spoken girls to press buttons on tape-recorders here. This was non-stop, bare-knuckle-ride, DIY radio. The first sports bulletin was at 6.30 a.m., so I had to be in with the sparrows to assemble the overnight interviews. These, an assortment of forty-second sound bites about last night's football recorded on little cassettes called carts, had been dumped on my desk by the night editor. Once you'd ordered the mini-interviews into categories of 'bland', 'pointless' and 'incoherent', you then had to type out a little script. At 6.25 a.m. you'd slide past the rather overbearing production secretary into the live studio, balancing your pile of little carts, making sure the studio door didn't thud shut during a live item about noise pollution. Then you'd realise you'd forgotten your script and make a commotion hurriedly setting down your carts before going out of the door again and past the still-eager production secretary to collect it. When it came to your slot, you'd enunciate your links well, if a little breathlessly, and lead into the carted interviews, which could be any or all of the following: in the wrong order; so badly edited that various words were cut off; or accidentally rewound to the end so that when the producer pressed 'Play' there was just dead silence. You could console yourself with the knowledge that the only people listening were probably barely awake anyway.

You had a bit more time to prepare for the lunchtime slot, which meant you were expected to go out with your Uher and get a face-to-face ground-breaking interview with a sports personality. If there wasn't an Arsenal striker's book launch that day and no Middlesex colleagues were answering their phones, this involved paying a passer-by in Marylebone High Street a tenner to sound like Gazza. That was the easy part. Then it was a question of editing twenty-five minutes of waffle down to three minutes of intelligible chat. Lacking proper training and any proficiency with the block and razor blade, cutting audio tape wasn't my strong point. Ten minutes before I was due to go on air, I'd have coils of the brown, straggly stuff entwined round my neck (what is it about radio and the potential for being strangled?) while I was on my hands and knees searching under the machine for a sliced-off tape-morsel containing the first syllable of 'hamstring problem'. Once I played out an interview with the 'p' of 'passing' accidentally chopped off. Luckily, my father could never find the wavelength for this station. Even more luckily, nor could Mary Whitehouse.

There were two perks of this job: one, you knocked off at lunchtime; and two, on provision of your driving licence you were supplied with a green Corporation car pass, which, though resembling a laundry receipt, was like an open sesame. The revered letters 'BBC' in the top corner gained me free entry to top First Division football matches, rugby internationals, airline business lounges and sold-out Madonna concerts for years afterwards. No one ever looked closely enough to realise that the small print stated merely that 'This pass allows the bearer to drive a BBC radio car with an extendable mast.'

CHAPTER 4 – 1990–93

SQUARE EYES

'I squirmed as our dozy batsmen threw in the towel,' lamented Geoff Boycott in the *Sun* after England had subsided by an innings in the fifth Test in Antigua, to lose the 1990 series in the Caribbean 2–1. But it wasn't a fair summation of the tour. In fact, after a stunning victory in the first Test in Jamaica, Graham Gooch's side had become favourites to win the series. They were ultimately robbed by a combination of the weather, cynical West Indian time-wasting in Trinidad and a serious hand injury to the captain himself.

Still, English cricket was on the up, buoyed by the performances in the Caribbean, beamed back to the UK live for the first time by Sky. Although Tony Greig's regular exclamations of 'Goodnight Charlie!' and Boycott's frequent ''e could 'ave caught that in 'is moother's pinny' did get on your nerves after a while, the colourful scenes and exciting play certainly alleviated the grey evening TV fare of *Wogan* and *Blankety Blank*. That is, if you could afford the £359.99 outlay for dish and installation, never mind the extra £199.99 for squarial and separate box you needed to receive Sky's rival BSB (who had the rights to the Benson and Hedges Cup). If the cost didn't put you off, then the wiring probably would.

There were nine camera angles (the BBC had just five), close-ups of an English batsman's fearful stare as a West Indian bowler thundered to the wicket, and 'com-cams' illustrating that Boycott did actually take his hat off when indoors. I asked him once why he always wore it, expecting him to say it was a precaution against getting sunburnt. 'The thing is, it can be goosty in t'middle,' he said, 'and t'wind blows me wispy bits of hair about. I don't want viewers distracted by that and not listening to what I'm saying.'

National sports coverage had expanded considerably. In addition to the advent of Rupert Murdoch's satellite TV, there was the remorseless swelling of weekend newspapers, with their sports, leisure and business supplements. Murdoch's *Sunday Times* led this trend, causing quite a circulation war with Tiny Rowland's *Observer* and a spate of back injuries among paper boys. A front page of *Private Eye* captured this development astutely. The society 'hostess' Pamella Bordes is pictured on the arm of Andrew Neil, editor of the *Sunday Times*, looking at him seductively.

'Yours is bigger than Trelford's,' she is saying, a reference to Donald Trelford, the editor of the *Observer* and ladies man.

'Yes,' Neil replies, grinning lustfully, 'and it has more sections.'

With the *Sunday Correspondent* also at the peak of its brief life, there were reams of newsprint on sport: reports, interviews, profiles, and columnists employed to comment on others' comment columns. Slightly out of the blue, I was invited to join in this incestuous little game, co-presenting a slot on BSB's weekend sports show *Press Box*, essentially commenting on columns' comment on columns. It was the height of journalistic navel-gazing, but was fun while it lasted. I was making acerbic remarks about sportsmen's debacles and writers' prose in the secure knowledge that none of them would be watching: BSB's total audience could have been accommodated in a two-car garage, including their vehicles. After a few months the station was bought out by Sky in exchange for a couple of Luncheon Vouchers, and that was that.

The summer of 1990 was hot and on the domestic cricket scene it was the Year of the Bat. This was easy to tell from the increasingly forlorn pay-off lines in my *Independent* columns: 'Simon Hughes composed his column suffering from dehydration in the Lord's dressing room ... composed his column while trying to remember what taking a wicket feels like ... while connected to an Interferential machine in the physio's room ... at a special introductory bricklaying course in Kilburn.' Note that none were composed '... from the *TMS* commentary box at the Edgbaston Test'. Despite a few strong hints, including taking my own microphone to The Oval in an attempt to offer insights into my Middlesex colleague Neil Williams on his Test debut, the access to that particular Holy Grail remained denied.

The orgy of runs in county cricket at least gave the bowlers a decent rest when their team batted – often a whole day putting your feet up. At Lord's I made full use of these breaks to initiate potential male benefactors or pretty female acquaintances – mostly the latter – into the delights of cricket. I'd sit them in the sun at the Nursery End, furnish them with a Pimm's, and point out a bowler's strange action or a batsman's idiosyncrasies, or explain the reason for a particular fielding position. This was where, I realised later, the concept of 'The Analyst' on Channel 4 was born. Keeping a viewer's attention with stuff going on 'off the ball'. Here, though, I was just hoping to keep the girl's attention long enough for her at least to agree to dinner later. Actually, all they were usually interested in was training my binoculars on Graeme Hick's cute arse or Devon Malcolm's lunchbox, and who could blame them? Just as I might be winning them over, there'd be a couple of quick wickets, I'd realise I was next in to bat and would have to make a frantic dash behind the stands back to the pavilion to get padded up. More than once I was wandering breathlessly out to the middle ten minutes later, shoelaces undone, shirt untucked, still fiddling with my protective gear. Having taken guard, I'd glance quickly up at the stand, on the pretence that I was looking round the field, to see if she was watching. Usually she would have departed. With my binoculars.

England had a successful, run-filled 1990 summer, led by

a fully recovered Gooch, who positively filled his boots in the Test series against New Zealand and India. Now the microscope was on them as they set out optimistically for Australia to regain the Ashes. Things soon went horribly wrong. Gooch himself was ruled out of the first Test in Brisbane, having injured his hand taking a catch in a state game. Allan Lamb, a man with one eye on the ball and the other on a deal, took over the captaincy. By the second evening, England's ropy batting had already put them in the mire. But it didn't help that their stand-in captain, 10 not out overnight, had spent the evening in a casino fifty miles away in company with high rollers Tony Greig and Kerry Packer.

Lamb was out in the first over the next day, England managed only 114 in their second innings, and Australia knocked off the 157 required to win without losing a wicket. It set the tone for the rest of the series, which England lost 3–0. There was careless England batting, morale-sapping injuries, and inappropriate capers, of which David Gower and John Morris's buzzing of the ground in a pair of Tiger Moths during the match against Queensland gained the most notoriety. If only England could have produced something artful and original *on* the pitch.

Philip Clive Roderick Tufnell, on his first tour, came to symbolise England's campaign. Tufnell, alias The Cat, had talent, and proved it with five good wickets in Sydney. But his comic attempts with the bat, his erratic fielding and his general neurosis turned him into a laughing stock for the Australian spectators. It was where the 'Oi, Tufnell, lend us your brain – I'm building an idiot' line originated. And, as far as the Australians were concerned, he never quite shook it off.

PIERSED IN THE BACK

About the time England were sinking to an ignominious end in Perth, my first marriage was sinking to an ignominious end in Brentford, and I was having my first real tangle with the press, in Switzerland. I had just had an encounter with St Moritz's famous Cresta Run – bobsleigh on a teatray – and lost. My right collarbone was broken. Leaving the clinic later that morning with my arm in a sling, I bumped into a tabloid sports journalist who had arrived to cover our attempts to play cricket on ice. He enquired what had happened, feigning concern. I explained about my accident, then asked him, quite emphatically, if he wouldn't mind keeping the cause of the injury to himself. That, of course, is just about the worst thing you can say to a seasoned hack: the dangled carrot the donkey just can't resist. At the first opportunity he rang up my current employers, the Middlesex secretary and captain Mike Gatting, and regaled the full gory details in the hope of a reaction. He then printed them in his column a couple of days later.

This lack of probity is not new in the press, of course, and seems to be handed down through generations of hackage. It's like a rite of passage – you're not a real journalist until you've quoted or revealed something you know you shouldn't have, and then defended yourself from the affronted victim with an 'I *told* them not to print that bit but they didn't listen.' I, too, eventually transferred from Sinned Against to Sinners United.

To some, though, manipulating the truth is like artistic skill or maths ability: it's simply in the blood. At a private cricket dinner I was speaking at that summer, I told a tame anecdote about Mike Gatting's genitalia. A youngish club member came up to me after my speech, saying how much he'd enjoyed it and asking me to expand on the story. Two days later a prominent headline in the *Sun* next to a topless bird declared: 'OUCH! DINNER GAG HITS GATTING IN THE BAILS'. The article elaborated on the Gatting story and suggested it had been ill-judged. 'Several guests walked out in disgust,' it read, which was a complete fabrication. It went on to claim that 'there were as many women as men listening and a lot were upset'. This, in view of the hearty applause my speech received, was also news to me (as was the presence of 'many' women; I hadn't noticed *any*). The story's author (and aforementioned 'youngish member') was a certain Piers Morgan, then showbiz editor at the *Sun*.

The cricket club wrote to me and politely apologised for the article, confirming the inaccuracies and regretting the abuse of a private function. A week later a pompous letter arrived from Morgan on *Sun* headed notepaper apologising 'for the ridiculously grovelling letter you received from Newick Cricket Club ... written by people who have clearly had a sense of humour bypass'. He went on to justify his piece, adding that, regarding people walking out, 'my own father found some of your comments so offensive that he went to the loo until you had finished'.

Obviously, this was a trivial matter, and, as far as Gatting was concerned, the story was old hat. In fact it was a cause for celebration: I had made it at last into the pages of the old *Currant Bun*. I was a Z-list celebrity. It indicated, however, the methods often employed to conjure a story out of nothing, and the unwavering conceit of those reporters when brought to book. To these men, stories become like drugs: they need their daily fix. Truth becomes largely irrelevant. As the hits get harder, they become more and more resilient to the side-effects.

Piers Morgan quickly rose through newspaper echelons and he's got some good journalistic qualities – wit, energy, imagination. His commitment to a cause is pit-bullish: once he's got his teeth into something he won't let go. But the arrogant belligerence that got him to the top of his profession eventually brought him down. Nevertheless, with a massive pay-off and a huge advance for his entertaining *Insider* diaries, he was laughing all the way to the Swiss bank.

IN VISION

A virtuoso performance by Graham Gooch enabled England to win the first Test of the 1991 summer at Headingley.

Single-handedly he kept the much-vaunted West Indian pace attack at bay for almost eight hours to make an unbeaten 154 out of England's 252. Amazingly, it was the first time England had beaten the West Indies in a Test match at home since 1969. There was a Caribbean feel to England's bowling attack by the end of the drawn series, too. It featured Syd Lawrence (of Jamaican heritage), Phillip DeFreitas (born in Dominica) and his Willesden High School colleague Chris Lewis (born in Guyana). Fourteen years on, the cricketers of Caribbean extraction have all but dried up in England. Willesden High School, now called City Academy, doesn't even have a cricket pitch or a cricket team. British-born blacks feel less affinity with the West Indies or their cricket team, which anyway is a pale shadow of its former self. They're more interested in football, basketball and DJ-ing these days. In cricketing terms there's been a slow extinguishing of the Caribbean light. Will it ever be rekindled? The 2007 World Cup, to be held in the West Indies, probably represents the last chance.

The summer of 1991 was a watershed as far as I was concerned. Quite apart from my marriage being annulled, it was my benefit year, the time when sportsmen try not to think about their future career or how to deal with the taxman, but are obliged to by people coming up and saying, 'What are you going to do after you've got your P45?' Then another job offer came out of the blue: a BBC producer rang in August and asked me to be part of their radio commentary team. At last! It was only for Hampshire v. Notts, the least interesting of the four NatWest quarter-finals that the BBC were covering, but it was a start.

Instead of researching a load of meaningless statistics, I prepared for my assignment by describing imaginary shots and amazing catches with a large carrot as a makeshift microphone. I reckoned if I came out with some flowery descriptions of the play I might get the *TMS* call-up for the Oval Test against the West Indies in a week's time. I laid it on thick whenever the radio coverage came to us, talking about

Derek Randall's batting being 'a national treasure walking the tightrope between triumph and calamity' and describing David Gower's innings as 'deliciously thin spun', even though he wasn't actually batting at the time.

The call came three days later on my new-fangled mobile as I was driving to Lord's, drinking a cappuccino.

'Hello, is that Simon Hughes?'

'Yeooucchhh!'

'Pardon?'

'Sorry, I turned left and just tipped hot coffee into my lap.'

'Crikey ... shall I call back?'

'No, no it's fine.' (Grimacing.)

'OK. Well, it's Alan Griffiths here from the BBC.'

(Brightly.) 'Hi!'

'I heard you commentating at Southampton and I was wondering if you were able to do The Oval.'

'The Oval. Brilliant. Yes, of course. The Test starts next Thursday, doesn't it?'

'Actually, I ...'

'Middlesex have got a three-day match beginning on the Friday but I'm sure I won't be picked. It'll be fine.'

'But I ...'

'Yes, and I can tell all the listeners what Phil Tufnell is really like. D'you know when he bats he's always saying, "He's not bowling too fast, is he?" and "I'm not backing away much, am I?" and then treading on square leg's toes, and ...'

'Look, sorry to give you the wrong impression. I'm not referring to the Test match. I'm thinking of the NatWest semi-final between Surrey and Northants in a fortnight's time. And this is for TV, not radio.'

'Oh, er, great!'

My radio commentary career had lasted precisely one match.

Now, you'd think a great organ like the BBC, which first transmitted live sport in 1937 and is the most renowned name in world television, with an annual income of £2.2 billion and a staff of thousands, would offer broadcasting novices a bit of training, so as to maintain standards, if nothing else. I was expecting to have to report to TV Centre at Wood Lane the week before, to meet the producers, be shown a few videos of how (and how not) to do it, and get an elocution lesson or two, declaiming 'How Now Brown Cow' or 'Bowl, Roll, Goal' in front of a camp bloke in a corduroy jacket. Not a bit of it. I was asked to report to the ground at 10 a.m. on match day for a 10.30 start. This, I assumed, was a prelude to sitting in the commentary box for most of the morning watching the experts at work and making notes before being allowed to have a little try during the midday news and a proper go behind the microphone after lunch. Consequently, I didn't make a special effort to be there particularly early. I was met by a stage manager, looking a little flustered.

'Simon ... phew, thank God you're here,' he said. 'Quick, follow me, you're in vision with Richie at the top and we're on air in twelve minutes. Got to get you miked up.'

I was led onto a balcony overhanging the pavilion where the great Benaud sat in Cream Jacket Mark XII surrounded by cameras and monitors propped on packing cases and held precariously in place by gaffer tape. I clambered across a riot of cables towards the empty chair next to him.

'Aha, morning Simon,' said Richie, offering his hand, but not getting up. 'Sit down and make yourself comfortable.' A little microphone was shoved up inside my shirt. 'Interesting article you wrote the other day about reverse-shwing,' he went on. 'I keep it in my briefcase for everyday reference.'

'Thanks,' I said.

'Now,' he said, 'once I've introduced the programme, we'll chat about today's teams. They'll be on the monitor in front of us. You OK with that?'

'Fine,' I blustered.

There wasn't time to say much more because the stage manager was giving us a thirty-second count to the opening titles. At zero the tinkle of the cowbell at the start of the famous 'Soul Limbo' theme tune crackled through little speakers at our feet. I felt the same surge of exhilaration you get when you strike a perfect three-wood down the middle and smiled knowingly at Richie, but he was looking at camera.

'Morning everyone,' he said, as the music faded out, 'and welcome back to a sunny Kennington Oval for this eagerly awaited NatWest Bank semi-final between Surrey and Northants. The weather looks fine, the pitch is good and I'm sure we're in for a great day. Now, the first thing I can tell you is that Surrey won the toss and have elected to bat. They're two very strong, well-matched sides and here to tell us about them I'm delighted to welcome the Middlesex quick bowler Simon Hughes ... Morning Simon.'

'Hello,' I croaked, like a *University Challenge* contestant. *Hello?* You've had 29 years 235 days to prepare for this moment – given that you didn't utter your first word, 'digger', until you were 14 months old – and the best you can manage is 'hello'?

But if there's one man on earth who can settle a mind-in-a-whirl, it's Benaud. Sitting there, poised and tanned, he's a soothing, nurturing presence in the cold isolation of live TV, encouraging everything to grow. (Geoff Boycott, I was later to find out, could be more like mildew.)

'Now let's have a look at the Surrey side,' said Richie, smoothing my path. 'Good batting line-up backed up by excellent bowlers. Waqar Younis's sandshoe crusher's a bit of a handful isn't it, Simon?'

I was off at a canter, giving the low-down on every player without much erring and umming or too many 'y'knows' and an acceptable level of hand gesticulation and head-wiggling; and I managed to come to a definite end when I felt gentle pressure from Richie's foot on my toe for the third time. 'Excellent. Thanks Simon. Right, now the umpires and players are out and everyone's ready. So it's time to go upstairs now and say good morning to Tony Lewis.'

Richie gave me an approving nod, unhooked his mike and rose from his seat. I felt an overwhelming wave of relief, a warm glow of achievement and a chill down my back. My shirt was stuck to it with sweat.

'Good stuff,' said the stage manager. 'Now, quick, we've got to get up to the com box. You're first on with Tony Lewis.'

There was just no time to be nervous. I was thrust straight past Boycott, Illingworth and Tom Graveney and into a seat next to the welcoming Lewis. I was connected to a mixing box via a pink earplug, and I was shown how to use talk-back. Toggling down on a button marked 'lazy' allowed me to talk to the director. With it in the up position I was broadcasting to the nation. You could also regulate the volume of yourself, your co-commentator, the director and the ground ambience in your earpiece. I noticed later that Boycott, in particular, had *everything* turned up very loud.

The director Alan Griffiths's constant burble in your ear was initially quite off-putting. He spoke mainly to the cameramen: 'Three ... four ... coming to seven, seven ... on you, coming to six ... wider six ... on you ... coming to five ... on you ... there's the non-striker for you, Jack ... running ... one, two ... *shot*! ... five, still on you, five ... replay coming ... wipe ...' He would occasionally indulge in a bit of banter with the commentators. He and Tony Lewis both hailed proudly from the Principality, and there was a 'swear' box for every time they mentioned Wales, or anyone from it. As two Glamorgan players – Steve Watkin and Hugh Morris – had had an influence on the summer Tests, it was getting quite full.

I learned to filter out the director's babble unless he said, 'Going to the news in ten ... quick wrap, Richie ...' and come the afternoon I had built up enough confidence to ask for the odd close-up to tell an anecdote. The story about Monte Lynch earning an unexpected England one-day call-up under Mike Gatting because when the selectors said 'Lynch?' he thought they'd said, 'Lunch?' apparently aroused some telephoned complaints from Surrey supporters.

Overall, there was no guidance about what to say: you were just plugged in and left to get on with it. There was an audible intake of breath from the assistant director when I said on air that perhaps the reason why the Northants batsmen weren't seeing Waqar Younis's deliveries too well was because a black hand was coming out of a dark background. But otherwise nothing was said to me before, during or after, apart from enquiring how many sugars I took in tea. This is how the BBC has always been, which, in sports production terms, is both its strength and its weakness. They don't lay down rules or cramp your style: they trust you, which is a good thing. Then again, they are too star struck to dare to criticise, when what that star needs most of all is candid advice. As a result, you got commentators like Boycott, who, while admirably straight-talking, tended to labour a point too much; or Trevor Brooking, who never finished his sentences; or Bill Beaumont, who spoke in a strange turkey-like mumble. Though at least none were like John Barnes, who was completely unintelligible and dressed like Liberace. It's also why some legendary BBC commentators – David Coleman, Peter Alliss, John Motson – are allowed to carry on way past their sell-by dates.

I enjoyed my first day of live TV immensely, thinking I'd done OK. It was a great help to me that I was still a current player as it gave me a confidence-boosting insight that I knew none of the other commentators had. The fact that I'd written columns about the game was another advantage. It's a useful aid when you're trying to find words for a fifth successive driven boundary or sum up an unexpected dismissal.

The proof of approval was in the invitation to commentate again. This was not, however, at the NatWest final, but at a late September fixture between 1991 County Champions Essex and Sheffield Shield holders Victoria. It was the day after a close friend's wedding in deepest Normandy, meaning I had to leave the reception midway through the eighties disco to drive to Paris to catch a dawn flight. Having hired a car from Heathrow and then driven like the clappers round the M25, I made it to Chelmsford for the 10.30 start. It was presumably the only time anyone has commentated on a cricket match wearing rather dishevelled morning dress. Fortunately, I wasn't required in vision this time.

THE WORLD MOVES ON

Summer/winter 1991–92 was the pinnacle of a good spell for the England team. The disciplined combo of Graham Gooch and Mickey Stewart was working. Having held the West Indies to a drawn series for the first time in two decades, they went Down Under and hammered New Zealand before progressing, with only the odd hiccup, to the World Cup final in Melbourne.

Using my benefit money (that is, cricket benefit, not funds from the DSS) I took myself off to New Zealand to chronicle their exploits for the *Independent*. I based myself with friends in Auckland, from where I phoned in match reports to Greater London Radio. This was not quite so straightforward when England were playing in Sydney, 2500 miles away. Their matches were shown live on New Zealand TV, but my friends' telephone was in a different room from the telly. To provide GLR with live updates I had one person watching the match in the lounge scribbling down the details and passing them to his wife to ferry to me on the phone in the kitchen. Exuding excitement at 'Botham's sizzling square cut through the offside' while staring at racks of condiments tested the acting gene I'd inherited from my father. I so nearly added that the shot had given the cover fielder Juniper Berries no chance.

I made it to the Melbourne final between England and Pakistan in person, but such was the level of media interest that there was standing room only in the press box. So I watched the first innings from the top of the Southern Stand – so high that the white ball is barely a speck on the green sward – then followed the England innings from the midst of an embryonic Barmy Army in Bay 13.

'Que sera, sera
Whatever will be will be
We've got to the MCG
Que sera, sera.'

At least GLR listeners could hear authentic match atmosphere when I phoned in an update from here, rather than an
eerie silence interrupted by the kettle boiling. Armed with
their football-club banners, the England supporters continued to be in good voice until Wasim Akram's lethal second
spell vaporised England's lower order and any lingering
hopes of winning the World Cup for the first time.

It was a portent of things to come. For much of the next
five years, the dynamic cricket was played by everyone
except England. Pakistan, inspired by Imran's legacy, had
their wizardly fast bowlers and swashbuckling batsmen; the
Indians unearthed the Little Master Sachin Tendulkar and
the unorthodox leg-spinner Anil Kumble; Brian Lara's genius
emerged to augment the West Indians' still-potent pace
attack; the South Africans returned strong and fit after their
isolation; and the Sri Lankans took one-day cricket by storm.
And then, of course, there was the little phenomenon of an
Australian beach-bum with bleached-blond hair and an ear-
ring: Shane Warne.

England remained stuck in a rut. The World Cup was the
old guard's swansong. Botham, Lamb, Gower and Gatting
had reached the end of the road, leaving a gaping hole in the
batting, and Gooch had become a bit set in his ways, in spite
of a new hairpiece. The bowling attack was, with the occasional exception, moderate; the tail was regularly sliced
through. A few rearguard actions were mounted, usually led
by the indefatigable Michael Atherton, but England won
practically nothing between 1992 and 1997, except media
vilification.

The explanation for this sorry state of affairs was straightforward: there was a disunity of purpose, a revolving-door
policy in selection and little coherent strategy. On a dust

bowl at Calcutta in 1993, India played three spinners; England played four seamers. There was only going to be one winner. (The coach Keith Fletcher wasn't the first to observe after spying on the Indian leg-spinner Anil Kumble that he rarely turned the ball and wouldn't pose a problem. With twenty-one wickets in three games, he was India's man of the series.)

At Edgbaston against Australia, England asked for a green top and were given a desert. They lost heavily. During the six Ashes Tests of 1993, England fielded twenty-four different players, including ten fast bowlers and seven debutants. Phillip DeFreitas, an Ashes winner in 1987, when he was tipped as a potential world star, had by 1994 been dropped *thirteen* times. In Tests against the West Indies, someone was always making their England debut. Atherton, captain through most of this period, made the best of a difficult job but selectors, some of whom were old and clueless, came and went almost as often as his opening partners. He had fifteen in all. ('Why are players too old to play Test cricket at thirty-eight,' said Botham, aged thirty-eight, 'but too young to select the team until they are collecting their pension?')

England's paucity of match-winning bowlers was so acute that they tried anything to take wickets: big black fast bowlers, short white fast bowlers, tall lanky swingers, loud-mouthed appealers, right arm, left arm, round arm and spinners galore. The former Australian wicketkeeper Rod Marsh was not impressed: 'All England seems to produce is pie-throwers,' he said.

If changing the bowlers didn't work, they'd change the ball. Or fiddle with it. Atherton himself was hauled over the coals for putting a bit of dirt on it. They tried munching on jelly babies so their sweetened saliva would polish the ball better and make it swing. Chewing gum, too. One naïve twelfth man brought out sugar-free gum during a long, mainly wicketless fielding session. That just about summed it up. England were a spent force.

County cricket, an anachronism riven by internal squabbling, was largely to blame. Financially it was bleeding the game dry, yet it was producing nothing but run-of-the-mill players, few of whom could make the substantial leap up to Test cricket. The eleven TCCB committees charged with running English cricket just went round and round in circles.

I had joined Durham in the summer of 1992. It was their inaugural first-class season and I wrote a diary of it, *From Minor to Major*, aided by my mother, who typed up my scrawled manuscript on an Amstrad (the war-issue typewriter had finally jammed). When it was finished, I sent it to a couple of journalists, and Richie Benaud. I heard nothing more from the journalists, but Benaud, while packing up to head back to Australia, still found time for an instant four-page typed reply. There was a nice quote for the front cover, some general positive comments, various typos and/or inaccuracies itemised by the page, and one astonishing admission. Referring to my mention that Botham and Gooch had suddenly walked out of the pre-World Cup final dinner in Melbourne, he wrote:

> They walked past my left shoulder as I was mentally going through the manner in which, as the main speaker at the dinner, I intended extolling to the 1500 guests present their virtues and those of the rest of the England and Pakistan teams present. Gooch, the England captain, and Botham, the great all-rounder, were, with Imran, the other captain, to be the main thrust of my speech. It was one of the more daunting moments of my past forty-four years in cricket. For a start, I reasoned they might have walked out because they had heard me speak once before…!
>
> The whole thing reads really well.
> Cheers, Richie.

The book barely sold, even in Durham, but it did get some critical acclaim from Michael Parkinson, who had somehow purloined a copy, and said it provided 'a fascinating insight into the tedious routine of county cricket'. That was the phrase, 'tedious routine'. There was nothing dynamic or enterprising about county cricket any more. It was stuck, like some English batsmen, with its feet in clay. A more appropriate title might have been *From Major to Minor*.

PRESS PERSECUTION

In a pre-election speech, Prime Minister John Major drew parallels with the peculiarly English delights of 'warm beer, old maids bicycling to Holy Communion through the morning mist ... and long shadows falling across the county ground'. Inadvertently, he had advertised county cricket's redundancy. Like the Conservatives, it was marooned in a backwater while the world moved on. Newspapers, becoming more vituperative by the day, gorged themselves. Ted Dexter was mercilessly ridiculed for a couple of unguarded remarks about smog and planetary orientation during England's awful tour of India. Dexter brought some imagination to the chairman of selectors role, and cared deeply, staying at home to watch domestic Tests on TV where he wouldn't be distracted by waffling administrators. But this was unrecognised by the press who had never forgotten his reference to 'our fast bowler Malcolm Devon', disliked his aloofness and took him down with pot-shots like 'DROP THE TED DONKEY'. Like Ray Illingworth after him, Dexter was caught unawares by the voracious Hydra the press had turned into since his playing days. He didn't last long after that.

Occasionally the press leapt to England's defence, notably during the contentious 1992 series against Pakistan when allegations of ball tampering surfaced. 'GOT 'EM BY THE BALL', declared the *Sun*, backed up the *Mirror*'s 'CHEATS'. (Geoff Boycott got closer to reality: 'Quit squealing. They [Wasim and Waqar] could have got us out with an orange,' he wrote.) But generally the Fourth Estate seemed to take

sadistic delight in England's failings, mainly through a communal cynicism prevalent in most press boxes, where Tall
Poppy Syndrome (build 'em up, knock 'em down) is rife. A
country's press is a reflection of its readers, but given the slat-
ing the players were receiving, a growing rift formed between
them and the media. The pleasant tradition on tour for the
team to invite the press to their fancy-dress Christmas lunch
was abruptly terminated.

It therefore wasn't the most opportune time to be embark-
ing on a career as a cricket writer. Nevertheless, in early 1993
I was put on trial as cricket correspondent of the
Independent on Sunday. I fitted the odd game of cricket for
Durham round attending England games. It was a good
arrangement, meaning I still had a bit of exercise and kept in
touch with the game while avoiding the tedium of four-day
matches to go and watch Test matches and produce full-
length articles. The Sunday writers seemed a nicer bunch,
too, more broad-minded and less hostile than the harassed
daily boys.

After his ball of the century to Mike Gatting, Shane
Warne, the blond, earringed modern face of Australia, was
the talk of the town. But one of my first pieces was about a
relic of an earlier Aussie era, Merv Hughes. He looked like a
caveman with his walrus moustache and heavy physique;
and, despite his mincing run, was a remorseless competitor,
prepared to try anything – bouncer, yorker, slow leg-break,
expletive – to take a wicket. A byword for sledging, Hughes
was well known for giving the batsman an earful, but he
could be witty, too. In a Test at home he let fly a volley of
abuse at the provocative Pakistani batsman Javed Miandad,
to which an exasperated Miandad finally retorted, 'You're
just a fat bus conductor.' In the next over a riled Hughes
bounced out Miandad. He accompanied the batsman's
departure towards the pavilion with a bell-ringing motion
and a triumphant, 'Ding, ding! Tickets, please!'

Merv the Swerve took thirty-one wickets in the 1993 Ashes,
only three fewer than Warne. England were routed 4–1, with

the consolation victory in the sixth and final Test their first win for eleven games.

It was proposed that I should retire from playing for Durham at the end of the 1993 season to take up the *Independent on Sunday* job full time. It was a tricky decision. It would mean trading a pre-season confined to a damp, cold, indoor school in Houghton le Spring for a two-month ordeal following England in the Caribbean. After much deliberation – all of two nanoseconds – I accepted. Unfortunately, someone wouldn't accept me.

CHAPTER 5 – 1994

BEDTIME STORIES

That someone was Simon Kelner, the goatee-bearded Mancunian I'd first encountered as deputy sports editor in the early days of the *Independent*. Then there had been a certain purity and originality in its pages. Now that the Mirror Group had taken over the troubled *Independent* titles, there was a change of emphasis. They didn't want in-depth features on African Aids epidemics or Greenpeace missions. They wanted articles about the good things in life – Porsches and Rolexes and Armani suits and holidays in the Maldives.

Kelner, something of a celebrity hobnobber, was hired as sports editor. He didn't want a cricket correspondent who finished ninety-third in the first-class bowling averages writing quirky articles about being hit for a hundred. He wanted an England player with authority. Derek Pringle (with thirty Tests to his name), then a *Daily Telegraph* columnist, fitted the bill. I was fired before I'd begun. One minute you're the cock of the walk, the next you're the feather duster.

I could understand the *Independent*'s desire to pull in readers with big-name writers. What I couldn't understand was Kelner's reluctance to explain the situation to me. I learned my fate leaving the sports department PA's flat at about 4 a.m. after a drunken evening out.

'Oh well, guess this is the end of a beautiful friendship,' she said.

'Why? It wasn't that bad,' I slurred. 'Anyway, I'll probably be in the office on Thursday.'

'What for?'

'Write my winter tour preview.'

'Hey, babe. D'you mean you haven't been told?'

'Haven't been told what?'

'Derek Pringle's got your job.'

Pringle himself was surprised I didn't know when I phoned him to confirm the reality the next day. His polite sympathy didn't help. I felt empty and unwanted, a sensation not eased by a terrible hangover. Even though the weather was vile, I went out to get some air. I contemplated all the journeys I'd made on behalf of the paper as I walked, and thought of all the columns and features I'd laboured over, the occasional flak I'd endured from a rare cricketer who read the *Independent* and was displeased with something I'd written. I wondered how an editor could be so callous.

At Notting Hill Gate I felt some empathy with a *Big Issue* salesman huddling in a doorway against the wind and rain. I paid twice the cover price for a copy, perused the contents page and even refrained from throwing it in the nearest litter bin. Loyal, unsung journalists had slaved long and hard, probably for a pittance, for some of these stories. I walked a little further up the road. *Then* I threw it in a bin.

Salvation was at hand. David Welch, the smooth-talking sports editor of the *Daily Telegraph*, was happy to take me on as a freelance. It was a lucky break as Welch had recently persuaded the *Telegraph* to publish a separate sports section on a Saturday and a Monday, so there was lots of space. It also had four times the *Independent*'s readership. The downside was that they already had their man lined up to cover England's tour of the Caribbean (Christopher Martin-Jenkins). I would be exchanging a privileged spot in the press box at Bridgetown, Barbados, for a deckchair at the Nairobi Gymkhana in Kenya for Ireland v. Holland in the ICC Trophy.

Still, it was an interesting place to go, and I made light of the fact that my first Nairobi hotel was a ten-storey hostel for jobless immigrants, and my second was still being built as I slept (or tried to). At least it had operational plumbing, which was more than could be said for the place all 350 players were billeted. Kenya's average daily temperature is 32°C and they'd all come back from matches at the same time baked in sweat and turn on their showers, causing the primitive water system to seize up. Not a trickle emerged. So they'd all go to the bar having left the water on, and the system would raise itself to tsunami levels and flood everybody's bathroom before seizing up again. As a result, it was a tournament of unprecedented player ponginess.

There was plenty of incident on the field. The Irish captain broke his arm before the first match: inspecting the wicket, he was run over by the roller. The Papua New Guinea team arrived at each venue armed with as many guitars and ukuleles as bats and broke into rich harmony at any opportunity, no matter how they were doing in the middle. The United Arab Emirates side was made up almost entirely of Pakistanis who had all had their UAE passports issued mysteriously on the same date in 1989. The Bangladeshi assistant coach wailed hysterically down the phone after his team lost their semi-final: effigies of the players were apparently burning in the streets of Dhaka. He later apparently tried to kill himself.

I grabbed the chance, while I was in Kenya, to go on a three-day safari in the Masai Mara (from where I filed a match report on Malaysia v. Bermuda, with the help, via telephone, of a local correspondent); to see the world-famous flamingos on Lake Nakuru; and to eat in a Nairobi restaurant called Maids, through which buxom local women paraded every few minutes to be 'selected' by male diners sitting in booths, who would then escort them to rooms upstairs. Bearing in mind the astronomical levels of HIV infection in East Africa, the establishment should have been renamed 'Aids'.

I wrote my reports in pencil in an A4 book and phoned them through to the *Telegraph* copytakers from my building site/hotel. The calls cost seven pounds a minute. On an echoing line and featuring names like Johan Samarasekera,

Manraj Poonawalla and predatory fielder Tan Kim Hing, the UAE v. Malaysia match report alone cost £210 to file. The Karachi-born 'Arabs' won the tournament, so earning themselves a Mercedes each and entry to the 1996 World Cup. They were an embarrassment in that and two years later had disappeared off the cricketing radar.

In the end I made it to the Caribbean for four Tests of England's 1994 tour. Thinking it would be valuable journalistic experience and that it would show willing, I went under my own steam, sharing rooms wherever possible to save on expenses. Usually this was with other journalists, but in Trinidad my roommate was a Lancashire anorak who went to bed every night at 9 p.m. wearing his county's one-day replica strip with 'Watkinson' on the back. And in Antigua it was a Thalidomide victim friend who had shortened arms and no feet. He was an excellent companion except that he was rather fond of his beer and kept waking me up in the night to help him have a pee.

I was there to support the *Telegraph*'s main cricket-writer, CMJ, and supply a 'side bar' piece for each day's play. In that eventful series there was no shortage of subjects: Curtly Ambrose's demon bowling, Alec Stewart's two centuries in a match, Phil Tufnell's habit of going AWOL. The snag was the time difference. London is five hours ahead of the Caribbean, meaning that soon after lunch in the Test it was deadline time in the UK and they were screaming for copy. I caused more than a few hairs to be pulled out in the office with my late filing and missed one edition entirely.

Fortunately, the big story of the series – Lara's record-breaking innings of 375 – happened before lunch. England tried everything to get him out, including Devon Malcolm plying the bowlers with fresh mango slices during play. Here was another attempt to get a shine on the ball (through fruity saliva) but the ploy just ended up making it sticky. Angus Fraser even tried a bit of verbal abuse after Lara played a false shot, though he accepted that sledging is pretty futile when a batsman is 340 not out. Despite seeing my bowling brethren being battered into total submission, it was a privilege to watch Lara's innings. When he reached 364 I was reminded of the wooden loo seat on my parents' upstairs toilet. It was there, aged eight, where I would sit every morning with the 1968 *Wisden*, studying cricket records. The figures 365 not out (the highest Test score, made by Garfield Sobers) and 499 (highest first-class score, by Hanif Mohammed) were embedded in my memory. In the space of six weeks in 1994, Lara broke both. At the time of writing, though, the loo seat is still intact.

The West Indies tour was a fabulous one to be on, loitering in paradise watching cricket full of intrigue and excitement: a sportswriter's dream ticket. I finished up writing for the *Financial Times* as well as the *Telegraph* and felt a fully fledged member of the press pack. The travelling cricket writers made me feel as much by welcoming me into their inner circle at an end-of-tour dinner, in a beautiful restaurant by the glistening Caribbean in Antigua. They called me Yozzer (a Lancastrian nickname for Hughes) and I called them Iggy and Reggie and Bonker and Toff. Drinking a rum punch looking out across the moon-dappled water, I felt part of an exalted little family.

RUDE INTERRUPTIONS

Six days later I was back in the real world, shivering against the cold in a wooden lean-to, covering Derbyshire v. Durham at Chesterfield. I'd been incorporated into the *Telegraph*'s cricket-reporting team, and it was my first assignment as a full-time sportswriter. The box was populated by an assortment of people: a bloke in corduroys from the *Guardian*, a young upstart from the Sunderland *Echo*, a whiskery chap who said he had been the Derby *Evening Telegraph*'s cricket correspondent for the last twenty-nine years, and various agency people. Ray Illingworth, England's new chairman of selectors, on an early season scouting mission, popped in for a few minutes. And then there was a man in a tweed jacket with his unruly hair kept in place affectedly by a tan fedora: Michael Henderson of *The Times*.

Henderson had been on the circuit for a few years and I knew him well. We sometimes had a drink after matches I'd played in and I admired his writing style, with its mix of witty observation, bombast and artistic reference. He was an opera buff who made regular pilgrimages to Vienna to hear his beloved Wagner. He was an entertaining press-box companion, becoming apoplectic at players' hapless efforts. 'Oh, what infernal tripe, Malcolm!' he'd exclaim, when the fast bowler had sent down his third wide long hop in a row. 'Come, come, Daffy, keep your legs together, you goon!' after DeFreitas had misfielded one. He carried on in this vein throughout a run-filled day, dominated by the hefty stroke play of Durham's Mark Saxelby.

I was absorbed in the play and made a few notes in a newly purchased A4 book, before beginning to scribble my report in pencil after tea.

'How much do they want from you?' asked the bloke from the *Guardian*.

'Six-twenty,' I replied.

'Not bad! I've only got three-fifty,' he said, looking a bit cheesed off.

My deadline was 7.30 p.m. Around 7.10 p.m. I began dictating my report to copytakers on the *Telegraph* phone. I was midway through, delivering the line 'Saxelby, trying his luck with Durham after four staccato seasons at Trent Bridge', when Henderson, who was still writing, accosted me.

'Good lord, man, you can't use "staccato" about a person's career!' he said.

'You can,' I hissed, putting my hand over the phone mouthpiece.

'I'm sorry, you can't. Do you know what staccato means?'

I regret to say this caused a vehement exchange of words. Maybe as a career journalist he was feeling vulnerable at the sight of another ex-player breezing into the press box; maybe

I was trying too hard to prove, on my first day in a new job, that I wasn't just restricted to a vocabulary of 'square cuts' and 'jaffas'. But I was affronted at this challenge to my knowledge of music.

'Actually I do,' I said. 'I learned piano to Grade Seven and played the church organ for three years.'

'Hello? ... I can't hear you properly ... What was that about your organs?' burbled the female copytaker in my ear.

'What does it mean, then?' Henderson went on.

'Jumpy, abbreviated,' I said.

'Well, you still can't use it about a player's career.'

'*Helloooo?*' The copytaker again.

'Oh, will you just hold on a minute!' I ranted into the telephone.

'There's no need for that,' she said.

I slammed down the phone. I was getting cross now. 'You *can* bloody use it about a player's career. There's no law about it. Staccato equals jerky. And that's what his performances were like.'

'It's an inappropriate use of language. It's not the right context. "Inconsistent" would be better.'

'I like "staccato".' And so it went on. I just made my deadline.

A little tentative about venturing into the press box on the second day of the match, I fraternised with the Durham players – my former colleagues – before play. But that refuge was soon off limits, too. Durham's new recruit, John Morris, with whom I'd always got on well, strode into the dressing room and started haranguing me for describing his technique as 'lazy' in my report. I sat outside on a bench and stewed.

It took only a week to welcome my career change, though. As a recent retiree I'd been roped in to play for the Duchess of Norfolk's XI against the touring New Zealanders. Not only did my bowling get a hearty tonking, but when I came in to bat at number eleven Umpire Peter Willey, an uncompromising character, said drily, 'Five balls to coom ... if you play well.' I lasted three.

IMMEASURABLE QUALITIES

I quickly adjusted to life behind the boundary rope. Actually, I found it rather enjoyable doing the rounds of county grounds, turning up two minutes before the first ball was bowled rather than two hours, and without the necessary burden of performance. I'd spend much of the day lolling in deckchairs flipping through the papers or chatting to lifetime supporters or the odd player who might be roaming around the ground. I politely declined their invitations into dressing rooms, remembering how protective many individuals were about their private space. I also knew there would be the odd prickly type within, annoyed by something I'd written last week, last month, last year. Sportsmen have elephantine memories.

Most days I didn't think much about work until after tea, when I'd phone the office to enquire about the allocated space for my report. They gave me generous amounts initially – 600 words or more. Quite right, I thought, for a brand-new correspondent so well connected. But as the weeks wore on this gradually declined: 550, 480, 360, 250. I began to take this personally. Was I not writing to the requisite standard? Was there too much waffle? I noticed they tended to cut my best lines at the end of paragraphs. Perhaps I was being too flippant. No one would tell me. You'd phone up for queries twenty minutes after filing, to be told everything was fine. Then you'd read your stuff in the paper and find they'd hacked out what you thought were all your best bits.

Still, the job was immensely pleasurable – being paid to watch cricket, having for fifteen years been paid to play it – and substantially easier than bowling for a living. But it was hard to gauge how I measured up. Your quality as a sportsman is illustrated by figures: the goals you net, the sets you win, the wickets you take. Your quality as a journalist is impossible to define: some think your prose is polished and insightful; others think it's a load of old tosh. There's no 'score'. It's all a matter of opinion. Experienced journalists are accustomed to it: they've had to live with this subjectivity all their working lives. Ex-cricketers used to the blunt truth of match statistics find it harder to handle.

BBC2 continued to cover a few Sunday League matches on which I was invited to commentate. I saw my role as offering tasty little nuggets of information about the players. Things like Peter Hartley of Yorkshire's scratch handicap at golf, and his nickname 'Daisy' – some days 'e does it, some days 'e doesn't. Or Jack Russell's compulsion to drive to the ground listening to the same military march on his car cassette-player every morning. My mum phoned up to say she found my comments interesting, as did my dad, after he'd enquired whether I was eating properly. But it didn't win me my coveted admission into the Test match commentary box. And not every player was favourably disposed to my attempts at viewer-enlightenment. Most county teams listened to the commentary in the dressing room (as opposed to England, who invariably had it turned down) and some were piqued by having an awful shot described as such. One bowler, whom I'd described as having his radar on the blink after he had sent down an assortment of unmitigated dross, approached me aggressively in the car park afterwards. 'Fuck me,' he said. 'I thought you were my mate!'

After a whirlwind romance (we got engaged precisely sixteen days after meeting), I married Tanya in June. Well, it had to be whirlwind: experience told me that the better a girl knew me, the less she was likely to commit to anything. I was an opportunist, as was emphasised by the news, three days before my wedding, that my recent Durham colleagues had been assaulted for 501 not out by Brian Lara. If I'd stuck it out as a pro rather than joining the press corps, I might have exceeded the most expensive bowling analysis of all time – 4 for 362 – by the New South Wales leg-spinner Arthur Mailey in 1926–27.

The summer was dominated by Lara's exploits in county cricket, and the furore surrounding Atherton's pocketful of

dirt. In the past year we'd seen how torrents of tabloid bile –
loud, self-righteous and often based on the flimsiest of evidence – had driven prominent political figures from office.
Now it looked as if it might happen in cricket. A brief
glimpse on TV of Atherton apparently putting something
on the ball incited the mob. The inference was that he was
cheating. 'THE SOILED SKIPPER' headline at the weekend
quickly turned to 'GO' and 'QUIT NOW' on the Monday,
and by the middle of the week virtually everyone was calling
for his head.

This absurdity was based on a ludicrous presumption: that
cricket still occupied the moral high ground and was a
byword for honesty and fair play, and therefore the England
captain should be a paragon of virtue. (In fact, English
cricket sacrificed that status – if it ever possessed it – around
the Bodyline era of the 1930s. England cricket captains were
now no more role models than TV newsreaders.)
Furthermore, the South Africans never complained about
Atherton's antics, and there was no evidence that he had
done anything to the ball. In any case, the hounding of
Atherton assumed he, a specialist batsman, knew what he
was doing. I, an ex-bowler, certainly hadn't a clue. I'd never
applied anything except suncream-laden sweat to a ball in
my life. Then again, maybe that's why I was rarely in the top
fifty in the first-class bowling averages.

Atherton toughed it out and was known as Iron Mike
from then on. With regard to the increasingly ravenous press,
it turned him from a man of few words to a man of practically none, which naturally put the newspapermen's backs up
even more. Whenever anything went wrong – which it did
fairly often – they were gunning for him.

GLASS CEILINGS

The scribes had every right to be outraged by England's performances in the first two Ashes Tests of the 1994–95 winter.

The Australians, under Bobby Simpson, planned thoroughly, and analysed every England player on video. Craftily, as usual, they had England playing in cold, wet Tasmania four days before the first Test in hot, muggy Brisbane. But the England set-up was still run largely by amateurs, and with a bowling attack ravaged by the remorseless demands of county cricket, the team stumbled to Australia more in hope than expectation. Phillip DeFreitas's opening delivery of the first Test, a wide loosener thrashed to the boundary by Michael Slater in the course of making 176, set the tone for the series. The preparation lacked meticulousness. The players did have a few tapes of the Australian players, but initially nothing on which to view them. The story doing the rounds was that team manager M. J. K. Smith had to be dispatched into a Perth shopping mall to buy a video-recorder. England were thumped in the first two Tests, with their nemesis Shane Warne taking twenty wickets.

'The days when Australia used to sledge have long gone, as sledging is a mark of respect,' bemoaned the *Independent*. 'Now all they do is snigger.'

'They are degrading the nation,' wrote the *Express*, supportive as ever.

'No pride, no guts, no contest,' wittered the *Mail*.

Atherton ought to have been issued with a black box recorder so that the authorities back home could at least pinpoint where the latest disaster had occurred, but it wouldn't have done any good. The feckless jobsworths at the TCCB, resembling a battery of chickens clucking over trivialities, were too busy discussing whether to rename themselves the ECB, the UKCB or the GBCB. JOKE might have been more appropriate.

Disillusioned with English cricket, I diversified a little, trying my hand at sports feature-writing. After a December weekend when England's sports teams had been hammered left, right and centre and it appeared likely that Atherton would be presented with a wreath rather than the Ashes at the end of the series, I was contacted by the *Telegraph*'s features editor, Sebastian someone or other. Could I, he asked, do a big piece explaining our lack of sporting prowess for the paper's Hop-Ed page?

'Hop-Ed?'

'*Op*-ed ... opposite editorial. Next to the leader page.'

'OK. How long?'

'Well ... say sixteen hundred words?'

'Wow. Sixteen hundred words. When d'you want it, next week?'

'Today.'

Apart from twenty overs into the wind against Viv Richards in full flow, it was the hardest six hours I've ever worked. Knee deep in faxed articles, reference books and notes from phone conversations, I assembled an argument suggesting our failings were all about attitude. We had individually talented sportsmen – Steve Redgrave, Nick Faldo, Linford Christie – but our teams lacked real desire and ruthlessness. They hoped for success; they didn't crave it. Sport was now a science in many ambitious countries, like Australia, where they had an Institute of Sport and a Cricket Academy. In England it remained predominantly a social activity. The government were paying lip service to the importance of sport, privately treating it as a pointless cul-de-sac. They allowed over twenty thousand playing fields to be sold off.

I bought the *Telegraph* the next morning, to admire my piece advertised prominently on the front page below the masthead: 'Seeds of Defeat: the reasons for British sporting failure'. And on page nineteen there it was, grandly laid out across the whole page under the apt headline: 'WHERE THERE'S NO WILL THERE'S NO WAY'. My byline was in capital letters, though regrettably there was no mug shot next to it.

It was my birthday and I took the tube to Docklands in high expectation of being lauded at the *Telegraph* sports desk Christmas lunch. More than 200 people had gathered at a restaurant in Wapping Lane: writers, columnists, ex-columnists, racing experts, photographers, sub-editors, marketing people, staff from other departments and the odd special guest like Desmond Lynam. I had no idea such a number were required to produce the sports pages. Most were gathered round a table plan to see where they had been seated. This, I discovered, was how journalists gauged their year's performance. It was a ranking system, like the publication of the first-class averages. Your proximity to the sports editor's table indicated how well you were regarded. I was on Table 2. Excellent, I thought, right in his hip pocket. The equivalent of top ten in the national bowling averages. In line for a pay rise. I'd meet some interesting people at lunch – John Motson perhaps, whom I'd seen at the bar, or Daley Thompson, who wrote a column. But then I noticed that the tables had been numbered in reverse order. The sports editor's was Table 22, at the front near a small rostrum. Mine was in the corner at the back. I was seated next to an old bloke who said he was the paper's powerboating correspondent. I learned a lot about the tides in the Bristol Channel, where, apparently, they raced a lot.

After the sports editor's speech, which dwelt mainly on the brilliance of the star writers on the paper, I edged towards his table to show my face. Just as I had distracted him briefly from a conversation with one of those stellar columnists, one of the paper's cricket stringers, cantankerous when he'd had a few, interjected:

'Hughes … I'll tell you something about that bloody Hughes,' he cackled. 'One season he bet me a tenner he'd take thirty wickets at under forty and he lost! Couldn't take thirty wickets at under forty! Crikey!'

I left the function shortly afterwards.

CHAPTER 6 – 1995

FLY ON THE WALL

I spent the early part of 1995 in India, covering England A on their six-week expedition across the subcontinent. The Sussex captain Alan Wells was in charge; the enthusiastic Etonian and former Sussex captain John Rupert Troutbeck Barclay was the manager. At last England were looking to the future, and the team was stacked with fresh-faced lads: Michael Vaughan on his first overseas tour, Nick Knight, Glenn Chapple, Dominic Cork. My wife Tanya, out for a fortnight's holiday, christened them the Fluffy Bunnies. This, I suggested, was largely due to her briefly relishing the company of males who had profusions of thick, glossy hair while living with one who didn't.

Despite their youthful appearance, the England A team exposed numerous frailties in the young Indians' batting and went through the tour unbeaten. Feeling some sympathy towards the Indians and also badly in need of some exercise, I bowled at a couple of their players in the nets after play. One was a left-handed slogger with a haughty demeanour; the other was a studious blocker with acne. I couldn't see either of them making it. Ten years later, the former, Sourav Ganguly, was captain of his country and had made 10,000 one-day international runs. The latter, Rahul Dravid, has a better Test batting average (57.86 at the time of writing) than the maestro Sachin Tendulkar.

With these being matches between A teams, the Indian Test grounds were mostly deserted. You were free to stroll around, which I did, filming the play from different vantage points with a camcorder I'd brought to make video diaries of the tour. I interspersed crudely filmed match action with player interviews, shot in quirky locations like the roofs of stands, and any local colour I could find. This included near accidents involving the team bus, a tiny twelve-year-old boy ferrying mountains of curry, noodles and nans into the dressing room for lunch, and a scoreboard spelling Middlesex's Paul Weekes 'Poll Vicks'. I also caught on film a large rat scuttling across the dressing-room floor in Delhi, and the attendant shouting, 'Don't worry, it's one of our members.'

Being young, most of the players were willing but uninspiring interviewees. Fortunately, John Barclay, a keen fisherman known to everyone as Trout, was priceless. When I asked him what he thought about the flighty Vaughan giving his wicket away for 20 in Madras, he said, 'He batted like a recently stocked rainbow trout: full of promise but falling for the first imitation, however inexpertly presented, that came along.' Barclay was breathlessly effusive about everything from the smelly accommodation in Ahmedabad ('I've never had buffalo grazing by a hotel pool before. Fascinating creatures!'), to the pitiable dribble of water from the dressing-room showers ('Well, I say, at least we've got a roof over our heads!'), to the players' competition to cultivate the best beard ('What fun! I'm afraid mine's rather pathetic, don't you think? More like a dirty mark. But Johnno's, by golly! He looks like Merlin!'). Trout was so perpetually effervescent it seemed only a matter of time before his head blew off.

Most evenings, having phoned through my match report, I reviewed the camcorder tapes, structured them into a little travelogue and recorded what I thought were humorous little voice-overs. I thought I was Michael Palin. These were mailed back to England to be properly produced and incorporated onto the video magazine *Cover Point*. This was a comprehensive monthly round-up of world cricket, featuring match action from the various international networks and profiles and interviews of new players, all put together in a rambling family house in Streatham. It had only about 1700 subscribers, but one of these was Steve Waugh, who pronounced it an invaluable research tool for making Australia invincible. As usual, we British were, this time inadvertently, making their task easier.

BOBBING ABOUT

I hoped my video diaries might get a rather larger audience when I took them to the BBC in April. I suggested producing the same kind of thing during the county season for *David Gower's Cricket Monthly*, the magazine show the Beeb had been obliged to create as part of the new TV contract. I'd roam around the country filming play and capturing local idiosyncrasies: the lament about the aphid epidemic over tea and flapjacks in the ladies' pavilion at Worcester; Big Geoff, the Derbyshire fanatic, sitting with his lumberjack shirt open to the navel in a chill wind supping a morning pint; spectators filing past the memorabilia in the Trent Bridge museum comparing Larwood's and Hadlee's bowling boots. Sort of *That's Life* meets *The Antiques Roadshow*.

'Nice idea,' said the programme editor. 'But no.' He did, however, hire me as a freelance reporter for Saturday's *Cricket Focus*.

Initially this was just a job writing and presenting scripts for county round-ups. This was a longer process than I'd expected it to be, taking three hours in an editing suite to cut action from various matches into a three-minute 'package'. Then I'd be dispatched to a tiny, airless booth like you used to get at seventies peepshows, to record my voice-over. Whole county matches were usually crammed into thirty-second chunks.

Still, they realised I was reasonably trustworthy, so I was invited to do the same, live, on *Grandstand*. This was great for two reasons. First, it was good to work on a programme that, back then, still had a point. The BBC maintained a decent sporting portfolio: Premiership football (*Match of the Day*), Test cricket, rugby union and league, Formula One, horseracing, golf and boxing. If you wanted to watch the major events, you knew where to find them. Second, TV Centre was an easy five-minute cycle-ride from my house. Finding the *Grandstand* studio was not so easy, though. It was hidden deep in the interior of TV Centre, which, just like that other BBC nerve-centre Broadcasting House, is a disorientating labyrinth of corridors and staircases. Signposting, clearly undertaken by the same people who formulated the South Circular, was terrible. There was Spur-this, Ramp-that, the sinister-sounding Dept 5024 and erratic lifts that seemed to stop at floors that didn't exist on the layout by Reception.

I was soon commissioned to film some player interviews for the Gower programme, and was amazed at the number of people required to record these. Cameraman, sound man, sparks, producer – who did little except carry the camera tripod – and assistant producer, who did even less. BB (Before Birt) the BBC motto on location was: 'Never Knowingly Understaffed'.

I gradually learned the cardinal rule of interviewing – that is, not making the questions longer than the answers – and even suggested a few personalities for the show myself. My old school acquaintance Hugh Grant, for instance. He and I could reminisce about our seventh-wicket stand of 19 for Latymer Upper against Alec Stewart's school, I said. The editor liked the idea (I bet I'd have had an even larger production crew for that item) but then poor old Hugh was caught in his car with Divine Brown, leaving me to fathom the most tactful way to approach him for the first time in eight years. ('Hello Hugh, remember me? That's right: the bloke who made you field third man both ends and never gave you a bat or a bowl. Listen ... so sorry about the blow-job thing, but would you be able to turn up at Lord's next Thursday for an interview for the David Gower programme? You can bring Elizabeth along if you like; show solidarity. I promise we won't talk about hooking and pulling.') I didn't make the call. Well, he had contributed only three runs to our partnership anyway.

The BBC still had the Test match rights (in a £60 million, four-year deal with Sky) and I was close to getting my voice on a Test match broadcast, on account of chatting rather too loudly with a spectator next to the BBC effects mike. One lunchtime I was invited into the commentary box to watch England's Rugby World Cup quarter-final in South Africa. They were 19–22 down to Australia with Boycott saying, 'They'll niver catch 'em, you know.' When England drew level he was still dismissive. As Rob Andrew's winning drop goal went over, Tony Lewis and David Gower were jumping up and down ecstatically. Boycott could only grumble – 'Ay, well, they won't beat New Zealand.' The most irritating thing about Boycott is he's (almost) invariably right.

The BBC's Test match coverage was pretty basic. They had half a dozen cameras, and Boycott and his car key, which he stuck in the pitch to test for moisture; except before a one-day match at Headingley where he was told not to by a jobsworth who didn't recognise him. 'Ee, you're about as mooch use as a chocolate mouse,' Boycott barked at the man. He was still smarting from being shunned as England's batting coach. 'I wrote them a nice, detailed programme,' he had said, 'but when it came to paying for it, they didn't want to know. So they've got John Edrich. He was a damn fine player but he never said 'owt.'

Sky were altogether more progressive. They had snapped up the recently retired Botham on a long-term contract – about twenty years, judging from the satisfied smile on his face – and had been wowing a small percentage of the nation with stump cams, stump mikes and especially 'Spinvision'. First introduced from the Caribbean during Australia's conquering of the West Indies, this illustrated with amazing clarity the ball revolving dizzily out of Shane Warne's hand. 'I'm glad they didn't have it in my day,' the former England off-spinner Vic Marks said. 'It would've just showed the ball coming out straight on. I would have got carted everywhere.'

SUPERSUBS

County cricket was a bit like the BBC, pottering along at its own pace, almost oblivious to the real world. This was both its strength and its weakness. There remained a genteel air about county games, the slow meander of matches accompanied by the polite clapping of Tupperware Man acting as a soothing antidote to the hurly-burly of modern life. The system unearthed few really good players, but when it did and they were finally selected for England, they turned up to a Test match knackered. The eighteen counties played a combination of four-day and three-day matches, often with a one-day match lumped in the middle. This was exhausting enough, without the better players trying to fit in some Test cricket as well. That summer Michael Atherton captained England and opened the batting in six Tests and three one-day internationals against the West Indies, but he was still required to play twelve County Championship matches (and eighteen one-dayers) for Lancashire. No wonder his back started to play up.

Warwickshire, adventurous rather than particularly talented, were the dominant team. Their captain Dermot Reeve's bare-faced cheek dovetailed with Bob Woolmer's more scientific approach. Woolmer rigorously tested each player, mentally and physically, videoed their batting techniques and timed their run-ups to the nanosecond. He constantly varied his methods, in contrast to the recently deposed England coach, Keith Fletcher, who, though a good judge of talent, rarely varied the same tried and tested warm-up routine. Woolmer was the Philips of cricket: simply years ahead. Or maybe it was just that everyone else was aeons behind.

Influenced by the traditionalist E. W. Swanton and his heir apparent Christopher Martin-Jenkins, the *Daily Telegraph* still gave the county game extensive coverage. Even a meaningless early season fixture like Cambridge University against Lancashire was granted generous space. I did the rounds: Fenners, Stockton, Canterbury, Nottingham, Hove, Edgbaston,

Chester-le-Street. Excellent for travelling expenses (thirty pence a mile), though not so good if the pitch was dodgy and the match finished early, as you didn't get paid for unused days.

Armed with my thesaurus, I took my writing seriously. Swanton himself had written me a nice letter after the India tour saying he'd enjoyed my match reports containing local colour as 'cricket is not played in a vacuum'. Encouraged, I spent most days sitting among the spectators, sampling the atmosphere. The moans, the groans, the post-lunch torpor, the blind nostalgia, the regular bemusement, the odd bit of irony, the occasional whiff of excitement (a player making his debut, a rogue dog on the field, a different sort of Battenberg for tea in the pavilion). It was like living in an Alan Bennett play. I roamed the boundary, gossiping with the players I knew, absorbing titbits about incidents or new recruits, while trying to keep a respectful distance. Occasionally I bought the less wary ones a beer after play. I laboured over my reports, trying to work in little details. I thought I understood the importance of writing to a specified length and keeping my language simple. I reckoned without the pedantry of one *Telegraph* sub, a fully paid-up member of the Apostrophe Protection Society. He seemed to pride himself on never being satisfied with the standard, length, subject, spelling or punctuation of anyone's material. A writer's copy was unrecognisable after he'd been at it, and my heart sank whenever I made a check call to the sports desk and he answered it.

'What's a "bandy-kneed stance"?' he'd ask.

'Well ... bow-legged,' I'd reply.

'So say "bow-legged" then.'

'It sounds rather rude.'

'Not as rude as "bandy-kneed", and that's not even grammatically correct, as is the case with a lot of your copy,' he said. 'Why don't you come into the office for a day? You might learn something.'

I did as he suggested. After all, the *Telegraph* was reputed to have the best sports section in Fleet Street. John Major swore by it, though I think Roy Hattersley swore *at* it (his beloved Yorkshire were having a rough time). It certainly gave cricket more time and space than anyone else. I was expecting furious activity when I arrived in the department one morning for some subbing experience. What I encountered instead in a large, open-plan office, was a game of coin bowls. Several of the sub-editors were on their hands and knees by the photocopier, under which one had bowled the jack, a 5p piece. Another sub's 10p was currently in pole position, nestling a couple of inches away, while yet another was noisily claiming his latest roll had been unfairly intercepted by a table leg. The football editor was trying to arbitrate as the third player lined up his final throw. Ringing phones remained unanswered.

'Bollocks!' the thrower exclaimed, when his coin pulled up short of the target.

'Wheball didn't allow for the virgin weave under Luscombe's seat!' proclaimed a fourth sub, the self-appointed commentator.

The deputy sports editor was sighted coming back from morning conference and they all hastened back to their desks. I was introduced to everyone, and seated at a free computer terminal. The screen was blank and not responding. It emerged that the machine had been violated by someone after he'd been asked to re-edit a rugby story for the third time. It was unusable until new components, only now available in Nigeria, had been sourced.

Having found one that worked, I was shown how to access news stories from the wires and cut them to fit particular slots on the page. I remained for the rest of the day, editing an assortment of little items, and returned on several subsequent afternoons. I was amazed at the number of cumbersome intros and cliché-ridden material constantly landing in the system, as well as the sheer volume of stories pouring out of every sporting orifice. On the Friday there was a contest to find the longest opening sentence. One totalling 121 words was the clear winner.

Most days that week I subbed a few stories, wrote the odd headline and fielded various complaints from journalists angry that their story had been cut, didn't have enough prominence or was missing its photo-byline. One even complained that his photo-byline made him look a bit jowly and couldn't we use a picture of him in his younger days. During the evening shift there were regular laments from football reporters, along the lines of: 'How am I supposed to get six goals, three sendings off and the quotes into a hundred and twenty words?'

The subs had one aim in mind: to avoid being allocated the dreaded Sport in Brief. This task, known as SIBS, involved collating the minutiae of golf scores in tin-pot overseas tournaments, ice-hockey results, table tennis, skiing and curling and sundry other detritus. It was the journalistic equivalent of emptying the bins. Last one in usually got landed with it.

Journalists I knew talked about sports editors as cantankerous ogres storming about the office exclaiming, 'You international piece of dogshit!' or 'Rendall wouldn't be able to recognise his penis if it had bunting on it!' and scrunching painstakingly designed page layouts into little balls and tossing them in the bin. But the *Telegraph* sports editor, David Welch, seemed a smiley, mild-mannered chap often conspicuous by his absence. Most days he was out lunching with sporting bigwigs or favoured columnists. He must have thought I was OK, as he agreed to a monthly column, player profiles whenever I wanted to offer them, and attendance at three of the summer's Tests as a colour writer. Hotel expenses and all. I was supplied with a company Tandy – a basic laptop to file stories. Enthused, I went out and bought a new thesaurus and a tin of orange paint. The latter I used to write favourite words I was intending to get into my copy on my study wall. 'Feckless', 'Luddite' and 'moron' all fitted easily into critiques of English cricket. Inviting friends to paint their favourites complicated the issue a bit. There was 'Leopardstown' (from James Brown, editor of *Loaded* magazine) and 'Floccinaucinihilipilification' (Derek Pringle), which not only stumped me but took up most of the remaining wall space.

'But what does it mean?' I asked, unable to find it in a dictionary.

'Estimating something as worthless,' he said. 'Like my contract with the *Independent*.'

I was feeling good about myself. Happily married and having just moved into a new house, I was earning on two fronts, my status was rising and my diary was full. With Tanya's encouragement and ideas, I had made an effective conversion from cricketer to journalist. There was no going back, emphasised by former playing colleagues and adversaries now addressing me as the more formal 'Simon' rather than the more familiar 'Yozzer' (anything was better than the irritated 'Christ *Hughes*!' from irked Middlesex supporters). 'Mmm, nice wheels!' they'd say as I parked my brand-new black BMW 323i alongside their Peugeots and Vauxhalls. I didn't admit that it was Tanya's.

People asked if I missed playing. I didn't. Fifteen years' bowling on the county circuit is quite enough to satisfy your competitive urges and render your knees a mass of scar tissue and floating bone particles; and while the mickey-taking banter in the dressing room is entertaining, it does eventually become a bit predictable. Life moves on, and you're stimulated by new challenges, such as the chance to reinvent yourself as a grown-up.

DEFLATIONARY TACTICS

The radio was on in the background one morning as I was flicking through the papers. It was a discussion about sportswriting on 5 Live. My ears pricked up. They were debating who was better qualified to cover sport: the career journalist or the ex-player. I recognised the voice of my sports editor, David Welch, arguing that it was healthy to have a mix. Michael Henderson, he of the Staccato Wars, said it depended on who the ex-players were. Some were good scribes, like

Mike Selvey and Mark Nicholas, and some weren't. 'Simon Hughes can't write,' he said disparagingly. 'He was a very poor player and he's an *execrable* writer.' I looked up the heavily emphasised 'execrable' in the dictionary: 'abhorrent; loathsome; of very poor quality'. Thanks.

I was not alone: Henderson also denounced Vic Marks, cricket correspondent of the *Observer*, as 'an embarrassment, palpably out of his depth'. But, after airing similar sentiments in a magazine, it was the third time Henderson had belittled my literary efforts in public. His outburst deserved a dignified, mature response. Better still, it deserved no response at all. I could still hold my head up high. Retaliation was just a sign of insecurity and all that.

So I let his tyres down. Well, actually, it was only one tyre, though by the time the story had done the rounds of the Trent Bridge press box I had whipped off all the wheels and left his car on blocks. As it turned out, that would have been preferable for all concerned, as then he wouldn't have tried to drive it to the ground. He didn't notice the flat back wheel as he set off down the road from the hotel, so caused considerably more damage than I had initially. I received a £200 bill and a stern written warning from David Welch that this was no way for correspondents to behave. Fair enough. There could have been a serious accident. But it didn't deter me from attempting to present Henderson with a car jack at the Cricket Writers' dinner. I was lucky he didn't try to hit me over the head with it. I was later to discover that to be lambasted by Henderson provided admittance to an exclusive club.

So I'd got the 'I've Been Hendo-ed' T-shirt. And after a week in Pakistan covering England's A tour during the autumn of 1995, I was for the first time a properly equipped sports journalist: I had the notebook, the dictaphone, the laptop, the contacts book, the current *Wisden*, the four-coloured biro and, most important of all, the Book of Blank Receipts. Journalists come in many forms: fat, thin, tall, short, lazy, industrious, perceptive, blind, heartless, sympathetic (rare), modest, conceited, educated, ignorant. Some are motor mouths; others are silent assassins. Most, in love or hate, are committed to their work. Very few are well paid, so expenses are their lifeblood. Ingenuity is the name of their game.

In addition to their hotel and travelling expenses, most sportswriters receive a daily allowance when they're on the road, to cover food, drink, taxis, etc. Mine at the time was forty pounds, but you didn't get it up front. You had to supply receipts to the office to claim it back. Now, the problem in Pakistan was the insanely cheap price of everything: a rickshaw to the ground was the equivalent of 50p, including tip; lunch – a curried vegetable slosh and chapattis – was 30p; a three-course evening meal, including as much lime and soda as you could force down (alcohol not being available in hotels), cost the grand sum of £2.80. Surprising as it may sound, it was impossible to get the waiters to amend the 37-rupee bill to 137. There was no alternative: it was straight down to a stationer's at the local market in Rawalpindi for a variety of cash-receipt books (8p each). For a small fee (10p), waiters or local journalists could be persuaded to fill in a few of these for amounts more in keeping with meals at home. Then at least you could reclaim most of the forty pounds you'd been pledged. Obviously, it was important to use the receipts in random order, and from different books, or the paper's accountants would pull you up for your blatant transparency. The Cricket World Cup was to be staged in Pakistan the year after that, and once word got round the press that I was in possession of reams of blank receipts, I was inundated with requests. I sold them on at a quid a go.

The cricket in Pakistan on the A tour was competitive, with every local kid trying to tear in and bowl like Waqar and Wasim or moola it over midwicket like Inzamam. It provided some entertaining match write-ups, superseded only by the entertainment in trying to file them back to the *Telegraph* from my new computer. The hotel phone sockets were either in some hopelessly inaccessible position like behind a fitted wardrobe or a lethal-looking assembly of naked wires. Connecting to England would clearly be a matter of life or death. One day, having tried to send from various people's rooms for the best part of two hours – keeping several players awake past midnight – I went to reception in despair. The man took me into the telephone operating room, basically a riot of copper wire floor to ceiling. Apparently picking one at random, he joined it to a terminal on my computer with something resembling jump leads. He pressed a few buttons, and, bingo, the copy was winging its way to England. Alas, it didn't make it into the paper: that day they'd run out of space.

With the lack of alcohol and the problems filing copy, the evenings in Pakistan were relatively solitary. Luckily there was some good stuff on hotel telly. You could choose between English Premiership football, Australian cricket, *Dallas*, kung fu movies, *Inspector Morse* and the Saudi Arabian weather forecast. This featured a sheikh in a headdress being Michael Fish. He gabbled away in Arabic for several minutes. It would have been intriguing to know what he'd said, since the weather maps never featured anything other than baking temperatures and cloudless skies.

RECORDING ERRORS

I scooped my first exclusive in Pakistan. My visit coincided with the arrival of Imran and Jemima Khan to begin their married life. A week after they'd returned to Lahore from their English nuptials (and acreage of press coverage) I visited Imran – a co-columnist on the *Telegraph* – at the cancer hospital he founded, and was invited round to meet Jemima. I would be the first media guest in their marital home.

Demonstrating my journalistic naïvety, I didn't take a notebook or a tape-recorder. There was a reason for this: no one had specified whether my visit constituted a formal interview. I felt that the presence of recording device/notebook would seem presumptuous and intrusive, and they might be a bit guarded as a result. I memorised a list of questions, rehearsing them to myself as I rang the doorbell of the relatively modest (by Goldsmith standards) villa by a busy main road. We sat and had tea, and Imran talked boorishly about his cancer hospital and belligerently about ball tampering while Jemima looked radiant and smiled sweetly. When Imran left us alone to check on his ill father her cut-glass accent belied an alert, independent mind.

After we'd said goodbye, I sat in the back of my waiting Ambassador taxi and furiously wrote down everything that I could remember from the conversation, not knowing which of it (if any) was on the record, a concept with which I'd always had a lot of trouble anyway. I often thought that if a person had to say that such and such was off the record, they ought not to be saying it at all. Infuriatingly, of course, these little morsels are often the most interesting items in a conversation. From these random recollections scrawled in the dark on a scrap of hotel notepaper I painstakingly assembled a 1500-word piece for the *Telegraph*'s feature pages and sent it via the hotel telephonist's Heath Robinson arrangement. It was immediately rejected by the features editor who said it was too bland. Offended, I faxed it to my wife Tanya for a sympathetic opinion. 'It's like a piece in *Hello!*,' she said. Eventually a third rewrite was accepted by the features editor, and after more rejigging in the office it went in the paper with quite a fanfare. It finished with the line: 'If anyone can survive this unusual culture clash, Jemima can.' Eight years later, they divorced.

Here in Pakistan in late 1995 was where England's cricketing future was being fashioned. The architect was Nasser Hussain, an adventurous selection as A team captain, bearing in mind he was born in India and had an anti-establishment reputation. Contrary to expectations, Hussain was a relaxed, approachable leader, who never shirked hard work or responsibility. He played it tough but fair, forged an excellent relationship with the coach John Emburey, and imbued in the other players a determination to succeed in a hostile environment. There were problems with grounds, with light, with umpires, but none swayed England from their primary objective – to win the three-match series – which they achieved 1–0.

In mid-tour there appeared a vision of what Hussain's England would slowly leave behind. Tim Lamb, chief executive of the TCCB, arrived for what was termed a 'fact-finding' week in preparation for England being based in Pakistan during the World Cup in the new year. Lamb and Hussain were Old England and New England juxtaposed. Needless to say, they never particularly got on. Lamb, whose public-school amiability and appearance evoked Morgan Leafy, the hapless Foreign Office hero of William Boyd's *A Good Man in Africa*, exchanged a few pleasantries and shook a few Pakistani hands. He did move mountains, too, but only in the sense of managing to get the schedule of an aerial sightseeing tour of the nearby Himalayas brought forward so he (and I) could get back in time for the start of play in the second A Test. Otherwise, he achieved little. Simultaneously, South African officials were carefully analysing every Pakistani venue and hotel for their team's participation in the World Cup, checking out net facilities, gyms and suitable restaurants. South Africa won all five of their group games in the tournament and lost narrowly to West Indies in the quarter-finals. England, by contrast, were woeful, and soon eliminated.

It was the culmination of an awful winter. At the root of it was a growing rift between the outspoken team manager Ray Illingworth and some key players. As soon as England got to South Africa, Illingworth informed the press that the opening bowler Devon Malcolm 'wouldn't frighten you, let alone the South Africans' and the bowling coach Peter Lever described him as a cricketing 'nonentity'. Malcolm, half fit and lacklustre in practice, didn't help himself, but Illingworth would sometimes spend practice days on the golf course with co-selector John Edrich, leaving captain Mike Atherton to organise nets (and practically everything else as well). The idea that Duncan Fletcher would ever overlook these responsibilities is inconceivable, illustrating how far England have come now. Or perhaps how far they were lagging behind then.

CHAPTER 7 – 1996

SLOW TRANSITION

The most important letter of my life – bearing in mind that I got engaged by fax – arrived on 23 January 1996. On publisher's headed notepaper it began, 'Dear Simon, I am delighted to be able to make you an offer for this book ...' and went on to specify how much (£6000) and how the money would be paid (in three instalments). It was triple what I'd received for writing a diary of Durham's first season, and the royalties of 7¹/₂ per cent on sales of the first 40,000 copies of the paperback seemed irrelevant. I'd have been happy with 40 sales, never mind 40,000. Actually, that's a lie. But the main thing was to get it written. After I'd cracked open a bottle of Spanish champagne.

I wasn't particularly keen on the title – *A Lot of Hard Yakka* ('yakka' is an Aboriginal word for work) – but my mum liked it, and so did the publisher, so I stuck with it. Anyway, it wasn't as naff as some of the titles that were around at the time (remember *Hick and Dilley Circus*?). The content would be the trials and tribulations of my life as a cricketer. People had recently been coming up to me saying how much they'd enjoyed my bowling (not only batsmen), and that I had seemed like a free spirit during my fifteen-year career. But I remembered being mainly consumed by anxiety. I wanted to relay the true feelings of a professional sportsman.

I was inspired by three sources: an article in the irreverent cricket magazine *Third Man* entitled 'Short Pitched Rubbish',

pleading for a really illuminating cricket book as an antidote
to all the superficial ghosted autobiographies; Nick Hornby's
Fever Pitch, which viewed his emotional development
through the prism of football allegiance; and a darker piece
of work, David Frith's *By His Own Hand*, a book exploring
the emotional traumas of cricketers and their suicidal tenden-
cies. By writing my story, I hoped to reveal the uncertainty of
a cricketer's life, and unravel the reasons for my see-sawing
career. If I didn't kill myself in the meantime.

I could still vividly remember my early experiences with
Middlesex – Mike Brearley's limp handshake and Mike
Gatting's bone-crushing one, and the mountains of food he
ate in pre-season training. I put together a synopsis and four
chapters and took it round to three publishing acquaintances. After brief consideration two rejected it, but the third, Ian
Marshall, the author of the *Third Man* article, took it on.

The *Independent* diaries I'd written through the previous
few seasons were invaluable. What they provided, apart from
quirky pay-off lines, was detail. The minutiae of a cricketer's
daily life – the strange routines, unsuitable food and weird
behaviour – are mainly hidden from the public. I wanted to
bring them to life. Sport reveals character, and I'd been in the
privileged position of seeing the greats of the game, warts
and all, from the inside. My opening line summed up my
agenda: 'I haven't set the world alight, but I've hung around
with people who have.' It sounds a simple sentence, but it
took an eternity to conjure up.

While I was mulling over that opening line, I wrote the rest
of the book. It took me about eight months, split between
two winters. Having read that most serious writers have a
daily routine, I fashioned one of my own:

9 a.m.: start work.
11–11.15: tea break.
1–1.45: lunch.
5.30 p.m.: finish work, 2000 words completed.

I never followed it. By the time I'd cleared up breakfast, read the paper, had a coffee and tidied the desk, it was the 11 a.m. tea break. A couple of phone calls, a fiddle on the piano and an argument with the next-door neighbour about excessive noise, and it was time for lunch in a Thai caff. If I started work before 3 p.m., I was lucky. That was on the days when the Cricket World Cup wasn't live on Sky.

I did at least manage to sustain a lesser target of 1000 words a day. It might not sound like much, but when your understanding of language and use of apostrophe's is as erratic as mine, and you're editing and re-editing phrases, trying to find precisely the right word, without sounding as if you'd looked it up, which you usually had, 1000 words can take all day.

(I've just looked at the clock: it's after lunch, of course. Those last two paragraphs have taken forty-five minutes to compose – including a cup of tea and a quick look at England in South Africa on Sky (third Test, 2005). That's a pathetic $3^{1}/_{3}$ words a minute!

Still, it's not as bad as James Joyce. Late one afternoon, a friend found the novelist slumped forlornly across his desk.

'How many words did you write today?' asked the friend, attuned to the writer's moods.

'Seven,' came Joyce's depressed reply.

'Seven! But, James, that's good … at least for you,' the friend encouraged.

'Yes,' Joyce croaked, 'but I don't know what order they go in.'

ALL FOWLED UP

Writing the book was a continuation of my conversion from player to journalist. It gave me a detachment from cricket, forcing me to look more critically at it. In his tactless way, Michael Henderson had been right: one of his beefs was that recently retired ex-players were generally too cosy with the game to be really analytical of it. I wanted to be regarded as a writer who had played cricket rather than a cricketer who could write a bit. It was a subtle but important distinction.

A crucial part of this transition lay on a graphics database at the *Daily Telegraph*: my photo-byline. Currently above my column they used a mug shot of me in a cricket sweater. It looked like a picture out of a county club handbook. It *was* a picture out of a county club handbook. Especially as I was intending to diversify into other sports, it had to be changed, so I took control of the situation. I went to a photo booth in Hammersmith station wearing a checked shirt and inserted £3.50. The results were appalling, not helped by the photographs becoming stuck together in my pocket. Summoning up some courage, I booked my photographer friend Tim and his studio for a morning. I assembled a few casual outfits, had what was left of my hair cut professionally in Chelsea instead of by a dodgy barber in Shepherd's Bush, and practised using Tanya's spare compact (I had a deathly midwinter pallor).

The appointed day arrived. I had slept badly and my eyes felt sore. I looked in the mirror after breakfast. I had the biggest sty outside the Association of East Anglian Pig-farmers. No matter what pose I adopted at the shoot or how much Tim dimmed the lights, I couldn't conceal it. The best of the pictures – the one that the *Telegraph* adopted – still made me look as if I'd had a night on the tiles.

'Well, actually, you always look a bit like that,' said Tim.

The use of the new photo-byline coincided with the launch of 'Sporting Relations', a new series of big Saturday features portraying the influence of a special mentor or coach on a leading sportsman's career. I bragged to the sports editor that, as an ex-cricketer, I could get into the mindsets of other sportsmen. They were always available and open with me.

I decided to start with a humdinger – how Liverpool's wunderkind Robbie Fowler had been influenced by the club's most prolific striker, Ian Rush. They were apparently like father and son. I was keen to analyse the depth and detail of their relationship. I also wanted to work in to the piece a famous copytaking error. The *Daily Star* reporter who had dictated, 'Rush and Hughes make a great strike force,' had been astonished to read in the paper the next day his line had materialised as 'Russian Jews make a great strike force.' I went to considerable lengths to organise interviews with both Rush and Fowler. I spoke to their agents and press officers and coaches. I sent letters and faxes and was finally guaranteed fifteen minutes with Fowler at 12.30 p.m. after training had finished the following Tuesday. Rush would be available for as long as I wanted afterwards.

I felt smug as I boarded an early train from Euston on the scheduled day. I'd gained access to two of the most celebrated names in English football. This would be a groundbreaking double-header. The Rush and Fowler story had, apparently, never been properly told. I soon discovered why.

I took a cab from Lime Street Station to Liverpool's modest training ground in the suburbs. I was in time to see the team playing a match among themselves and then watch Fowler do half an hour's extra penalty practice. The press officer who'd 'set up' the interviews was nowhere to be found. So as Fowler headed towards the changing rooms at the end, I approached him.

'Hi, Robbie. I'm Simon Hughes from the *Daily Telegraph*,' I said confidently. 'Are you OK to do the interview we arranged in a minute?'

'No,' he said, still walking.

'Oh … right … well, shall we do it after you've had a shower?' I said, shuffling alongside him.

'No, I'm not doing it,' he announced truculently, as if he'd just been asked to cut off his testicles for charity. Perhaps no one had warned him I'd be coming.

That was that: seven words, counting 'no' twice and 'I'm' as two. Bearing in mind this was scheduled as a 1500-word article, I had to hope Rush could supply the other 1493.

I grabbed him briefly in the windy car park and he was reasonably chatty, in a rather monosyllabic way; but he was, of course, in a rush. His comments gave me another paragraph.

The vast bulk of the article was supplied by my taxi driver. An Irishman apparently well acquainted with the players, he took me past Fowler's current mock-Tudor house, Fowler's previous mock-Tudor house, Fowler's grandmother's shop, and Fowler's 'pitch', the yard opposite a terraced street in Toxteth where he practised his dribbling as a kid. The taxi driver recounted numerous anecdotes, most of them unprintable. Still, it was thirty-five pounds well spent. He should have given me a picture of himself as well. Then he could have had his photo-byline above the piece instead of mine:

'FOWLER IN A RUSH by Patrick O'Riley of ABC Cars'.

BUMBLING ALONG

It was inevitable that my first serious piece of non-cricket journalism was football-related, bearing in mind the suffocating growth of the 'winter' game, its tentacles entwining themselves around every sporting artery. Ten years earlier, with corpses from Heysel still fresh on the slab, football attendances at an all-time low and Botham and Gower in excelsis, the gap between football and cricket was narrow. Now it was a chasm.

It was June. A Test series (against India) was under way, but the buzz was all around the Euro '96 football tournament. Papers were full of it, with supplements and pull-outs; two comedians, David Baddiel and Frank Skinner, waffled on about it on *Fantasy Football League*; *Loaded* magazine's 500,000 monthly sales were based on its liberal supply of a lad's three basic requirements – football, beer and birds; Chris Evans mentioned footie in every breath on Radio 1 and played the Lightning Seeds anthem ('It's coming home, it's coming home, football's coming home …') ad nauseam. The Lord's Test was halted at one point by the umpires until the hubbub surrounding the drama of England's penalty shootout with Spain in the quarter-final had subsided. Gareth Southgate's penalty miss in the semi against Germany briefly silenced Chris Evans, but it guaranteed Southgate pizzas (and infamy) for life. From that point on the football hype has never abated.

It satisfied a need, even an urge, in an era of instant gratification. It fitted into a modern lifestyle of pre-cooked meals and satellite TV and 'having a good time'. Football also filled the void created by the decline of religion. It provided an allegiance, a loyalty, satisfied a desperate desire for belonging in people's lives. The press conference announcing Alan Shearer's world-record £15 million transfer to Newcastle was attended by more people than went to the first two days of the Lord's Test. England footballers had become the modern rock stars. England cricketers were mere roadies. If that.

But after heading down lots of blind alleys, the TCCB had taken one important turn: they had appointed a professional England coach. David Lloyd, known universally as Bumble after a bouncy, cartoon character with a big nose, was an excellent choice. A man of wide experience, he had been a player, a coach, an umpire, a broadcaster, an after-dinner speaker and presenter of Channel 4's gardening programme *Fruity Stories*. 'I'LL MAKE ATHERTON BLOOMING BRILLIANT' was the headline in the *News of the World* across a picture of him in the shrubbery brandishing a garden fork. He positively fizzed with energy in everything he did. A born motivator, he plastered the dressing room with words in capital letters, like 'COMMITMENT' and 'WIN!', and played recordings of Churchill's speeches and 'Land of Hope and Glory'. He had highlights videos of each player set to music and played them in team meetings to make individuals feel good about themselves. He enthused about his players to reporters in his trademark Accrington burr: 'Alistair Brown, openin' the innin's, woon-day internashionul, 'ome ground. Bottle!' He videoed every ball of the Indian tourists' warm-up games and devised little plans for each of their players. He quickly recruited full-time nutritionists and train-ers. Unfortunately, he didn't have full-time England players.

Atherton had championed the idea of England central con-tracts in his captain's report, but it fell on the deaf ears of the Acfield Committee and was rejected. All the England players were still obliged to play for their counties whenever pos-sible. This would count against them for the awkward series against Pakistan in the second half of the summer.

India, in June and July, was less of an obstacle, but England's success in that series was almost completely over-shadowed by the circus surrounding Dickie Bird's last Test. There were television documentaries, radio programmes, two books, souvenir posters, interviews and farewell dinners for the umpire. He was the one English cricket figure that infil-trated the mainstream. His book later sold a million copies, the profits from which he used to widen the entrance to his car port. 'I joost can't get me new Jaguar in!' he proclaimed to me excitedly. But his quirky chatter betrayed the fact that he was very lonely. You'd often see him dining alone in a fish-and-chip restaurant up the road from Headingley. He was a tragi-comic figure – rather in the mould of his hero Tommy Cooper – who had nothing else to live for apart from cricket. 'If after retirement I plonk myself into a chair and sit in front of the telly, I'll be dead inside twelve moonths,' he said.

Imagining a television scoop for the BBC, I sneaked my camcorder into the Lord's pavilion on the first morning of Dickie's final Test, grabbed a brief word with him as he emerged from the umpires' room and followed him through a standing ovation in the packed Long Room. I was instant-ly apprehended by a steward, taken to see the beak (MCC secretary Roger Knight) and had the film confiscated.

Disaster struck on the third day. The two Indian batsmen, Sourav Ganguly and Rahul Dravid, the youngsters I'd dis-missed as ordinary on an A team tour, had scored 131 and 95, respectively, in their first Test innings. 'You could see the signs then that they were going to be future Test stars,' I lied in a piece for the *Sunday Telegraph*, and waxed lyrical about

Ganguly's magical wrists and Dravid's immaculate technique. Knowing the deadline for the Sunday paper was unfamiliarly early, I assembled the piece by 5 p.m., leaving enough time to check it over. With five minutes in hand, I was poised to send it from my Tandy, when it all disappeared from the screen. I switched off and on a couple of times. Nothing. Not a dickie bird. Now, you know the feeling you get when you realise you've locked yourself out and all the windows are bolted? And the sausages are about to burn. And it's your mother-in-law's house. Yes, that's about it.

I tried to remain calm. I thumped the laptop a few times, dropped it, shouted at it hysterically, poked about inside it, accidentally spilled tea on it. Surprisingly, none of that worked. I was forced to ad lib my piece down the phone, annoying the pricklier writers in the press box who liked complete silence while composing their prose.

BLINDING ADMISSION

June's sporting squeeze meant England's series victory over India went almost unnoticed. At least England v. Pakistan had the stage to itself in high summer. Not the encounter on the field, but the one in the High Court. There Ian Botham was attempting to hook a verbal bouncer from his old adversary Imran Khan into the gallery. Botham, with Allan Lamb, was challenging Imran for depicting him as a racist and accusing him of ball doctoring.

It was an unfortunate diversion for Atherton and Lloyd to have to attend court on the eve of the first Test. It was an intriguing one for me because I had been invited on *Newsnight* to try to explain the case. The prospect of being grilled by Paxman in front of two million people was a little daunting, so at home I scoured newspaper cuttings of the case and rehearsed what I was going to say. I then took an age going through my wardrobe, eventually settling on a favourite blue and white striped shirt by Paul Smith. I looked in the mirror. There was a small bump on the left side of my chin. A zit was developing. The white head was just about visible, and it was starting to make the skin around it feel tight. I tried in vain to coax it out. I squeezed harder. That just made my eyes water and the spot worse.

Sitting in a BBC car, I reassured myself it would be OK. I could sit at an angle to the camera, keeping the spot in shade. The butterflies began as I was led down various BBC corridors by a producer in a headset, treading carefully over the cables radiating across the *Newsnight* studio, where Paxman was sitting leafing through the running order. The general hush was broken by the cameras squeaking across the shiny floor like grotesque daleks, rehearsing their positions.

A woman with a clipboard led me into make-up. 'Mmm,' she said, 'better find you another shirt. That stripy one will strobe badly.'

The make-up girl switched on some bright lights above a large mirror. The spot had become Vesuvius. 'Bashed myself opening the car door,' I said.

'Looks more like you've been squeezing a spot,' the girl replied, and dabbed an astringent lotion on it, before covering it with concealer. The red lump had become a brown lump. A runner brought a plain beige extra-large shirt which billowed round my body like a spinnaker.

I was shown into the green room to sit beside another of the show's guests, an enormous African man in orange tribal dress there to discuss his continent's plight. I introduced myself.

'I'm Bueche Mattress,' the man replied politely.

'Unusual name,' I said. 'What's the origin of it?'

'I made a lot of money selling mattresses in Dar es Salaam,' he said.

Summoned into the studio, I found the blinding spotlights made it awkward negotiating props and cables strewn across the floor. I was ushered to a cheap-looking chrome chair with slightly stained upholstery. Several cameras were pointing at me, slightly to my left. My spot was going to be in full view.

With them on one side and Paxman on the other, I felt like I was about to face a firing squad.

In fact, the interview went surprisingly well. I wasn't distracted by Paxman's necessary but slightly disconcerting habit of looking down at his notes or gazing into the distance, listening to the producer through his earpiece while I was talking. People say men can't multi-task: he was surfing tomorrow's papers, absorbing instructions, following gestures from the floor and performing an interview all at the same time. Gentle pressure on my foot and a winding-up motion under the desk was my cue to stop.

'Excellent, you were absolutely great,' he said afterwards. 'Really good to get some cricket on. The show can be a bit grim sometimes. Anything about old Beefy's going to stop 'em switching off. I can't see him winning this one, though.'

He was right: Botham lost the case. His strength – an unshakeable belief that he is always right – is occasionally his weakness. He always wants the last word. The anecdote I tend to use to illustrate this is the occasion he ordered 'dolecetti' cheese in an Italian restaurant. When the waiter looked blank and I'd twice corrected it to 'dolcelatte', Botham reacted by saying, 'How many bloody Test wickets did you get?' I repeated this story to him a couple of years later in a tour bus after watching *Beef and Lamb in a Stew*, their winter roadshow, at a Guildford theatre. 'D'you know,' I said, 'I've got loads of laughs telling that story about you asking for "dolecetti", and me correcting you, and you asking me how many bloody Test wickets I got. People love it.'

He looked distinctly unimpressed. 'Well, how many bloody Test wickets *did* you get?' he retorted.

AT HOME WITH THE BENAUDS

On the field England's submission to Pakistan was meek. 'They were as solid as eleven jellies in a hurricane,' bemoaned Boycott in the *Sun* after their capitulation at The Oval to lose the series 2–0. They seemed destined to make one step forward and two back. The sense that the English game was still hamstrung by dithering committees was reinforced by the interminable time it took to pass judgement on Ray Illingworth's indiscreet comments about Devon Malcolm in his book. He was eventually fined £2000 by the disciplinary committee of the TCCB, which comprised thirteen jobsworths. The trial of the Kray twins had a jury of only twelve.

I touched on this theme more than once as I strived to complete my book, *A Lot of Hard Yakka*, by the November 1996 deadline. I hadn't set out to be overly critical of the blazers that ran the game; I just wanted to tell the story. But I found a recurring theme of parochialism and jobsworthiness. This in-depth analysis of the last fifteen years also revealed another thing: my own astonishing lack of discipline and professionalism as a cricketer. At least I now understood why my captains became so infuriated and my father had no hair left.

I was lucky that my lifestyle – a wife in a highly paid job allowing me a cushy winter – gave me the scope to complete the project. And when I say cushy, I mean cushy. To the question in a national Census survey which asked how many hours a week one devoted to one's main employer, I answered, 'Eight'. This amounted to one piece a week for the *Daily Telegraph* in the off-season. It was a level of output that nudged me only fractionally nearer the sports editor's table at the department's Christmas lunch. I had escaped the witless banter of the powerboats correspondent, only to be landed with the chap who covered amateur golf, who by 4 p.m. was somewhat inebriated and suffocating me with his tannin breath and his exhortations to follow the Walker Cup.

I worked from home until Christmas, then spent eight weeks in Australia and New Zealand over Christmas and into 1997. I'd call it 'research', since I did attend two Tests of the Australia–West Indies series mindful of the upcoming Ashes. Most people would call it 'holiday'. After testing the sand on various different Sydney beaches for a week, I turned up at the Melbourne Cricket Ground and made a beeline for the Channel 9 commentary box, suspended from the roof of the stand at the members' end. I'd been invited by Richie Benaud, 'if you're passing Simon', having again worked with him on one or two televised county games during the summer. I think he'd been quite taken with me, because I had done something on air that people warned me not to do: I had asked him a direct question.

'What d'you think makes a good captain?' I said to Richie, watching Somerset's bowling being plundered to all parts at Taunton.

Far from being put out, he was sprightly in response. 'Captaincy is ninety per cent luck and ten per cent talent,' he said. There was a pregnant pause as the camera alighted on Somerset's ailing skipper Andy Hayhurst. 'But don't try it without that ten per cent.'

As commentary boxes go, Channel 9's was an institution, with a broadcast trendsetting reputation (the cartoon duck walking solemnly off when a batsman is out for nought, for instance) and an assembly of the most distinguished – and, Benaud excepted, most outspokenly biased – commentators in the game.

Play was in progress and hearing Tony Greig's strident tones describing some lamentable bit of batting, I entered the box rather gingerly. Benaud was, as usual, hunched over his laptop. Ian Chappell was chatting to Bill Lawry in the summariser's seat. I tapped Benaud lightly on the shoulder. He turned round, smiled when he recognised me and rose to shake my hand.

'Morning, Simon,' he said, 'so glad you could make it.'

Within a minute we were immersed in the subject of flippers (the spin bowler's version, not the frogman's), a ball had been rustled up and Benaud was going through a leg-spinner's complete repertoire, flicking deliveries across the box at Chappell, who, as an occasional leggie himself, enthusiastically flicked them back. One narrowly missed

Greig's head as he was commentating on a wicket. 'That's the Ear, Nose and Throat specialist Curtly Ambrose with another Australian vectum!' he exclaimed. Then, turning to Lawry, he added with undisguised glee, 'Gee, this current bunch of Aussie selectors couldn't pick your nose, Bull.'

For some months, Benaud had been encouraging me to produce some TV features on the cricketing themes I wrote about – reverse swing, leg-spin, captaincy. 'You really must do it,' he'd said; 'it'd be absolutely mavellus.' He'd even offered Tanya and me dinner at his Sydney apartment to discuss it. We eagerly accepted.

You'd expect the *éminence crème* to have a luxury pad in some exclusive Sydney suburb with security gates, white marble floors to match his jackets, expensive mahogany furniture, a garden with floodlit palms and a glistening pool. But no. Chez Benaud is nothing like that. The flat is several floors up in the type of unspectacular seaside apartment block normally found in Eastbourne. The front door is secured by half a dozen locks, and opens into a long, plain hall adorned with a few old cricket scenes. It leads to a functional sitting room furnished with two simple settees and a glass coffee table in between. There is a cabinet with sliding glass doors in which knick-knacks and a few books are displayed. There is no music playing and the only sound is the hum of the V8 engines rumbling along the coast road below. The enclosed balcony does have stupendous views across Coogee Beach and out to sea, but it doesn't encourage Richie downstairs for an early morning dip.

'Why?' I asked.

'I can't swim,' he said, not joking.

Richie shares the flat with his immaculately presented English wife Daphne, a former assistant of E. W. Swanton, who also acts as a sort of PA, organising their diaries. During the day a secretary comes in to deal with correspondence and filing. This is very important, because Richie is an information junkie, never knowingly under-prepared. This probably stems from his 1950's apprenticehip as a crime reporter. He rises most mornings at six to begin sifting through the bombardment of faxes, emails, cuttings and letters, keeping himself up to date with all the cricket news and gossip around the world.

After a glass of his favourite Chardonnay, he and Daphne took us out to dinner. It was a simple Thai restaurant just back from the seafront. We squeezed round a small square table, and over dim sum (which for some reason they call dim sim in Australia) I asked him how he started in TV.

'While all my 1956 Australian team-mates went round Europe after the tour of England, I stayed behind for three weeks to study television,' he said with that famous sideways glance, developed because, as a model pro, he wanted to keep his television earpiece out of sight. 'They set me up a special course and I experienced everything – drama, news, entertainment, an outside broadcast at Newbury with Peter O'Sullevan. My first time behind the mike was the 1960 South African tour for BBC Radio, then I did the England–West Indies series for TV in 1963.'

From then on he was a permanent fixture at the BBC, until he transferred to Channel 4 when they won the Test match rights in 1999. So, when *he* says Shane Warne is one of the best leg-spinners the game has ever seen, it means something. And when *he* suggests you go away and make some TV features about cricketing skills because *he* would be interested in them, you don't need a second invitation.

EARLY WARNING SYSTEM

First, though, I decided to investigate the Warne phenomenon, given that the Australians were due in England the following summer. So, after a few days' testing the sand on some Melbourne beaches, I borrowed a friend's bike and cycled the twenty kilometres from his place to Warne's home opposite Brighton beach in the city's southern suburbs.

This was more like a superstar's home: a grand mock-Victorian villa with panoramic sea views, surrounded by high walls and security gates. I could just make out through the hinges a couple of BMWs and a Maserati on the forecourt, not to mention a blonde sunning herself on the pool deck. The pizza-delivery bike parked outside rather ruined the overall image.

I pressed the button on the intercom.

'What's up, mate?' barked Warne through the speaker. 'Forget your helmet?'

'Huh?' I grunted.

'Aren't you the bloke from Speedy Pizzas?'

'No … I'm Simon Hughes, from the *Daily Telegraph*. I've been trying to arrange an interview with you through Austin, [Warne's agent]. Could you spare a few minutes?'

'Look, I'm sorry mate. I'm a bit busy right now,' said Warne. 'Er, you gonna be at the Adelaide Test?'

'Yes, actually.'

'Well, look, we'll hook up there, no problems.'

This was a significant advance on my recent attempt to try to interview Curtly Ambrose after breakfast in a Melbourne hotel.

'Hi, Curtly,' I said brightly, 'mind if I talk to you for a minute?'

'What about?' he said sternly.

'Your fantastic spell at the MCG.'

'Probably not,' he said.

'OK … how about later?' I ventured.

'Definitely not,' he replied.

I took these rejections to heart: I thought my ex-professional-cricketer status would bypass players' animosity towards the media. In fact, they treated me like any other press pipsqueak.

I pursued Warne hard – out of fascination as much as professionalism. He was completely modern – earrings, clean shaven, a bottle-blond pin-up – and yet he was a throwback, employing old-fashioned cricketing sleight of hand to spin balls in different directions. He even had what he called a 'pickpocket' delivery that spun into the stumps behind the batsman's legs. A light-fingered maestro had subverted the pectoral macho man in Australian bowling psyche.

I was rewarded. After a couple of reminders Warne was as good as his word, padding down two flights of hotel stairs in his socks to chat to me in my room prior to the Adelaide Test. He was an effusive interviewee, chatting away in unguarded fashion as if he'd known me for years, rabbiting on about his art, and the importance of beating the Poms to every Australian, and the vast influence on his life of the former Aussie leg-spinner Terry Jenner.

I would soon witness the potency of their relationship. Earlier that day I had wheedled my way into Australia's net practice through my friendship with their coach Geoff Marsh and captain Mark Taylor. There were four bowlers in Net 1: Glenn McGrath, Shane Warne, me and a fat old bloke lobbing up innocuous leggies.

'Who's that fat old bloke lobbing up innocuous leggies?' I asked Taylor, who was standing near by.

'That's the Spin Doctor Terry Jenner. You *can't* talk about him like that!' said Taylor, defensively. Whereupon Matthew Hayden launched a Jenner offering over a distant wall. 'Well, perhaps you can,' added Taylor.

Later, when Taylor batted, Jenner (who, truth be told, could still land a useful leg-break) bowled a couple of deliveries, then explained to Warne that he was bowling from a bit wider on the crease to the left-hander to create a bit of an angle. 'I used to do it when I played against Sobers,' said Jenner. 'You might get a miscue or an edge against the West Indies lefties.' Warne practised this variation for a while, until he was happy with it.

The next day in the first innings of the fourth Test, Warne was on in the seventeenth over. He went wider of the crease fourth ball to the left-handed Brian Lara, who, slightly disorientated, could only ladle a simple catch to mid-on. In his next over, he tried the same ploy to the left-handed

Shivnarine Chanderpaul, who edged the ball to slip. Warne rushed up the pitch to be engulfed by excited colleagues, then turned towards the radio box in the pavilion where Jenner was commentating and nodded acknowledgement. 'Marvellous bowling by Warne. He planned for that,' said Jenner on air, betraying a satisfied smile.

Warne's bowling turned the match and the series. The West Indies' fifteen years of world domination were well and truly over.

A GRAND EXPERIENCE

My cushy winter hadn't finished. A week after arriving back from Australia I was on a flight to Brazil, again with Tanya (her client paid for it). I was going to write a colour piece about the Brazilian Grand Prix focusing on the revamped Jordan team, whose sponsors (Benson and Hedges) she represented. Afterwards we'd tack on five days in Rio, all expenses paid. Accompanying us were four 'journalists' from *Loaded* magazine – the editor and founder James Brown, his assistant Martin Deeson, two other writers and a snapper. They had also been flown out to do a story about Jordan, though their primary intent was to get loaded in Rio. We were all Formula One virgins.

The Brazilian race was held in sprawling São Paulo, the world's second-largest city, a vast concrete metropolis of apartment blocks, endless seven-lane highways and flyovers but no obvious landmarks. It's like six Birminghams knocked together, with cuter women. The circuit, Interlagos, is on the southern fringes of the city, built into its one and only hill. The first thing that hits you at the track, even before you've stepped out of your minibus, is the noise: the scream of the engines, punctuated by the pop-pop-pop of the turbochargers, rends the air. The sound is so much more intense than it appears on TV. It makes your whole body tingle. The cars were buzzing round the track in clusters, testing aerodynamic settings. This was at eight o'clock in the morning two days before the race.

Formula One is pass-obsessed. There are a hundred of them permitting varying permutations of access, and they all cost a fortune. No pass, no passage. There are swipe gates at every entrance or staircase which emit a welcoming bleep if the correct piece of plastic is inserted, and a rude klaxon if it's incorrect or invalid, making you immediately feel like a shoplifter. Our passes were special (and cost as much as a timeshare in Majorca): they gained us access to the inner sanctum, the paddock. This is the area behind the pits, where all the drivers, owners and mechanics flit between their garages and their motorhomes, exchanging gossip, catching up with old friends, eyeing up pit babes in skintight jump-suits or accidentally on purpose leaving a pile of particular tyres in view as a red herring to other teams. We mingled freely among them. It was like being able to wander about backstage before a Rolling Stones concert, watching Jagger and Richards and the roadies preparing for the show.

Having heard much about the glamour of the Formula One paddock, replete with gleaming motorhomes, I was a bit surprised to find the one at Interlagos was an unremarkable stretch of tarmac to one side of which were what looked like a collection of park-football changing rooms: the garages. The lack of space had reduced each team's headquarters to a modified coach with a plastic awning tacked on to the side acting as a restaurant. There was a hierarchical nature to their layout: they were lined up in order of their finishing positions the previous year, which meant Williams at the head, Ferrari second, Benetton third and so on. They have to be parked precisely in delineated zones. If so much as a back wheel is overlapping the relevant white line, the team is fined. Bernie Ecclestone is a remorseless ringmaster.

We were escorted into Jordan's 'restaurant', bedecked in Benson and Hedges yellow, and served a sumptuous breakfast. At the next table, the team's new driver Giancarlo Fisichella, a diminutive Italian with the upper half of his racing jumpsuit tied round his waist, was in consultation with his chief mechanic. Then a short, trendily dressed man with funny round glasses, a shock of grey hair and long, sickle-shaped sideburns strode in: Eddie Jordan, the Irish team owner.

'Ah, you've arroived at last. Good on yas!' he exclaimed to all of us. The engine noise had abated, allowing the rat-tat-tat of his Irish blarney total domination.

Jordan escorted us into the team garage. It was about the size of a small classroom, with a subdivided area at the back full of technicians studying telemetry on computer screens. Three yellow cars were lined up out front. They were in bits, as mechanics tinkered with engine parts and cleaned and polished body panels and individual components. Everything was spotless. 'Garage' seemed an inappropriate word. It was more like being in an operating theatre. It had a hermetically sealed feel.

Eddie Jordan handed us yellow sponge earplugs and urged us to put them in. It was good advice. A mechanic inserted what looked like a Kalashnikov wired to a computer into the back of one of the half-cars and there was some low-level whirring before the engine burst into screaming life.

'They're just burning off the excess oil,' I think Jordan shouted above the din.

Later he let me examine the cramped-looking cockpit. I pointed to the little coloured buttons in the centre of the steering wheel, and asked what they did.

'Don't ask me technical questions in front of the engineering boys,' he scolded. 'All I'm good at is finding them the money to let them play with their toys.'

It was an understatement. The team had forty-eight sponsors. We were with the most important one (B&H), which gave us extra privileges, like being in the garage when the cars arrived back in eerie silence after practice (the engines had been cut) and hobnobbing with Jordan and his drivers (who ate pasta and drank only mineral water) at the hotel in the evening. Fisichella kept smiling and saying, 'I very 'appy,' which seemed to be the only English he knew. Ralf

Schumacher, the team's other young driver, spoke little except to his manager.

The atmosphere of camaraderie in the paddock had become tight lipped by race morning on Sunday. Eddie Jordan had no time to tell us about his regular tennis matches with Bono back home, or what his band, the Pitstop Boogie Boys, would be playing after the race. He was hurrying, grim faced, from one consultation to another. The drivers emerged from their neck massages, bottle of water in one hand, helmet in the other, and headed for their last-minute briefings. Sponsors' representatives were checking their logos on the car were correctly positioned. By late morning the sound of screaming engines had ceased. An intense lull pervaded the paddock.

I decamped to the media centre to watch the race. Thirty rows of desks were fully occupied by journalists from forty countries who stared at monitors suspended from the ceiling. A nicotine-laced fug hung over the room as people massed at the bank of windows alongside the grid to watch the start. As the five red lights illuminated one by one, the engines' revs crescendoed until all you could hear was one shrill roaring. And then they were off down the straight, jockeying for position, round the first left-hand bend and out of sight. Everyone went back to their desks and followed the race on the monitors. It seemed odd to have travelled 8000 miles to watch the main event on telly. But despite a decent view of half the circuit from the media-centre balcony, it is impossible to know what's happening except by watching the TV coverage. It's the same at every circuit.

A grand prix media centre is the most stressful place I've ever had to work in. You're trying to follow the race on the telly and analyse the lap sector times on another screen and focusing back on the jockeying cars wondering why everyone had suddenly gone 'Oooooh.' People had warned me Formula One was boring. Here there were red flags, breakdowns, crashes and spectacular skids, and then the race was aborted. So they all lined up to start again. Then, at the end, there are press conferences to listen to and press releases to read and Japanese people yelling into radio mikes next to you and Portuguese smoking acrid cigarettes and phones ringing and 400 fingers tapping away on rackety laptops. You can't hear yourself think, and because of the restart and the time difference it's now 10 p.m. in England and they're screaming for copy.

We repaired to the Jordan motorhome after the race for a soothing ale or two, acknowledging a grinning Fisichella still proclaiming, 'I very 'appy' (he came eighth; Ralf Schumacher didn't finish), and chatting to relieved/realistic team personnel. Several hours later we were ushered inside an exclusive São Paulo nightclub open only to the VIPs from the race. There in a lounge area at the back was the slight form of Jacques Villeneuve, looking like a perpetual student with his untucked lumberjack shirt and round glasses, exchanging small talk, and on the dance floor was the tall, slim figure of David Coulthard, in grey shirt and black jeans, jigging about to thumping Europop among a gaggle of adoring girls.

'Hey James, hey Martin, great to see you!' Coulthard called out when he saw the boys from *Loaded*. He'd been featured in their magazine before and *he* regarded *them* as minor celebrities. Coulthard beckoned a waiter over and ordered champagne all round. He more or less ignored the women.

The *Loaded* contingent certainly didn't ignore the women once we'd flown down to Rio. Their daily routine was as follows. Wake up late morning at our Copacabana beachfront hotel. On to sand for a spot of beach football and ogling the girls in their dental-floss bikinis. After a liquid lunch, the evening involved knocking back several caipirinhas, Brazil's national drink – an evil potion of rum mixed with lime juice and sugar – before trying their luck in Help!, the largest nightclub in the southern hemisphere. This was an appropriate name not because you needed assistance finding a willing female. Conversely, a panic alarm would have been useful to fight *off* the hordes of beautiful girls (mostly hookers). Most would then head for a 'love hotel' until dawn. Food, time of day and normal bodily functions were largely irrelevant.

This performance continued unabated for about seventy-two hours, by which time the pace was visibly slowing. It was exhausting just hearing about their escapades. When it was time to depart after a fabulous stay in a beguiling city, three of the four were virtually comatose. It occurred to me that if England were truly serious about regaining the Ashes, the thing to do would be to get the *Loaded* boys and a phalanx of Brazilian girls to hang out in the Australian team's hotel for a couple of days before the first Test. (That is, after all, virtually what used to happen. England didn't have *Loaded*, but they had the next best thing: Ian Botham, a master at leading the opposition astray while possessing remarkable stamina himself.)

Certainly England needed to do something exceptional, since they'd had an appalling winter. They failed to beat Zimbabwe in two Tests and lost all three one-day internationals – being routed by a chicken farmer, Eddo Brandes, in the last of them – causing David Lloyd's 'we flippin' murdered 'em' observation after the first drawn Test really to come home to roost. The *Sun* proposed sending the whole England team in a rocket to the moon.

When they went on to New Zealand, they were powerless to prevent the Kiwis' number eleven Danny Morrison from keeping them at bay for almost three hours to draw the first Test. The *Sun* superimposed sheep's heads on the England players' bodies under the headline 'EWE'LL NEVER GET 'EM OUT'. In the last sixteen Tests they'd achieved only one win. Fortified by Atherton's determination, though, they fared a little better from then on, clinching the Test series 2–0. The press vilification abated somewhat, but the stated intent of Lord Ian MacLaurin, the newly elected chairman of the renamed ECB, to make England the best side in the world by 2007 was looking utterly deluded. When Ireland meted out a hammering to a Middlesex side containing five of the England squad in an early summer round of the Benson and Hedges Cup, it could be said that England weren't even the best side in the UK.

CHAPTER 8 – 1997

THUMBS DOWN

The Australians arrived expectantly in early May 1997, finely tuned and drilled, but irked by a spread I had contributed to the *Daily Telegraph*. This, a list of pen portraits of the tourists, was, at a glance, innocuous. But alongside the descriptive text about each player were symbols ranking their performance in three categories – entertainment value, fitness and sledging levels. They got a thumbs-up in each category if there was a positive assessment (i.e. the player was very entertaining, very fit, quiet as a mouse), a thumbs-down in each if the opinion was negative (i.e. he was boring, fat or loud). A third symbol, thumb horizontal, implied they were neither especially good nor especially bad in that category. I awarded Steve Waugh two horizontal thumbs, since I believed he wasn't particularly entertaining or particularly fit, and one thumbs-down (he was an arch sledger).

When the time came to print this layout, the *Telegraph* graphics people, for reasons of space, and unbeknown to me, edited out the horizontal-thumb signals. So every judgement was either thumbs-up or thumbs-down. It caused quite a scene when I wandered past the Australian players' balcony during their rained-off game at Durham.

'There's that fuckin' prat who says I'm useless,' Steve Waugh called after me, in that indirect way he employs when he's sledging opponents.

'Uh? What do you mean?' I said, wheeling around.

'I was the only one in the team you gave three thumbs-down to,' said Waugh, clearly aggrieved.

It was true. The two horizontal thumbs next to his name had been scaled down rather than up. Effectively I had summed him up as dull, unfit and verbose.

'Yeah, and he gave me two thumbs-down, the bastard!' said Shane Warne, joining in.

'It's a fuckin' disgrace. I thought you were a responsible journalist,' Waugh went on. His forbidding tone made me feel distinctly uncomfortable surrounded by his team-mates. I could appreciate the impact of his sledging (though he preferred to call it mental disintegration).

'Yeah, and he had me down as fat!' Mark Taylor exclaimed.

'Well you can't argue with the truth, Tubs,' Glenn McGrath replied.

It lightened the mood a bit and I tried to explain that it was due to situations beyond my control. I presented Waugh with a placatory copy of my new book, which after a bit more humphing he accepted begrudgingly.

It was a rather deflating experience after the encouraging events of April. *A Lot of Hard Yakka* had been published, and received unexpectedly glowing reviews. This was in spite of the 'publicity' campaign. Three weeks before publication, the publishers had sent the book to a number of journalists for review purposes. Half of them had either retired or moved on. Two were dead (John Arlott and Brian Johnston). A few copies did find their way into the right hands, though, and Mike Selvey set the ball rolling in the *Guardian*, drawing attention to my revelations about the original ball-tamperer, 'Amazing' Grace. Mention of her, wrote Selvey, a former Middlesex colleague of mine, 'will drain the blood from cricketers from Birmingham to Brisbane'. He added that I had been a 'pillock' as a team-mate – 'bumptious ... brazen ... impudent' (no doubt true) – but that I had written 'a brilliant commentary about the life of a county cricketer'.

One or two of my former colleagues were hurt by the book's material. Phil Tufnell complained that he had been unfairly portrayed as neurotic, oblivious to the fact that as he spoke he was wringing his hands intently. John Emburey said, 'How could you reveal that I was well endowed? That's pisshole!'

'Well, at least I didn't say that you were poorly endowed,' I replied, and he shrugged resignedly.

Mike Gatting, who had come in for a fair bit of gentle stick in the book, seemed reassuringly unperturbed.

It was ten years since Gatting had proudly clasped the Ashes to his breast in Melbourne, and he was now a national selector. It was a good cue for a piece about him. I invited him to lunch at a restaurant near his Enfield home, where he berated me about focusing so much in my book on his food intake. As he was talking, the waiter, who had accidentally brought two portions of fried skate, made to remove one. 'Don't worry,' said Gatting, 'I'll eat them both.' He did so, then demolished an enormous plate of lamb and veg, accosting the passing waiter with 'Is there a ration on greens?', then wolfed down spotted dick and custard (his favourite) and a considerable quantity of Turkish delight. It reminded me why in the dressing room we nicknamed him Jabba, after the blob in *Star Wars* that eats anything that moves. The total gusto with which he devours food makes it a spectator sport worthy of an admission charge. Needless to say, most of the section was about that.

Reflecting county cricket's umbilical link to eating, I compiled a guide to the players' lunches on the first-class circuit for the *Telegraph*. In spite of the England side now being more diet conscious, the standard of food around the counties was generally appalling. An opponent at Northampton said, 'Unless I was starving, I wouldn't eat in their dining room,' and the fare I sampled at Cardiff consisted of thin soup, desiccated meat and synthetic-tasting scones and cream. Even the orange squash was disgusting.

Australia's answer to Gatting – David Boon, captaining Durham, and very fond of his tucker – saw the piece. 'The Australian Board have sent nutritionists into every kitchen at home and ensured what we eat is appropriate – pasta, rice, salads,' he said despondently. 'There are no sandwiches or cakes at teatime, only occasionally those muffin things people say are supposed to be good for you. Big Merv [Hughes] was forbidden from eating anything at tea, and one time he'd disappeared. They found him hiding in the dunny troughing a whole pile of stuff on a salver.'

TOSSING AND TURNING

It was a big summer. Labour won the election, the newly divorced Princess Diana was photographed on Dodi Fayed's yacht, and, after much hand-wringing, the BBC TV sports department invited me to be their Test match roving reporter. This was the real deal. My voice, maybe even my face, would be on proper, live Test match coverage. I'd be recognised in the street. I'd get voice-overs for life insurance. It was Australia as well. At last I could leave at home the spare radio microphone I always took to Test matches just in case one of the *TMS* commentators died when I was in the vicinity.

I should have been salivating at this exciting career development, and I was, in a way. But there was a fair degree of trepidation mixed in as the first Ashes Test at Edgbaston approached. My first job would be to pre-record an interview with the captains at the toss. After the thumbs-up, thumbs-down saga, and other negative press around Mark Taylor's lack of form, I wasn't looking forward to encountering the Australian captain. Though I was quite friendly with his opposite number, Mike Atherton, having played against and socialised with him both at home and abroad, he wasn't known for his effusiveness in interviews. I had a sleepless night racking my brains for questions other than 'Are you going to win?' and 'Do you wish you'd called tails instead?' What if I dried, and there was an uncomfortable silence and Steve Pierson, our genial stage manager, said, 'Cut!' and they

had to toss up again? What if the coin disappeared down a
crack in the Edgbaston pitch? When I did eventually fall
asleep, I dreamed that I was about to ask my first question
but had mislaid the microphone, like a cricketer's recurring
nightmare of being next in to bat and unable to find gloves
or box. I couldn't eat breakfast, arrived at the ground just
after 9 a.m. and strolled about rehearsing the questions to
startled TV engineers doing last-minute checks.

But when the moment came, I was surprisingly cool,
despite the shock of seeing Atherton freshly shaved (well, it
was the first Test). I think it was the match referee Ranjan
Madugalle who relaxed me. I had coached him when he was
a schoolboy in Sri Lanka and he was like a long-lost half-
brother. He had a cheery demeanour and we were chatting so
freely I nearly missed my cue.

Taylor won the toss and said he'd bat. 'Aw, there's a bit of
live grass on it, but it should be all right once it dries out after
lunch,' he said. He was right. The problem was that Australia
were all out by then. Gough's first ball of the match fizzed
past Taylor's outside edge – in contrast to the first ball of the
previous Ashes series which Michael Slater had lashed for
four – and the Aussies were soon 54 for 8. By the end of day
two, England were 449 for 6, a lead of 331. On Sunday
evening they were celebrating an astonishing nine-wicket win.

It was one of those matches when everything went right
for one team and everything bombed for the other. Gough
made the ball talk, Caddick overcame his introspection,
Ealham winkled out the tail, Hussain batted with imperious
majesty for more than a day to score 207. Even Atherton
blitzed a fifty. The Australians nicked everything that moved,
McGrath could bowl nothing but long hops and half-volleys,
Gillespie went off injured, Warne was innocuous. 'Warne
can't grip his balls!' declared the *Sun*'s back page. The vocal
Edgbaston crowd accompanied England's victory charge
with a joyful, 'They're coming home, they're coming home,
Ash-es coming home.' The next day's papers were full of jin-
goistic fervour.

But Edgbaston was a wake-up call for Australia. At Lord's, McGrath regained his aim with a vengeance, routing England for 77 in a rain-ruined draw. And at Old Trafford the previously run-less Steve Waugh made two centuries. The toss was crucial there, and Taylor took a gamble by opting again to bat first on an obviously juicy pitch. It threw me off my pre-match questioning, but it turned out to be a clever ruse, because the huge dents in the damp pitch made by the England bowlers' run-ups on that first day created the perfect rough for Warne to weave his magic later.

The Australians also used the media to advantageous effect in this series-turning match. It was customary for a batsman who was already out to give the post-match interview. My BBC camera crew and I were therefore surprised when Steve Waugh, who was 102 *not out*, and still in his pads, bounded up to the interview point at the top of the pavilion. 'That's the most difficult Test wicket I've ever played on,' he said on air, grimacing, well aware the England players would be watching on their dressing-room telly. The following day they perceived gremlins where there were none and subsided to 162 all out.

After this, a catalogue of indifferent batting, missed chances and ill-judged selections (like picking the diminutive Gloucestershire seamer Mike Smith at Headingley rather than the hit-the-deck Andrew Caddick, or giving Adam and Ben Hollioake their Test debuts on the same day at Trent Bridge) cost England dear. Boycott could be heard regularly lamenting, ''E couldn't have got ma moom out.' The Australians, it must be said, were also rather good. They won the series 3–2, a scoreline that flattered England by dint of winning the last, meaningless Test at The Oval. The *Sun* wasn't deceived, referring to England as 'Messrs Bumble, Fumble and Crumble'.

With each passing defeat Atherton grew more morose and tight lipped, as the job of captaining a starless England became increasingly exasperating (it didn't help that he lost five tosses in a row). There were calls for him to resign, or at least get someone else to flick the coin, and he was sorely tempted. Mervyn Hardy, a cricket-mad JP I knew in Durham, had a better suggestion: 'What we need,' he said in a letter to me, 'is someone who can bat, bowl or field like Boycott's mother.'

TOUCHY RELATIONS

I spent the Ashes in the BBC commentary box. Despite offering various feature ideas, I was required only for pre- and post-match interviews so hung around at the back watching the great and good at work. Boycott always dressed colour coordinately, as if he were attending a wedding (as the series wore on, funeral attire would have been more appropriate). He invariably disappeared after his commentary stint; if it was a Saturday to chat up Sue Barker, who'd be presenting *Grandstand* from the cricket and who flirted with him good naturedly. He'd return precisely sixty seconds before he was due on again. Then he went through his little routine of hanging up his jacket and hat, turning his sleeveless pullover inside out, neatly folding it and draping it over the back of his seat, before removing the black BBC-issue foam microphone shield and replacing it with his personal yellow one. He was fastidious with a capital 'F', forensically labelling his water glass and at lunch sticking rigidly to the Hay diet – no mixing of carbohydrate and protein. He wouldn't touch the lunch if it had been standing outside for more than five minutes.

The cream-jacketed Benaud made a little nest in the corner of the commentary box where he'd set up his laptop, and lay out his copies of *Wisden* and Tom Smith's *Cricket Umpiring and Scoring* and his Tupperware container of home-made banana sandwiches. Except when commentating, he rarely moved from this position all day. Gower, a chinos man, received numerous visitors with the same cheery bonhomie and laugh like a Cortina with a slightly dodgy battery trying to start. While acknowledging Boycott's excellence as a broadcaster, neither conversed much with him off air (Gower once stamped on his precious straw hat in sheer irritation). Jack Bannister's Ronnie Corbett-like ability to make amusing anecdotes run in to each other during his regular visits defused the occasionally awkward atmosphere in the commentary box.

I was struck by the different ways the commentators wielded their microphones. Boycott gripped his tightly round its neck and held it still and bolt upright while talking as if playing a resolute forward defensive. Off-mike, he bemoaned England players' technique, muttering, 'What sort of a fookin' shot were that?' Gower waved his mike about rather more airily, while Benaud treated his reverentially, cradling it in his hand and laying it down carefully after he'd finished speaking as if it were a precious ornament.

Occasionally, if you sought it, he offered little morsels of advice. He pointed out that, when interviewing, it would be better to hold the microphone in the hand *furthest* from the camera, to avoid reaching across the 'guests'. He said I was prone to begin a question with 'It must be …' or 'You must …' or 'They must …' which was more of a statement. And he recalled one interview I'd done as the players ran on, while I was positioned with my back to the pitch so I couldn't see when play was about to resume. 'Never, *ever* let them do that to you again,' he said.

My lack of employment during the day allowed me time to do lunchtime signings of my new hardback book. The success of these varied. At Old Trafford and The Oval I got an excellent response, and Trent Bridge was reasonable, but at Headingley they mostly said 'Bloody 'ell! Sixteen ninety-nine? Think I'll wait 'til it cooms out in paperback.' They did me proud at Lord's, erecting a stall with an awning with covers of *A Lot of Hard Yakka* displayed everywhere. I was signing away madly for nearly an hour, mainly for thirty-something men who said it was for their son. Just as I was helping pack away a few unsold books, two stylishly dressed middle-aged women approached. They didn't look the type to buy my irreverent tale of sweaty jockstraps and boys on tour.

'We'll have one each, please,' one said, betraying a slight North Country accent. 'Could you write "with love"?'

I dutifully signed and handed them over. They looked at what I'd written briefly, then handed them back.

'Oh, sorry, we thought you were Ian Botham,' the other lady said, and they departed empty handed.

Botham did have a book out, *The Botham Report*, written by the *Mail on Sunday*'s Peter Hayter (son of Reg, the godfather of sportswriters). The book's theme was 'What is wrong with English cricket and how I intend to put it right', and it certainly didn't pull its punches, mostly blaming the people at the head of the game during the last decade – men like Ray Illingworth, Raman Subba Row and Ted Dexter – for its ruination. At an exclusive little dinner to launch the book, I suggested to Botham maybe floodlit cricket would be a good thing in England, encouraging people to go to matches after work.

'Nah, it's too cold, pitches will be damp from the dew, the lights won't be good enough,' he said. 'It'll never work.'

I met him in mid-pitch before the Headingley Test, two months later. 'You'll never guess where I was last night,' he said, beaming.

'Where?' I replied, imagining it would have been one of his amazing parties at his beach house on the island of Alderney.

'Edgbaston, day–night game, Warwickshire v. Somerset. Fantastic, beautiful night, fifteen thousand people. I always said it was a great idea.'

'But Beefy, I thought you said that floodlit cricket wouldn't work,' I said, my masochistic streak coming out.

'No. What I said was the *floodlights* might not work. Cloth-head!'

FEET OF ENDURANCE

I had a fascinating summer aside from the cricket. Continuing my Sporting Relations column, I cornered Tim Henman and his coach David Felgate for half an hour at Wimbledon, did a training session with Steve Redgrave and the other members of our oarsome-foursome at Henley, and visited Prince Naseem Hamed and his trainer in their Sheffield gym.

On the Saturday of the Austrian Grand Prix I entered a commentary box containing Murray Walker and Martin Brundle. The first job was to get rid of the chairs.

'If there are four of us in here, they'll just be in the way,' said Murray, surveying a broadcasting box the size of a downstairs loo.

'What if you want to sit down?' I said, helpfully removing them anyway.

'We don't. Ever!' replied Murray proudly. Murray and Martin did it standing up.

That was the initial surprise. The next was the amount of loosening up Murray went through before describing the qualifying session. Erect in jeans and muddy trainers, he cleared his throat, inhaled deeply, flexed his shoulders, stretched his arms, slapped his thighs, clenched and unclenched his fists, did some knee bends. It was a better limbering-up routine than Ian Botham ever managed.

It was six minutes to transmission. I looked along the line of thirty identical commentary boxes, suspended like little cable cars under the roof of the grandstand. *Thirty* commentary boxes! Every other team was sitting down. Murray was making final adjustments to his crib sheets plastered on the windows and monitors, flicking through pages of technical information on another screen, peering at the pits for any sign of activity, speaking very loudly to the producer (slight deafness is a feature of most older commentators), stretching some more. And the race itself wasn't until the next day.

Four minutes to transmission. I wondered where Brundle had got to, at which point he strolled in, an aura of calm in his wake. Now the room was feeling warm with four of us squeezed in – Murray, Martin, me and assistant producer Ted Kravitz, whose main job was to hold up laminated signs saying, 'Ad break in thirty seconds' or 'No More Commentary'.

I put on the headphones they'd given me, the kind worn by men guiding aeroplanes to their parking bays. The theme music finished. Jim Rosenthal introduced the show and led in to the commentators. Cue Murray. 'It is a great day and this is the most visually stunning circuit in the world, full stop,' he said emphatically, and rabbited away, delivering all sorts of anoraky observations ('D'you know only nine-tenths of a second separated the first fourteen cars in practice this morning'). Brundle applied gentle pressure on Walker's shoulder when he wanted to interject.

A car emerged from the pit lane. Murray interrupted his own ramble, his voice at once rising half an octave in anticipation. 'Do I hear an engine? Indeed I do. Now who is it, who is it? Ah, it's Tarso Marques – now I know why he's out first in his Arrows. Because he'll get some TV exposure that way.' There was a pause. Then Brundle said, smirking, 'Well, Murray, Tarso Marques would have created a lot of exposure if he'd gone out in the Arrows because he drives for Minardi.' They both laughed off-mike.

Walker's boyish enthusiasm, despite his age, his trousers-on-fire style of commentary, made mistakes inevitable. But instead of trying to cover them up, or gloss over them – as Richie Benaud does unconsciously, making you doubt he made an error at all – Walker endearingly drew attention to his, apologising and referring back to them. He brandished his microphone like a weapon, yanking it away from his mouth as a cue when he felt the pressure of the hand on his shoulder intensify. Brundle, smooth, deft, just a touch supercilious, was the calming influence.

Qualifying over, I took the tunnel back under the circuit to the media centre, a journey requiring four different passes to complete. Murray was hot on my heels and into the press room, nodding acquaintance everywhere, to collect lap-time sheets and team press releases. Later I saw him nipping in and out of team motorhomes, assimilating gossip, checking facts, catching up with old friends. I realised, watching his typical day, why he wore trainers to work. He thoroughly lived up to his surname.

Watching him at work was uplifting. He demonstrated that you didn't have to be a star performer to commentate with authority about your sport, just show willing and initiative. Also, he demonstrated that total enthusiasm is more important than total accuracy. If, like me, your mind's like a sieve, that's a reassuring thought.

Going to Formula One races gave me an interesting perspective on cricket. It was such a dynamic environment, embracing technology, vast corporate sponsorship and mass support. Race weekends are a kind of pilgrimage, drawing crowds of 100,000-plus to anonymous spots in central Europe to watch their heroes, with many fans camping or sleeping rough in surrounding fields. Most had come to see a man whose control of a 200 m.p.h. machine was superhuman: Michael Schumacher. Trapped in a baking cockpit for two hours, he retained supreme control of his vehicle and his emotions and never, repeat never, broke sweat. (Nor did his brother Ralf, a fact I could confirm after working out next to him for a good forty-five minutes on a hotel gym exercise bike before one race.)

Grand Prix drivers are odd paradoxes. They drive £2 million cars that do 0–100 in 2.8 seconds, earn sackfuls of lolly – £1 million a race in Schumacher's case, which equates to £700,000 an hour – and they're always surrounded by very rich men and extremely beautiful women. But the expectations from sponsors, owners and supporters are so high that they are obliged to endure lives of almost total abstinence: no sex, no drugs, no rock and roll (though not all observe this rule). Consequently most are as dull as ditchwater. They are just extensions of the cars they drive –

pristine, computer-engineered, characterless. There is no scope for personality. Schumacher even keeps his three dogs in his hotel room, sometimes. It is said that the screaming noises at a Formula One racetrack are the sounds of million-aires crying. Maybe it's really the drivers.

A LOONY KINGDOM

A fortnight after attending the Austrian Grand Prix, I was watching four more renowned sportsmen warming up for a race. This time there were a good deal fewer than 100,000 spectators. In fact, there were only two: me and a man walk-ing his dog. You had to be a loon to be out in this weather (steady drizzle) at this hour (7 a.m.). But, then again, most international rowers are loonies. They get up before some of us have gone to bed, flog up and down the river in horrible weather pushing their heart rates to inhumane levels, then hasten to the gym to put themselves through the sort of phys-ical punishment only found in Chinese torture chambers. Having vomited and eaten a round of toast, they're back on the water again for another hour of lowly paid masochism. It's all right, though. They get evenings and Sundays off.

I'd come down to Henley to watch King Loon (Steve Redgrave) – a man who the previous summer had asked to be shot if he was spotted once more handling an oar, and was now back doing precisely that every day – and Lieutenant Loon (Matthew Pinsent), a disciple of the King and more or less his equal. It was the S&M of British sport. They'd been joined in the boat by Laid-back Loon (Tim Foster) – a bright, casual lad with blond rock guitarist's hair and a slim frame which belied surprising power – and James Cracknell, a Herculean figure who appeared to thrive on thrashing his body virtually to death and was known aptly as 'Crackers'. Great Britain's premier coxless four.

Coming from a sport whose male participants only regu-larly exercised one muscle (five letters, beginning with 'p'), I could appreciate the rowers' daily routine as the ultimate contrast:

> 7 a.m. Arrive Leander Club. Haul boat on to the water and complete 40 km at varying speeds.
> 9.15 a.m. Breakfast: scrambled egg on toast, bacon, tea.
> 10.30 a.m. Gym: hard weights for one hour (or 20 km on the rowing machine).
> 12.15 p.m. Another 20-km burst on the river. Each man, therefore, had rowed the equivalent of London to Brighton before lunch.
> 2 p.m. Take boat out of water.
> 2.30 p.m. Lunch.
> 3.30 p.m. Bed. (Where Pinsent was currently lying, ill. So would you be if you had to do this every day.)

And there were still three years to go before the Sydney Olympics.

A weakling in the land of Hercules, I wanted to try to sample their training. So I started with the egg and toast bit and then I joined them in Leander's cramped, decrepit gym for power training. Strip lights hung by a thread, paint peeled from the ceiling, no one had dusted for several years. Redgrave and Cracknell were taking it in turns with Foster to lift weights I couldn't even roll, watched over by Jürgen 'You-Must-Do-What-I-Say' Gröbler, their coach, constantly tapping his watch. Gröbler challenged Cracknell to do 270 bench pulls of a 60-kilo bar. With much heaving and grimacing, he managed it. The others couldn't do as many at once, and I could lift only twenty in total. They had withering loads on the leg and shoulder presses, which I could hardly move, and did squats and pull-ups in between.

'They aren't daunted by my and Matthew's presence in the crew,' Redgrave whispered, as the new boys, Cracknell and Foster, raced each other over 2000 metres on the rowing machine. 'I hope they see our partnership in positive way, as an opportunity for achievement.' Clearly they did. Both recorded personal bests of under 5 minutes 40 seconds. I managed a woeful 7 minutes 38 seconds and afterwards suffered convulsions and had to go for a lie down. Professional cricketers, who invariably complained about one morning of sprint training a year, didn't know they were born.

ARRIVALS AND DEPARTURES

Being the BBC's post-Test match reporter and therefore fairly inactive during the day, I had asterisked 6 September in my diary as a red-letter day. It was the NatWest final at Lord's, where I was given the chance to commentate to a national audience. I'd prepared by going to watch both teams – Essex and Warwickshire – the week before and had a notebook full of potential anecdotes and observations.

Then Princess Diana was killed, and her funeral clashed with the NatWest final, so the match was cancelled. Well, postponed to the next day, anyway. This posed problems for the cricket production crew. The BBC were broadcasting the funeral, so the trucks, equipment and personnel that should have been at Lord's were transferred to Westminster Abbey. Instead of organising my pre-match interviews, our ever-willing stage manager Steve Pierson, a man who shook your hand every time he encountered you, even if the previous occasion was only ten minutes ago, was on duty in the Abbey. He was operating Elton John's autocue for his special tribute version of 'Candle in the Wind'.

Steve was back on more familiar duty at the NatWest final on the Sunday, lining up cameras and mikes for me to interview my nemesis Neil Smith, the Warwickshire captain, at the toss. Smith kept looking in the direction of where he'd deposited my slower ball to win the 1989 final, which was quite off-putting. Later, I did some commentary, trying to offer as much insight as I could about the players, most of whom I'd competed against. I sat at the back of the box, then located in the Warner stand, after one stint, thinking I'd done well. Next to me was the BBC bigwig, Jonathan Martin, head of sport, who'd popped in to say hello.

'First rule of commentary: if you can't add to the pictures, don't say anything,' he said drily.

The following week, three important things happened. Various cricket committees met and, after the cheese and port, threw out most of the recommendations of Lord MacLaurin's *Raising the Standard* document, including an England elite being centrally contracted to the Board. Meanwhile, Glamorgan won the County Championship, under the tutelage of a certain Duncan Andrew Gwynne Fletcher, the former Zimbabwean all-rounder, whom Glamorgan had hired on the back of his success coaching Western Province to a similar title in South Africa. And my wife Tanya said she was pregnant.

Her tummy grew bigger and so did my head when *A Lot of Hard Yakka* was shortlisted for the William Hill Sports Book of the Year award. It was getting towards Christmas and various men's magazines had promoted it as a good seasonal buy. I suggested to the publisher that they should organise me a few Big City bookshop signings. So I did one in Tunbridge Wells and one in Kenilworth. Then they arranged one at the Leadenhall Market branch of Waterstone's in London EC1. It was the lunch hour in the city and there were loads of people milling about, most of whom were sports fans who earned £16.99 roughly every 5½ minutes, so I expected a lot of interest. I was set up at a little table twenty yards from the door with a stack of a hundred books ready and waiting. A lot of people passed by, a few looking at me quizzically or flicking through the book until they realised there were no pictures in it, after which they put it back. By 2 p.m. I'd signed and sold three, and one man had come up to me saying he'd bought the book the week before but decided he didn't like it, so could he have his money back? So there were ninety-eight left when I gave up.

The William Hill award, which Nick Hornby won in 1992 with *Fever Pitch*, setting him on his path to stardom, is sport's version of the Booker, without the prestige, the money, the TV coverage, the celebrity audience, the sumptuous banquet or the opulent venue. Otherwise it's exactly the same. It was held at Sportspages, a small, warren-like bookshop off the Charing Cross Road. Journalists, publishers and agents were crammed around bookcases and display tables and in every nook and cranny, waiting for Frances Edmonds, author, broadcaster, translator and wife of left-arm spinner Phil, to announce the winner. The other candidates included the *Guardian*'s Richard Williams's excellent book about Formula One and an entry from the ex-England fly-half Stuart Barnes.

I thought mine might be in with a small chance, but I consoled myself with the thought that it was an honour just to be nominated. Still, the suspense was terrible. Frances really milked the moment – she was a forerunner to the way evictions are announced on *Big Brother* or *Pop Idol* – lingering over 'And the winner is ...' for ever, until she at last exclaimed, 'Simon Hughes's *A Lot of Hard Yakka!*'

It was the proudest moment of my life. Other occasions had been more exciting – Lord's finals (5), weddings (2), winning a Blue Peter badge (1) (for a model I'd made with a friend) – but here it was me alone, with all my own work (well, give or take the editing and the typesetting, and Tanya's tolerance of me consumed by it every minute of the day). I lapped up the attention for several hours. I lapped up quite a few glasses of champagne, too. I was a cricketer-who-could-write-a-bit no more. I envisaged it would secure me lucrative book deals, appearances on late-night arts shows, offers for the movie rights. They might ask me to write the screenplay myself, like Hornby did with *High Fidelity*. I could command a substantial pay rise at the *Telegraph* and my own weekly column. I could write about sport the way A. A. Gill wrote about food, incorporating my other half into the prose: 'Thorpe prestidigitously circumnavigated the suppurating mould of the legside field, as the Blonde terebrates feckless underlings.'

It didn't get me any of that. But it did get me a place at the sports editor's table at the Christmas lunch. The journalistic equivalent of finishing top of the bowling averages with 62 wickets at 21.4. Hallelujah! The other premier-division guests included Michael Parkinson, who wrote a monthly column, Paul Hayward and Sue Mott, treasured and accomplished writers, Sir Paul Fox, the man who created *Grandstand*, Lucinda Green (née Prior-Palmer) and, next to me, Sebastian Coe. It was, then, rather unfortunate that the Docklands Light Railway was playing up and I was forty-five minutes late. At least I didn't make the embarrassing faux pas that one of the *Telegraph*'s racing staff had made when he'd fawned all over Britain's double 1500 metres gold medallist the year before. 'Oh, I used to love your running style,' he had said. 'You were fantastic. Especially when you pissed all over that smug cunt Seb Coe in his own event.' He had thought he was chatting to Steve Ovett.

The lunch broke up about 6 p.m. with the traditional circulation of the Bloops of the Year, a sheet of unconsciously flawed copy filed by the paper's correspondents, and smartly edited out by hawk-eyed subs. Undoubtedly the best was Lucinda Green's assessment of a steed: 'He is not wide between your legs, but being deep girthed he has plenty of room for hearts, lungs and stamina ...'

CHAPTER 9 – 1998

MUCKY BUSINESS

The year began with a feast. A fish restaurant in Nairobi, 500 kilometres from the sea, is perhaps not the obvious choice of establishment to entertain two former England captains, being roughly equivalent to barbecuing a lamb on a spit in the middle of the Indian Ocean. But the food was surprisingly good. Mike Gatting certainly enjoyed it anyway, and convinced Graham Gooch to tuck in. The pièce de résistance was the crab curry. It came whole in a bucket, covered with spicy red gravy. The waiters brought us hats and large bibs like doctors' scrubs and presented us with a collection of implements. It was as if we were about to perform an operation. Which, in fact, we were. Extracting the flesh from the sauce-covered shell was at least as hard as a kidney transplant and twice as messy. We finished up splattered with gravy, and Gatting had it in his beard and all round his mouth. He looked like a child who had just played war games with tomato ketchup.

Gooch and Gatting, by now both England selectors, were in Kenya as manager and coach of the England A team, en route for Sri Lanka. Apart from influencing the next generation of England players, Gooch was doing his best to drive Gatting to hitherto unattained levels of fitness, to maximise his chances of scoring the seven centuries he needed the following summer to reach a hundred hundreds. I joined them in the hotel gym the following morning.

'Come on, Pie, just five more sit-ups,' urged Gooch, who

himself had a weakness for doughnuts, cackling at Gatting's laboured efforts, 'and you won't have to stoop to playing against the universities for those runs.'

'I'm trying, Zap, I'm trying,' retorted Gatting, his face puce and contorted in agony. 'That's a bit rich, anyway. I've only got three tons against the universities. You've got about twelve.'

Gooch hung his head in mock-shame.

With 197 Test appearances between them, there was a vast reservoir of experience to pass on, and several young aspirants keen to lap it up. The most exciting of these was a strapping lad from Preston who in the first match in Nairobi had already made the most of the thinner air (the Kenyan capital is 5000 feet above sea level) and his own withering power: Andrew Flintoff had hit five enormous sixes and lost two balls. His boyish face and slight shyness betrayed his age (twenty). 'I love Elvis records and occasionally I go to theme nights,' he told me, leaning against the pavilion, 'but I can't grow me sideboards long. It's all just bum-fluff.' Just how much he'd make fielders' fingers tingle when he was big enough to shave didn't bear thinking about. There was an essence of Graeme Hick about his driving, and an uncomplicated, Botham-like approach in general. You sensed he had the potential to be something special. Judging by his early Test match form in the following couple of years, however, he seemed to have gleaned more from Gatting and Gooch about eating than batting.

When I'd returned from Kenya, David Welch, the *Telegraph*'s sports editor, asked me to have lunch with him. I thought it might be to talk about being taken on the paper's staff proper, so I sought the guidance of a few journalists about how I should react. The best advice I was given came from Peter Hayter, nicknamed Reggie after his dad, at the *Mail on Sunday*:

'When Welchy mentions a proposed salary, cough.'

'Cough?'

'Yes, it worked brilliantly for me. I was called in to see my sports editor last year after a good run of exclusives. Out of the blue he said, "We'd like to put up your pay. How does fifty-five thousand sound?" I spluttered and choked with pleasure. "OK, OK, we'll make it sixty-five," he said.'

In fact, Welch wanted to talk about a new Monday column he'd created for the sports section, 'Heroes and Villains'. As I tucked into a salmon teriyaki he said he'd like me to do it once a month. Fine, I said. He poured more wine. As he was an inveterate gambler mainly interested in athletics and horseracing, two sports I knew nothing about, I never found having conversations with him either easy or particularly enjoyable. Eventually I managed to get him on to the subject of my pay. I was getting £125 a piece. In my mind the target was my BBC fee of £200 a day.

'Well, we can probably manage a hundred and fifty,' he said, as I took a swig from my glass.

I coughed, as directed by Hayter, even dribbling a tiny bit of wine into my lap.

'Don't you like that Chilean Sauvignon blanc?' he said. 'Perhaps I'll order the New Zealand.'

As it turned out, I couldn't do any writing for a while because in early spring our first child, Callum, was born. I played a full part in the process – at the business end – and broadcast the fact to friends afterwards.

'I helped with the delivery!' I proclaimed to Tony Pastor, one of the BBC cricket producers I'd befriended in the summer.

'Bet it was down the legside,' he replied.

Tanya had a bit of trouble with the breastfeeding early on. There was a wealth of literature about being pregnant, but hardly anything on what to do when the baby had been born. The only advice I could unearth was from Jeremy Hardy's *Being a Parent – How Men Do It*, which suggested encouraging your partner with exhortations like: 'Don't you want him to have any immunities, then?' and 'My mother breast-fed me until I was seven.' 'If she does give up and change to bottle feeding,' Hardy went on, 'she must be made to feel guilty and a failure.' I hid the book in an upstairs cupboard and hosed powdered milk down Callum when Tanya was in bed.

Naturally, I put sport on the telly whenever I was in charge of the baby, and arranged my old sports kit around his carrycot, hoping that by osmosis he'd develop the stunning natural talent that I thought I had, until I came up against people who really did possess it. But he was sick on one of my cricket sweaters. Then, when my malapropism-prone mother-in-law came over and talked about having heard an interview with 'David Beckenham' and seen an exciting match between 'Manchester United and Vanilla', I realised poor Callum didn't have much of a chance.

WATERY END

I was back at work in April, covering the Boat Race. I'd always loved the special flavour of the event, ever since Harry Carpenter had said on TV, 'Ah, isn't that nice: the wife of the Cambridge President is kissing the cox of the Oxford crew.' In addition to writing a colour piece for the *Telegraph*, I thought I'd do a book on the Great British Sporting Summer, now that my April-to-September life wasn't totally devoted to cricket. It would feature all the major events – the Boat Race, the Lord's Test, Royal Ascot, Wimbledon, the Open – and a few less well-known ones: the Devizes-to-Westminster canoe race, the National Conker Championships, BMX racing in Cheddar Gorge, etc. It seemed like a good idea at the time.

Equipped with notebook and long-lensed camera, I positioned myself on the embankment just beyond Barnes Bridge. I thought I would really be able to sample the atmosphere there, as the large crowds egged on their crew with just a few hundred yards to go. As the boats approached the bridge, I moved close to the water's edge and crouched down to get some really dramatic, low-angled shots of the race. It was neck and neck and I was snapping away furiously as the crews passed, largely unaware of the huge bow wave created by the flotilla of following craft. I saw it out of the corner of my eye as it approached. I started backing hastily up the embankment, lost my footing, slipped and went straight under. The water immediately turned the embankment into a skating rink, and though I scrambled to my feet I couldn't clamber out and I was dumped on by several further waves, one of which rammed the camera lens into my temple. Filming the Boat Race was turning out to be more dangerous than facing Malcolm Marshall. I only escaped thanks to the efforts of a group of students on the bank. They formed a human chain to drag me out, trailing mud and weeds. The camera was ruined and I threw it away. The book idea went with it.

Seeking the sights and sounds and smells of an English spring, and a generally more hospitable experience, I went to the first county game of the season at Canterbury. It was damp and freezing. The birds were croaking with laryngitis, the bees were drowning in flooded hives, the buds were frost-bitten, and the air was laden with the aroma of newly paint-ed sponsors' logos. Puddles lay on the outfield and, apart from the playing staffs sheltering in the pavilion, the ground was more or less deserted at the scheduled start.

Kent's overseas player Carl Hooper had driven into the ground, taken a quick look from the warmth of his metallic-blue BMW, and driven out again, declaring himself unavail-able. 'Too cold, man,' he mouthed through the car window. Eventually the rain relented and the Kent team emerged for a throwing drill using the 'Fieldwell', a large frame hung with coloured plastic squares, designed by their batsman Alan Wells, for target practice. Points were awarded for hitting certain colours. Wells aroused hoots of derision by missing the frame altogether.

The rain soon returned, play was called off for the day and the visitors, Middlesex, returned to their city-centre hotel to play cards. Their new Australian coach, John Buchanan, said he would take the chance to read some of my book, which I was pleased to learn was on his bedside table, even if it was just as an insomnia cure. Buchanan soon gained first-hand experience of the appalling ills of the county system and found he was powerless to do anything about it. Player-power and biddable committees conspired to relieve him of his post just when he had started to make a difference.

COME IN NUMBER 23

The next sporting event I attended was the ultimate contrast to dank, dreary Canterbury. It was indoors, for a start, and attended by some 18,000 delirious fans, happy to shell out $300 or more for one final glimpse of the richest sportsman on the planet and his 'head and shoulder fake'. Having piloted the Chicago Bulls to five NBA Championships in seven years, Michael Jordan was being paid £50 million for one final pop at the title before he retired. Part of this came from Nike, his sponsors, for whom he had created a global brand (Nike Air), leading to him being christened His Royal Airness.

I had secured a press pass to be courtside at Newark to watch one of the final play-off games between the Bulls and the New Jersey Nets. And 'courtside' it is, too. The press get the very best seats, centimetres from the playing surface, from where you look up in wonder at the size and athleticism of these superhumans, and feel the wind as they glide past, and are startled by the squeakiness of their shoes, and see the odd sweat droplet land on your notepad (presumably now highly auctionable on eBay).

I had seen Him play live before, at an exhibition match in Paris, so I already knew of His incredible prowess on the court, of His ownership of a fleet of Ferraris and Lamborghinis, in the boots of which He always kept signed basketballs in case He was stopped for speeding ('Gee, thanks, Mr Jordan. Have a nice day!'), and in front of one of which an infatuated teenage girl had recently lain down and demanded to be run over by Him. (OK, I'll stop capitalising the 'h's now: it's boring, but I wanted to try it because when I'd attempted it in my *Telegraph* piece, it was vetoed by the subs who claimed the paper's God-fearing editor Charles Moore wouldn't approve.)

I had seen Jordan, in front of 14,000 fans in Paris, cradling the ball with his back to the hoop, bouncing it casually as if he were in a school playground, then suddenly jigging and weaving past three Greek defenders, leaping beyond the clutches of a fourth, and, apparently hanging in mid-air, facing the wrong way, flicking the ball over his head and into the basket. It was Pelé and Nureyev rolled into one. 'Mmm, I suppose you could say that was a little mustard on top of the hot dawg,' he said, smirking afterwards at a press conference attended by about 300 people.

That game was for fun. In Newark, it was for real. The Bulls were two up in the best-of-seven final series. The lights were down, the music was rising to a crescendo as each player was introduced individually. 'And finally, people, here comes the king himself,' the announcer boomed, 'the man who averages an incredible 30.12 points a game, the man with the most MVPs in history, the man with five NBA titles and more than 32,000 points, the man who *is* basketball. People! You're in for a treat tonight. Come in no. 23. Myyyyyyykkkallllllllll Jorrrrrrrrrrrrrrrrrdannn!' The crowd went hysterical as he swaggered onto the playing surface.

His performance lived up to the billing. The body swerves, the swivels on a dime, the feints, the dribbles, the electrifying changes of pace, through-the-leg transfers, slam dunks, the amazing 'hangtime', as if suspended from the ceiling, were all there in abundance. They didn't happen by chance. Even in the twilight of his career, Jordan still practised harder than anyone else, arriving on court two hours before games to rehearse the jinks and jumps, to perfect the free-throws.

The real Jordan genius, though, was invariably saved for the end of a quarter. Here, the clock is ticking down, 20 seconds to go to the interval, 19, 18, 17, 16, the score 46 all, Jordan standing mid-court, idly bouncing the ball from hand to hand, waiting, waiting. He is challenging players to confront him, but no one does. He seems untouchable. At eight seconds to go, he has exploded into action, weaving, bobbing, tongue out, biceps rippling, ducking under tackles, leaping from virtually under the basket to score with that famous fading jump shot. The scoreboard clicks to 48–46. The clock clicks to zero. The buzzer sounds. The crowd are delirious. Most remarkable of all, everyone in the arena, and more particularly on the court, *knew* this was going to happen. Yet no one had the power to prevent it. It has a sense of total inevitability about it. 'Michael's eyes look right through you, as if he could read your brain,' said Jayson Williams, one of his opponents that night. 'He's like Medusa that way.'

One of the bonuses of covering American sport is that the press are allowed in the locker room, in stark contrast to English sports where it is a no-go zone. It wasn't a bonus for Jordan, though. Eight camera crews and a score of rubber-necking journalists jostled around him as he was towelling himself down in there afterwards. Men like Dennis Rodman and Scottie Pippen – American superstars in their own right – dressed quietly next to him, barely noticed. Twenty minutes later, Jordan, having changed into a sharp cream suit, left the room dogged by reporters and photographers, poking lenses and microphones up his nostrils as he stopped to sign autographs for a man in a wheelchair. 'Er, where am I?' he muttered to his minders as they hustled him through the bowels of the arena to a waiting Mercedes.

I met him briefly later in a private room at a Manhattan hotel. He daren't go to the public areas: he would have been mobbed. I asked if there was anywhere he could find peace. He reclined in his armchair and crossed his legs. 'The basketball court for me is, during a game, the most peaceful place I can imagine,' he said. 'Being out there is one of the most private parts of my life. I'm untouchable out there. When I'm playing serious basketball, it's like meditation.' Jordan was beyond fame. The only place he could escape unwanted attention was in front of 20,000 people on court. His life was the definition of a goldfish bowl.

I got up to go, shaking his vast hand and marvelling at the smoothness of his shaved dome, his colossal shoulders, the southern lilt to his voice, the penetrating stare. He had a presence, an aura, that I have only experienced in one other person: Vivian Richards, who had a similarly imposing physique, confident swagger, and devastating inevitability. I left reflecting that Jordan is the same height as Angus Fraser (6 feet 6 inches) and roughly the same age (early thirties then). But his earnings were 500 times more. Jordan's exceptional prowess, consequent wealth and unparalleled fame right across America and the Caribbean made him one of the biggest single reasons for the demise of West Indian cricket. And he has made 23 the most sought-after shirt number in world sport.

HELPLESS PREY

Jordan's great mate – perhaps the only person in the world to whom he could properly relate – was Tiger Woods. As I stood watching him and the other players tee off in the Open at Royal Birkdale, it was tempting to think what life as a golfer might have been like. Twelve years on the European Tour rather than trundling around the county cricket circuit would have surely guaranteed me a luxurious property on the Algarve, a slot on A Question of Sport and a lifetime's supply of Pringle sweaters. But I'd never have lasted that long. The solitude, an inevitable attack of the yips, the attention span of an eight-year-old and an obligation to wear polo necks under checked jackets would have soon made me a basket case.

It was amazing, given the constant pressure he was under, that this hadn't yet happened to Tiger Woods. I (plus about 75 assorted media) walked the course with him, during his second round at Royal Birkdale. 'I love this golf course,' he had said, a picture of contentment after his first-round 65. 'It is extremely difficult but fair. There's no blind trouble; it's all right in front of you.'

But now the trouble was above him, below him and all around him. Thursday's balmy conditions had given way to slanting rain and buffeting winds. Crowds massed round the first tee and Woods, emerging for his afternoon start, had to fight his way to it. A police cordon, looking like a parade from *Dixon of Dock Green*, complicated rather than eased his passage through a sea of celebrity-hunters, then he was obliged to stand and wait until the group in front had moved on.

At last it was time for him to tee off. There was a rumble of thunder as he addressed the ball, and I remembered that golf adage that you should always hold a two-iron above your head if there's lightning around because even God can't hit a two-iron. Woods stroked his drive crisply up the middle, then led a gaggle of officials, journalists, photographers, TV people, radio commentators, ball-finders and security men down the fairway. Black-anoraked men kept the media in check; marshals in purple jackets recruited from the British Army Golf Association escorted Woods from dawn to dusk, maintaining a beady eye on the public. Everywhere he went people gawped and lenses pointed at him from the long grass. He was like a rare beast roaming through a safari park.

The rain bucketed down, the air was horizontal, bunkers gobbled balls, putts swerved round holes, at one point play was suspended. Woods, exuding a magnificent aura, with his statuesque physique, confident stride and richly expressive face, kept his cool. He was heeding the wise counsel of his surrogate older brother, Mark O'Meara. They'd spent the previous week together in Ireland practising, fishing, and talking about dealing with the spotlight. On that vile second day at Birkdale he smiled, he grimaced, he played bump-and-run shots under the wind. When his resolve slipped on the ninth and he had a huge slog with a driver, hooking the ball into the rough, he scolded himself and soon resumed normal, consistent service. Despite sacrificing the tournament lead, he sailed through the press conference as his idol Michael Jordan might have done. He was humble, honest and humorous.

I cornered him at the back of the press tent afterwards. I wondered how he coped with all the attention. He drew an immediate contrast with South American footballers. 'Remember after the 1994 World Cup in the States what happened to that Colombian player [Andrés Escobar] who'd scored an own goal? He got shot for it. I don't see that happening in golf if I hit a bad shot or something.'

And there you have it. Golf might be a solitary profession, but the only responsibility the players have is to themselves. It might turn them a bit cranky, they might put on weight and lose their beautiful wives to someone more attentive. But it's not a matter of life or death.

RESTLESS WHISPERS

Covering an elite golf tournament is exhilarating. You're made to feel like a VIP, being permitted inside the ropes, and as close as you dare to the players – some will even chat to you on the way round – and you can stare in wonder at their power, their precision and their appalling taste in knitwear. And you get a decent bit of exercise, instead of being stuck in a press box all day.

Despite the privilege of attending every England Test match, I was vexed by my inactivity there. All I did was agonise over a couple of dull questions with England's and South Africa's captains at the toss. Alec Stewart had taken over from an exhausted Atherton for England, which made for slightly longer but more predictable answers, and Hansie Cronje was equally platitudinous: if only we'd known what he was really up to! Then there'd be nothing much to do for about eight hours until, at close of play, it was time to see how many times Graham Thorpe said 'y'know' in a two-minute sound bite. Why do we do these interviews? I still haven't really fathomed it.

Having heard the tale of Garth Crooks and Gordon Strachan, I tried to keep my interview technique simple. Crooks, working for the BBC, with a reputation for being rather verbose, was trying to get some after-match comments from Strachan, then manager of Coventry. Twice he knocked on the dressing-room door and was politely told to come back in a little while. Eventually he became desperate: 'I'm really sorry, Gord, but we need to do this soon. We're off air at five-thirty,' said Crooks.

'OK, Garth,' said Strachan. 'I've got to do an interview for Sky first. You go down to the touchline and start asking your first question, and I'll be down in two minutes to answer it.'

The commentary boxes were extra cramped that summer, chiefly due to the regular presence of tabloid reporters and legal representatives hanging around Boycott after his suspended sentence for allegedly assaulting his girlfriend Margaret Moore. I found the story unbelievable. I couldn't visualise him assaulting anyone, unless they had underestimated his final tally of first-class runs (48,426). And I couldn't imagine that had been the topic of conversation on holiday at the Hotel du Cap in the south of France. I watched the reactions of the other commentators to him on his first day back after the scandal. They were neither overly friendly nor noticeably antagonistic. It was all very matter of fact. Benaud just said, 'Morning, Geoffrey,' and went back to his correspondence. Professionally, they all carried on as if nothing had happened, though I sensed that privately they were uneasy.

Boycott breezed about as if the incident had never taken place. He was even in fine form.

'Eee, that's joost Humpty-Dumpty bowlin',' he said after one appalling over from someone.

'Funny, I've never seen Humpty Dumpty bowl,' Jack Bannister replied good naturedly.

'No,' replied Boycott, 'but if he'd seen that he'd have fallen off the wall.'

I mainly gave the commentary box a wide berth and spent much of the day distracting the BBC videotape operators who fed action replays into the coverage. They were housed in two converted Transit vans connected by a metal walkway located in the ground's car park. There was a pleasant camaraderie here, in contrast to the respectful distance between the occupants of the commentary box. You could laugh at commentators' faux pas, which came through loud and clear ('Strangely, in slow motion, the ball seemed to hang in the air for even longer' – Tony Lewis; 'If you can get somebody out before they get in ...' – Boycott). You could also look at players' idiosyncrasies close up. You could replay and freeze shots of gorgeous girls that cameramen focused on between overs. You could even position the computerised magnifying glass, used for adjudicating on disputed catches, over their cleavage to make all but the flattest chests look like Jordan.

Hanging around in there gave me ideas: if not to start a porn channel then at least to use the various gizmos to explain the more baffling aspects of cricket. Egged on by producer Tony, often referred to as Scally, who'd graduated from doing the death knocks on the Liverpool *Echo* to being something of a whizzkid at the Beeb, I suggested to the editor putting together a few features: maybe an A–Z of cricket jargon, to illuminate the game in the tea interval or during rain breaks. I said it might be a persuasive influence when negotiations for the next TV contract began shortly. The idea fell on deaf ears. So I stuck to asking utterly pointless questions of captains: 'So this match is make or break, isn't it?' And getting utterly predictable answers: 'Yes ...we need to win it and that's what we'll be aiming to do.'

CAUGHT ON THE BOUNDARY

Trent Bridge was the make or break match that summer of 1998. England were 1–0 down against South Africa with two to play, and further behind in the national consciousness after the Football World Cup in France, the Open Golf and the British Grand Prix the previous weekend. Attending the Grand Prix Ball (prior to the race) just underlined cricket's third-rate status. Everyone arrived in stretch limos, there were genuine celebrities everywhere – Ewan McGregor, Elle Macpherson, Stirling Moss ('Oh! Kate's grandpa,' said a Sloaney model at my table) – dancing to Jools Holland and his band, and raffle prizes like 'Body contouring by liposuction for up to two areas of the body'. I thought of various cricketers who could have benefited from that.

The Trent Bridge match, Andrew Flintoff's Test debut (batting at number eight and playing mainly as a bowler), came to a head on Sunday afternoon when England set off in pursuit of 247 for victory. Allan Donald was blisteringly fast, especially in his second spell when he went round the wicket, but Atherton and Hussain were resolute. At 82 for 1, Atherton gloved a bouncer to the wicketkeeper but the New Zealand umpire Steve Dunne remained unmoved. Donald, who had followed through past the batsman, had to trudge all the way back to his mark. The next ball flew off the edge for four. Donald stood, inches from Atherton, and roared his displeasure. Atherton stared back impassively. Then Hussain was dropped by the wicketkeeper off the same bowler.

It was gripping stuff which I watched, riveted, from the top of the new Radcliffe Road Stand that Sir Garfield Sobers – once a Trent Bridge favourite – had officially opened, though not before he had agreed a good fee. Having faced Donald a number of times and discovered that his speed gives you nerves of jelly and feet of clay, I marvelled at the way the England batsmen stood firm. With Donald spent, they coasted to victory the next day.

The match was a watershed for the umpires. Dickie Bird paid a social visit, and even bought a drink (hardback sales of his autobiography were currently at 350,000). 'Just took delivery of my new powder-blue Jaguar XJ6,' he said proudly. "Ere, d'you think I'll pull the birds in that?' But umpires still in their day job weren't so happy with their lot. I ran in to Merv Kitchen, who had just officiated alongside Dunne in the Test, dejectedly getting into his car (an ordinary saloon) at the end. 'Can't say I enjoyed that Test match, Yozzer,' he muttered in his Somerset burr, reflecting on a couple of errors highlighted by television. 'I think it will be my last, I'm afraid.' I sympathised and asked why. 'I don't think I feel up to the job no more,' he said, and alluded to a couple of South African batsmen he'd wrongly given out caught. 'When I looked at the replays later I realised I'd made a mistake. It's terribly depressing, and I've had some awful mail – offers of special prescription glasses, hearing aids – which just makes it worse.'

He drove off sadly, leaving me in a bit of a quandary. Did he see me as a working journalist or an off-duty television interviewer or an empathetic former player? Was he speaking to me on or off the record? I had no idea. I did know it was an interesting revelation that could form the basis of a column about the invidious pressure on umpires. I also knew that the slot in the *Telegraph* to which I often contributed, entitled 'Talking Cricket', had been renamed 'Talking Bollocks' by some members of the cricket press because it was invariably waffle. It seldom broke new ground. Here was an opportunity to do so.

Sensing Kitchen might get cold feet about publicising his comments, I wrote up our conversation as sensitively as I could, but without phoning him. I buried his comments in the middle of the piece, thinking it wouldn't draw too much attention to them. That was both feeble and naïve. Recognising the rarity of a decent news story from my direction, the *Telegraph* subs gave the piece ostentatious back-page treatment and a headline which read: 'HEAT PROVING TOO MUCH FOR KITCHEN'.

I had already concluded that Merv, an umpire with whom I had always got on well, would never speak to me again, but then Allan Donald declared on radio that umpires like him who were so obviously racked by self-doubt had no business standing in Test matches. Now *no* umpire would ever speak to me again. Donald was consequently fined £600 for his remarks about Kitchen and threatened with imminent suspension from the final Test, which many would see as being my fault. Now no *player* would ever speak to me again.

Luckily, Donald was spared the suspension and played in the final Test; and everyone spoke to me, at least when I was holding a BBC microphone. England won it, thanks, in part, to some appalling decisions from Umpire Javed Akhtar. The episode was, I realised, the closest I'd come to influencing the course of a Test match. England had staged a stunning comeback to win the series 2–1 and for the first time in the summer got cricket on to the front page ... below a picture of Anthea Turner posing naked with a python.

OUT OF SIGHT

The BBC had taken some satisfaction from England's series win and the unprecedented live transmission of euphoria in their dressing room. Three weeks later, a rude awakening confronted them. The Test match rights for the next four years, for which they had assumed they were a shoo-in, were awarded to Channel 4 and Sky. The BBC got nothing. I immediately imagined ECB voices saying to BBC executives, 'Well, chaps, your commentary's fine but that toss interviewer ... *ye gads.*' In fact, the reason for the change was that Channel 4 had delivered a slick presentation involving current players – Hussain, Dean Headley and Thorpe – and promising innovation and energy, while the BBC's effort was complacent and cobbled together at the last minute.

There was initial shock in the Beeb's sports department, which had, in recent years, seen the departure of football, rugby, boxing, motor-racing, the Derby, the Cheltenham Festival and the Ryder Cup. It had covered Test cricket uninterrupted except by war since 1938. The shock turned to anger in some, introversion in others; while one outed himself as gay.

It happened like this. We were on a cricket production team outing to the movie *Out of Sight* starring George Clooney. It was one of Jennifer Lopez's early flicks and she looked smboulderingly seductive throughout.

'Cor, I fancy a bit of that, don't you?' I said to the producer next to me.

'I'm more of a Clooney fan myself,' he said.

'Why?' I asked.

'Haven't you realised?' he whispered. 'I bowl around the wicket. I couldn't tell anyone before or I wouldn't have been allowed to film in a cricket dressing room again.'

It seemed to me an excellent qualification for working for Channel 4, but he never applied. Encouraged by Tanya, I did straight away. We both imagined the ideas the BBC had rejected might be more favourably received at Channel 4. I wrote to their head, Michael Jackson, mentioning words like 'jargonbusting' and 'analysis' and outlining a convoluted suggestion involving a sketch board to illustrate field settings: a sort of Peter Snow of cricket.

It turned out to be a meeting of minds and soon I found myself in the Piccadilly offices of the appointed production company, Sunset and Vine, discussing (slightly sceptically) the idea of voicing items from the videotape truck, and who the commentators might be. Mark Nicholas and Richie Benaud were already signed; other names bandied around were Wasim Akram, Michael Holding, Tony Greig and Ian Smith. Quite a multicultural selection. Significantly, there was no Geoff Boycott. He'd recently had his guilty verdict upheld in the girlfriend-beating case and even the *Sun*, that distinguished pillar of moral values, had jettisoned him from the payroll. Despite his peerless commentary, his brilliant précis of situations or incidents, his one-take pieces to camera, his fascinating relationship with Ann Wyatt, sometimes referred to by colleagues as the Black Widow, as she often delivered him to the door clad head to toe in dark Chanel and then disappeared God knows where before picking him up at the close, he faced broadcasting exile. No serious operator would touch him with a barge pole now. So he signed up with Talksport.

But that came later. First there were the Ashes. After beating South Africa, England had high expectations of finally regaining the urn. In exuberant mood, Darren Gough said, 'We have a pretty good chance against Australia. Myself, Gus Fraser and Dominic Cork are a pretty good attack. I've heard people calling us the Dream Team.' Perhaps those people were the Australian batsmen, since neither Fraser nor Cork posed them any problems, although Gough himself was still a decent force. Andrew Caddick, not a favourite of the captain Alec Stewart, was left behind despite taking a hundred wickets for Somerset.

An even bigger problem was in the slow-bowling department. England sent two off-spinners to Australia (Robert Croft and Peter Such) and no left-armer, obviously influenced more by Muttiah Muralitharan's 16 wickets to win The Oval Test for Sri Lanka in September than by Croft's analysis of 0 for 211 during the summer's Tests. A spread-betting firm, City Index, conceived a market entitled 'Wish you were 'ere, Tuffers' which enticed punters to gauge how many runs Croft and Such would concede in the Tests before they took a wicket. The answer turned out to be only 55, but neither made any headway until the series was lost.

England, hampered again by injuries and the loss of all five tosses, were totally outclassed. The batting, with the exception of Mark Ramprakash and Hussain, was fallible; the bowling, bar Headley, lacked incisiveness. England were even hammered by Australia's second XI before the fourth Test. Stewart, captaining, keeping and batting at the pivotal number-four spot, had far too much on his plate. The Ashes had been sacrificed by the third Test, Australia won the series 3–1 and the Sydney *Daily Mirror* gloated: 'Is there anyone in England who can play cricket?'

CHAPTER 10 – 1999

OCCUPATIONAL HAZARDS

Our son Callum was approaching his first birthday. He had more teeth (seven) than words. They say having kids changes your life, and it's true. I would have missed most of the Australia v. England one-day series on Sky if I hadn't volunteered to get up in the dark to give him his milk. I still missed some of it because the little bugger had worked out how to switch channels to watch *Teletubbies*. If I tried to switch it back to the cricket there was a performance rivalling any Dominic Cork appeal for LBW, and I was stuck with Dipsy and Po prancing about instead of Gough strutting his stuff or Warne spinning his web.

One morning it dawned on me how similar the programmes were. Teletubby land was a green sward with herbaceous borders like the Adelaide Oval (one of Sky's commentators, Allan Border, was known as 'Herbie'). Their colours mirrored the pyjamas worn in one-day series and Teletubby house was a modern take on a cricket pavilion with lookouts and automatic doors, making gatemen redundant. Inside are all the things you're familiar with in a modern English cricket pavilion: beds, a toaster, large amounts of custard (chief sampler G. A. Gooch, the England team manager) and a machine that hoovers up all the leftovers (Mark Taylor/Shane Warne).

When the dust had settled on England's travails, David Welch invited some of the *Telegraph*'s writers to a lunch at Canary Wharf to discuss coverage of the Cricket World Cup,

the big event of the summer. I offered up a few ideas, including a big interview with Sachin Tendulkar, who had seven
$1 million sponsors. Ninety-two-year-old Jim Swanton, the
Telegraph's esteemed former cricket correspondent, immaculately turned out in checked blazer, I Zingari tie and braces
pulling trousers up to his nipples, was sitting opposite me
and was more concerned with my casual attire (open-neck
shirt and suede waistcoat). 'Hughes, your prose is acceptable
but your dress isn't,' he said. 'D'you know you can buy ties
in those Tie Rack places? They even have them on station
platforms!'

There were still a couple of months to go until the World
Cup. The host broadcaster, the BBC, used the time wisely.
Despite it being akin to attending their own wake, they
recruited a fabulous array of commentators, and my producer friend Scally created the most sumptuous opening titles.
Shot on 16mm film, they featured stylised shots of all the
major players, as well as computer animations of branches
growing out of bats and red roses entwining round stumps.
They would have done for *Gardeners' World* as well.

Others did not use the time so efficiently. The ECB failed
to attract the sponsorship they'd promised and produced an
opening ceremony at Lord's consisting of a few Girl Guides
waving flags and a £9.99 box of fireworks which shrouded
the whole ground in acrid smoke, to add to the drizzle that
was already falling. Utterly limp? It wasn't as good as that.
I've seen more dramatic openings of a packet of Rice
Krispies. I suppose we should have suspected as much when
they announced their 'celebrity' World Cup ambassadors as
John Kettley and the cast of *Goodness Gracious Me*.
Furthermore, the pre-World Cup concert was cancelled due
to lack of interest, and the World Cup song, produced by
Dave Stewart of Eurythmics fame, didn't mention the words
'cricket' or 'World Cup' and wasn't on sale until halfway
through the tournament.

By that time, just to add further irony, England had been
eliminated. Oh, and at that opening ceremony, Tony Blair's

microphone didn't work initially, and his speechwriter hadn't done his homework. 'Yes, I remember that first World Cup final back in '75,' the PM said when we could finally hear him, 'West Indies versus Australia, when Roy Fredericks hit the first ball of the match for six.' Actually, it was in the fifth over and he fell on his wicket doing so. Still, it *was* Tony Blair. You expect him to get his facts wrong.

At least England won their opening game. But my mind was already on the match the next day between India and South Africa. I had interviewed Sachin Tendulkar in a bog-standard hotel in Leicester, and written about how the fortunes of the willow prince over the next six weeks would influence the Bombay stock exchange, the hopes of the BJP to remain in government and the mood of his entire nation. I had watched him practise and realised that the two great batting gods of the world, Tendulkar and Lara, had vastly different attitudes. To Lara, a net was an occupational hazard, whereas to Tendulkar it was the laboratory to create clinical perfection. Lara destroyed bowling attacks; Tendulkar dissected them.

But as a member of the BBC commentary team for the match, I wasn't thinking about Tendulkar or his likely duel with South African speedster Allan Donald. I had a restless night mulling over how to get my mouth round the trickiest name in world sport, Ajay Jadeja. Sounds easy, doesn't it? Ja-day-ja. Try saying it a few times quickly now: Ajay Jadeja, Ajay Jadeja, Ajay Jadeja. It's as good a tongue twister as red lorry, yellow lorry, and it certainly found out Tony Greig. Here's a bit of his commentary on India v. Australia from the MCG: 'And Jadeja is dijappointed ... Jadeja is ji ... da ... I'll come again, Jajeda is didda ... OK, Ja-de-ja looks downcast.' And that was without using his first name.

I was lucky that I wasn't on commentary duty when Jadeja came into bat, and that his innings didn't last long. By then a much more interesting topic of conversation had arisen anyway: earpieces. Both Donald and Cronje wore them to be linked in the field to the coach Bob Woolmer in the pavilion.

It was a clever idea and it set me thinking. With such a device you could have soothing music piped through to you to nullify the noise of Australians sledging or Indians and Pakistanis incessantly appealing. You could get reruns of the *Goons* if you were batting with someone who never gave you the strike. If you had a little microphone attachment as well, you could congratulate a wicket-taking colleague or tell him about the gorgeous blonde near the sightscreen without having to run all the way in from the boundary to do so.

But earpieces were instantly forbidden by the ICC, so that was that.

I moved on to Dublin, where the West Indies were more inconvenienced by a bitter gale than by Bangladesh. (The Windies had hot soup brought out at the drinks interval.) Then it was Edinburgh for Scotland v. Bangladesh (I got all the top matches), which was chiefly memorable for being the first time Richie Benaud had ever met his arch impersonator Billy Birmingham, he of the *Twelfth Man* series fame, who, in perfect Benaud-speak, reads out the Pakistani team: 'Double-deck Abbas, Peanut-butter Jaas, Second-hand car Yaas, Hafeez Hand-missing, etc.' Their meeting was round the back of the rickety BBC commentary box. It was brief.

'How d'you do, Richie?'

'Morning, Billy. Fine, thank you. Now if you'll excuse me, I'm rather busy.'

The World Cup then moved on to a picturesque ground in Amsterdam where Kenya played South Africa, and the aroma of barbecuing steaks blended intriguingly with the unmistakable sweetness of dope wafting from the temporary stands. Disappointingly, there was no live sex going on in specially constructed booths, so, given the mismatch in the field, we had to make our own entertainment in the commentary box. This largely focused on getting specified phrases into the commentary. My challenge was 'ring of fire', a legacy of a curry the night before with Scally and the BBC production team. It was a relatively easy metaphor, given twitchy Kenyan batsmen confronted by the fearsome pace of Allan Donald and a predatory slip cordon. Barry Richards had a much tougher test: to get 'helmet washing' into his commentary. Remember we were transmitting well before the watershed. Richards may not be a premier-league wordsmith, but he's very quick witted. The moment the Dutch groundsman was beckoned on to the field by the umpires to sort out a muddy patch, he declared triumphantly, 'Aha, there's Amstelveen's head groundsman *Helmut Vorshing* with the sawdust.'

Finally, we were in Derby for Pakistan v. New Zealand, where Imran Khan, when he wasn't on his mobile giving radio interviews about the crisis in Kashmir, was scathing about England's narrow mindset, which he believed stemmed from the county system. 'If I had listened to the coaches at Worcester I would have remained a medium-pacer with the keeper stood up. They said I had a decent in-swinger and I shouldn't try to bowl too fast.' And 362 opposing Test batsmen would have been thankful.

England's World Cup campaign was abysmal. It initially stalled because of a dispute over match fees; then there were pockets of unrest over attendance at various sponsors' events; and generally there was little coherent strategy. The players seemed to find the whole thing a bit of a chore. When, on 29 May, Zimbabwe mysteriously beat South Africa (a game that to my knowledge has never been investigated by any of the various match-fixing inquiries), England were put out of their misery, having failed to reach the second stage of the tournament for the first time. Howls of derision ensued: mug shots of eight English batsmen were laid out in the *Sun* under the heading 'GUILTY OF WRECKING ENGLISH CRICKET'. Alec Stewart (captain) and David Lloyd (coach) fell on their swords.

CHANNEL HOPPING

It was hardly an ideal time for a new television channel to take over responsibility for the English game. But, six days after watching Australia beat Pakistan with embarrassing ease in the World Cup final, I headed for Taunton and the first Channel 4 *Cricket Roadshow*. The train was crammed with hippies. I wondered if these people, given the channel's alternative reputation, had been recruited as a wacky backdrop to the show. No, they were destined for the Glastonbury music festival.

At an official function in April, the ECB chief executive Tim Lamb had welcomed Channel 4 as English cricket's progressive new partner. He trumpeted 'a new era for the game', while on a screen behind him, live from Sharjah, Robert Croft's off-spin was simultaneously being deposited onto the pavilion roof by Pakistan's Ijaz Ahmed. Yet, by midsummer, there was some excitement about the new arrangements. Channel 4 had invested in extensive media and billboard promotion, had unearthed an energetic theme tune – Lou Bega's 'Mambo No. 5' – and had some interesting gizmos up its sleeve. These included a gadget that used the stump mikes to detect if the ball had touched the bat, and a graphically superimposed red stripe down the pitch in line with the stumps to help adjudicate LBWs. And, after the World Cup shemozzle, the reassuring thought was that at least things couldn't get any worse for England. A dangerous assumption...

Taunton was abuzz that late June morning. This was due less to the new programme or the New Zealand tourists being in town than to the fact that Channel 4's giant outside-broadcast trucks had taken over half the county ground's car park, creating traffic chaos outside. Mark Nicholas loquaciously introduced the show, beside Richie Benaud, seamlessly transferring his trademark cream jacket and raised eyebrow cross-channel, and a bunch of schoolkids. The new England captain, Nasser Hussain, was interviewed, declaring that 'I expect my players to have fire and passion.' Sybil Ruscoe (a woman on a cricket show!) chatted to Hussain's father and Dermot Reeve did a lively fielding drill. Towards the end I interviewed some of the New Zealanders on the pavilion balcony. It was pretty low brow: I was mainly interested in whether their good-looking quick bowler Geoff Allott had done any modelling. He said he hadn't. 'Well, I fancy you anyway,' I said spontaneously. This was proclaimed to have opened up the final taboo – latent homosexuality in cricket. The show pulled itself back together with a prediction of the forthcoming series between New Zealand and a new England. Benaud, though, cautioned would-be England backers: 'I have one rule, and I always stick to it: never bet on anything that can talk.' As the series progressed, it proved to be wise advice.

Five days later, at Edgbaston, we were doing our first Test, though only for an evening highlights programme. Sky were transmitting it live. Those who hadn't followed developments would have been surprised to switch on BBC1 at 10.58 a.m., hoping to hear Benaud saying, 'Thanks, Tony. Morning everyone,' to find instead the opening of the Scottish parliament. The highlights format was a useful exercise that gave the Channel 4 team time to experiment with the new equipment. It was a bit like having a net. I had been axed from doing the toss interviews, in favour of the former Kiwi wicket keeper Ian Smith. I was initially miffed until it dawned on me that it was the equivalent of cul-de-sac journalism: two minutes of dead ends. Instead I alternated with Dermot Reeve in the videotape van (twice the size of the BBC one), situated in the car park, putting together thirty-second featurettes about the play. We were instantly dubbed the Vanalists. We were quite competitive, each trying to point out something cleverer than the other.

In a match played in fast forward, England had ended the second day needing 200 to win with nine wickets in hand. This proved less problematic than Channel 4's second *Roadshow*, broadcast before the Saturday's play. There were various technical problems and my interview with a couple of journalists in the press box caused considerable chagrin among the rest, who preferred a peaceful Saturday morning picking holes in rivals' columns. I redeemed myself by handing back to our host, who was wearing a white T-shirt under a dark jacket, by saying, 'And now back to Mark Nicholas, who is obviously commemorating the fact that today is Tom Cruise's birthday.' The hacks in the press box laughed, but, Nicholas understandably, managed only a forced smile. It caused a slightly awkward atmosphere in the commentary box until England, through nightwatchman Alex Tudor's swashbuckling 99, swept to victory.

All was rosy in England's new garden, except in the view of Michael Henderson, just initiated as the new cricket correspondent of the *Telegraph*, who complained about Hussain's diction. 'Someone who went to a good university has no excuse for speaking in that ghastly Estuary sludge,' he wrote indignantly. Generally positive vibes emanated from elsewhere for the next three weeks, mainly because there was no Test cricket.

The *Roadshow* moved on to Durham the following Saturday. I arrived by hovercraft, train and taxi from Carnoustie, where I'd been covering the Open for the *Telegraph*. Tanya had impressed on me the importance of wearing smart shirts on TV, and, to avoid unsightly creasing, I hung up my favourite blue Prada in the train from Edinburgh and draped it over the back of the luggage trolley at Durham station. But a sudden gust of wind blew it off and straight under another passenger's trolley, leaving huge creases and a dirty mark right across it. I had to wear it under an anorak on the show, despite a temperature of 26°C.

I headed straight back to Scotland and the golf after the show, arriving in St Andrews – where the *Telegraph* team were put up – in mid-afternoon. With time to kill, I wandered round the old town, admiring the twelfth-century ruins, the quaint cottages and the 'swimming pool' cut out of the cliff. *Star Wars* was showing in the cinema and when I went to buy a ticket, the cashier said, 'D'you want stalls or circle?' St Andrews is quite a step back in time.

The following day was that crazy Sunday when the tournament leader Jean Van de Velde squandered his five-stroke lead with his paddle in the Barry Burn on the eighteenth. 'Oh, someone go and get him and talk some sense in him,' said Peter Alliss as the Frenchman proceeded to take his shoes and socks off to retrieve his ball. But no one did and he ended up losing the three-way play-off to Paul Lawrie.

It was all rather at odds with the extraordinary sporting achievements of the French in recent months. They'd won the Football World Cup, consecutive Rugby Union Grand Slams, Zinedine Zidane was Footballer of the Year and a French-inspired Arsenal had done the Double. Their sportsmen were highly skilled, but the foundation of their success lay in the sophistication and assiduousness of French managers and coaches. People like Arsène Wenger and rugby coach Pierre Villepreux were fascinated by their sports, regarding them less as art and more as science. They brandished computer printouts rather than big sticks in training. Everything was monitored and measured. The coaches created a stable base on which the flamboyance of players like Zidane and the rugby fly-half Thomas Castaignede could flourish. But, as Van de Velde proved, Gallic flair left to its own devices can end up self-destructing.

AUSPICIOUS BEGINNINGS

Thursday, 22 July 1999 was our big moment on Channel 4: a live Test match for the first time. England v. New Zealand at Lord's. The only place to start. Joining Mark Nicholas and Richie Benaud in the commentary box were Dermot Reeve, Ian Smith, Wasim Akram and James Whittaker, formerly captain of Leicestershire. They sat regally surveying the field from inside the Lord's media centre, doing half-hour stints of commentary. I sat in a giant darkened truck behind the indoor cricket school, surrounded by screens and people called Stacker, Storming and Barnsley. Our boss was Gary Franses, a career cricket producer and master planner, and our safety valve was director Rob Sheerlock, recruited from Channel 9.

He was the ultimate oxymoron, a calm, modest Australian. With a unique ability to sit in front of forty-two screens listening to five people at once and virtually pre-empt what commentators were going to say, he held everything together.

The general consensus was that Channel 4 might show the game from odd, low angles, with a house music underlay; that there'd be a camera in the showers, commentary using words like 'wicked' and 'cool' and a presenter who was a cricket-loving transvestite. I have no reason to assume Mark Nicholas was wearing anything untoward beneath his immaculate Richard James suit, but everyone's fears were banished as soon as the players emerged and Richie Benaud said, 'Morning everyone, and what a marvellus day it is at the headquarters of cricket for this second Cornhill Test between England and New Zealand ...'

We had one simple aim: to make cricket coverage more interesting and informative. The motivation was to undermine the trend for watching cricket on TV with the sound on mute while listening to the *TMS* radio commentary. We wanted the material on screen to be so interesting that people were compelled to increase the TV volume. So within a few minutes they saw for the first time the 'red zone' (the red stripe down the pitch) and the listening device to detect edges that we christened the 'Snickometer' (and its slightly nerdy inventor and operator 'Snicko'). We also enhanced the permanent little graphic in the corner of the screen – known in the trade as the 'ticker' – which tells you the score. Although, ironically, it wasn't as effective as it should have been in the Hughes home. When Tanya called down from upstairs to ask the Test score, her mum glanced at the numbers on the screen and shouted back, 'Eighty-four minus three.'

During that first day's play, either I or Dermot Reeve popped up every so often between overs to give brief explanations of wickets or players' psychology, with our nimble-fingered sidekick Damien Dexter running short video sequences using a little box of tricks in front of him. Together we developed split screens of two bowlers, illustrating their different styles, or of batsmen getting out twice in a similar way.

We were live all through lunch, during which the slot I'd called 'jargonbusting' attempted to define cricketing vernacular. The first day's phrase was 'through the gate', which was eminently appropriate, given how England batted. If they weren't missing straight ones or offering slip-catching practice, they were diving out of the way of Chris Cairns's slower ball, which promptly landed on the stumps. 'WHO'S A SILLY DUCKER' was the *Sun*'s headline the next morning, alluding to Chris Read's embarrassing misjudgement. Having won the toss, England closed at a dismal 183 for 9.

I was determined to try to demystify the game, and wandered up and down the pitch before the second day's play, explaining the unique Lord's problems of batting on a sloping surface, part-sympathising with the England batsmen. Various producers and other bystanders congratulated me afterwards on the first proper explanation of the Lord's slope they'd ever seen on TV. But Alan Mullally, walking past towards the dressing room just as I was finishing, said, 'What a load of fucking shit!' (This from the Aussie-born guy who took his surfboard on tour to [landlocked] Zimbabwe.)

I spent almost the entire day in the videotape truck. (Dermot Reeve soon tired of the idea, realising it constrained his grand ambitions involving commentary and marketing girls.) Despite the claustrophobia, I really enjoyed putting together little vignettes, and there was a never-ending stream of subjects. However, I began to feel a bit isolated, sensing a 'them (the commentators) and me' situation developing.

The press reaction to Channel 4's first two days' coverage was hugely flattering. Most were highly complimentary, waxing lyrical over its tone and innovations; 'and thank you Simon Hughes, a.k.a. the Analyst', wrote Ian Wooldridge in the *Daily Mail*, 'for at last explaining the intricacies of the Lord's slope to the layman'. I toyed with the idea of planting that cutting in Alan Mullally's hand, but, seeing as he'd had a long and fairly unrewarding day on said pitch, I decided against it.

The *Guardian* was generally positive about the coverage, but took a hard line on Mark Nicholas, suggesting he was a parody of Roger Moore with 'his ludicrous bouffant hair looking like someone on the pull in St Tropez', and claiming that he had 'a laminated veneer of self-regard'. Nicholas looked sheepish all day, clearly hurt by the insult (it *was* rather harsh). Giles Smith, in the *Telegraph*, was a little kinder: 'The camera loves him,' he wrote, 'and its love does not, shall we say, go unrequited.' This was a succinct assessment of someone who had at last found his niche. With his suave good looks, his confident articulacy and his deep love of the game, he was born to front cricket on TV.

The signs were there, even as a teenager, that he was destined for a career on screen. One evening in 1977, after he and I had played for the same Middlesex Under-19 side at the Cambridge Festival, he'd asked if I had a comb he could borrow. I remember this both for the image-consciousness it revealed in him even then and for the revelation that I had sufficient hair at that time for anyone to imagine I might own such an item. I didn't, as it happened. Neither Mark nor anyone else has ever asked me for one since. His mane of hair and his frequent grooming of it, often tossing his head back like a proud horse, earned him an early nickname – 'Elvis'. He had others, too, notably 'Jardine', after his slightly grandiose style of captaincy at Hampshire, though mostly people referred to him simply as 'MCJ'.

With our acting backgrounds, our decent rather than top-notch cricket careers, our journalistic endeavours for the same paper, and our constant knocking at telly's door until we were finally let in, we have followed remarkably similar career paths. He, with his natural charm, dapper style sense and patrician air, found his rightful place beneath the bright lights of the TV studio. I, with my self-deprecation, non-conformist dress and sweat-glistened pate, was definitely more suited to the gloom of the VT truck.

The bosses at Channel 4 were delighted with the performance and reaction after the first couple of days on air, and
threw a lavish party on the Friday night of the Lord's Test,
attended by a lot of the executives, many wearing untucked,
large-collared shirts and trendy square glasses. They wouldn't
have been quite so happy when the match ended soon after
lunch on Sunday – leaving acres of airtime to fill – with an
England defeat. Having done a few post-match interviews, I
stayed around chatting to the man of the match, New
Zealand's Matt Horne, with whom I'd played club cricket in
Auckland. He was distinctly unimpressed with the England
players' attitude. 'Whenever we lost a wicket and a new batsman walked to the crease, they just said, "Oh, here comes
another tail-ender!" which made us all even more determined
to stay in,' he said. English arrogance underestimated Kiwi
doggedness.

That was certainly how Boycott had seen it, watching from
his home in West Yorkshire. If there was one thing the
Channel 4 coverage was perceived to lack, it was an authoritative critique of England's performance, so I visited Boycott
to interview him for the Saturday Roadshow. He lives in a
stone farmhouse, just off the M1 near Wakefield, which, he
told me proudly, was 303 years old. I noticed the unlived-in
sitting room festooned with pictures of him, old bats on the
walls, balls, bronzes and other mementoes of his career: a
shrine to himself. There was a cleaner ironing his shirt in the
kitchen, then his partner, Ann Wyatt, emerged, stick thin
with a bouffant hairdo and heavy make-up: she looked like a
character out of Thunderbirds.

While the cameraman set up, Boycott gave me a guided
tour of the garden, switching on the 'water feature' (a little
waterfall), showing me the specially created bunker and
raised green where he endeavoured to reduce his golf handicap, and pointing out a wooden cross in the flower bed.
'Felix! One of my cats. I love cats. They coom and go as they
please, don't need no looking after.' They were loners, like
him, I thought, and fickle with it.

We sat down in the shade of a tree: he dapper as ever in a lime-green jacket, yellow tie, cream trousers and boater. He began to lament the art of English batsmanship and spoke loudly, almost stridently, when the camera was rolling:

'I don't know what was in their 'eads. Most of 'em played nicely for a few minutes, then suddenly tried to hit one over midwicket or dab a wide one to third man. We seem to have lost the art of batting for a *whole* day. Not blocking, but sensible batting. It's not good enough just to argue, "It's the way I play." They're not tough enough mentally, don't play smart cricket.'

He carried on in this vein, adding, when the cameraman was changing tape, 'Fook me, I could make roons against that attack with my sweeping broosh.' Back on camera, he delivered a fulsome parting shot:

'At Old Trafford, I'd go into the dressing room and say to the batsmen, "Go out there and bat all day." If you get out to a stupid shot, you are not playing in the next Test or going to South Africa. If they think that's unfair pressure, then I'd say, "Hey, my dad went down pit ten hours a day, five days a week, fifty weeks a year and every day he didn't know if the roof were gonna fall in on his 'ead. Now that's pressure."'

It was hard to disagree. The problem was that there was no one in the England camp to say it. Hussain, the captain, was injured for the Old Trafford Test (Mark Butcher stood in), and there was no other figure of authority. That was illustrated when Alan Knott approached the 'international team's director', Simon Pack, an ex-army friend of Lord MacLaurin, offering to help the young wicketkeeper Chris Read.

'Who do I talk to about this?' asked Knott.

'I don't know,' said Pack.

'Well, who's in charge of England's coaching?' asked Knott.

'There isn't anyone in charge of coaching,' said Pack.

The ECB's capacity for disorganisation was proving limitless.

BOTTOM OF THE WORLD

The third Test was a grind. Perhaps taking Boycott's observations literally, England staged a go-slow. Atherton laboured more than two hours for 11; Hick, whose recall Michael Henderson described to startled *Telegraph* readers as 'buttock-clenchingly grim', managed only one more; and Peter Such, whose Test batting average of 6.09 hardly inspired confidence with him coming in at number ten, hung about for seventy-two minutes without troubling the scorers.

Talking to some of the players in the bar, I learned of the terrible atmosphere in the England dressing room. The injured Hussain wasn't talking to anyone because he didn't want to subvert Butcher's captaincy; Stewart wasn't talking to anyone because he didn't want to bat at number three or keep wicket; Thorpe was morose because he wanted to be captain; and Ramprakash was sullen and introverted because there were rumours that this was his last chance. Not exactly a set of moods conducive to positive cricket.

Rain rendered the match a tedious draw, and in an attempt to lift the mood during the last day, I put together a few slightly more obscure pieces down in the truck: looking at how batsmen kept their concentration going between balls; plotting the distance fielders had to move between overs, etc. While Richie was perpetually complimentary, always saying, 'Well, that's absholutely fashinating,' Ian Smith put my offerings into perspective. When he was next cued to hand down to me he said, 'Well, now it's time to go down to the Analyst again, so why don't you go off and make a cup of tea.'

Apart from that, the only lighter moment was during an extended rain delay. We'd gone off air and Barry Richards, who'd joined us for the day, mentioned Don Bradman's response when asked how many he might have made against the current England attack.

'Oh about sixty,' said Bradman.

'Only sixty?' was the interviewer's surprised reply.

'Well, I am eighty-nine,' retorted Bradman.

Channel 4 were receiving lots of encouraging letters and emails from viewers, and 'the Analyst' seemed a popular slot. This was a handicap as I walked onto the field to play in Nasser Hussain's benefit match in Billericay; my first game for some months. I had to open the bowling against the full Essex XI, including Peter Such, whom I'd angered by describing his skills as 'redundant' in my *Telegraph* column. He clonked me for several fours, and came on to bowl when I was batting, while the close fielders all 'analysed' me, muttering, 'Mmm, the problem is he doesn't move his front leg much,' or 'Looks like he's got a weakness outside off-stump.' It dawned on me how lucky I had been to play in an era without super-slo-mo cameras and magnifying glasses ... not to mention 'analysts'. I'd have been exposed as an erratic chucker who frequently lost his run-up and whose batting consisted of the obdurate block and the hopeful waft. My innings at Billericay was mercifully brief.

Derek Pringle and I talked with Hussain in the bar afterwards, and he was interested in players we had seen who might be worth taking on tour to South Africa. Among others, I recommended Yorkshire's Gavin Hamilton, suggesting he 'could become a Thorpe who bowls'.

The fourth and final Test was at The Oval. Hussain was back and assisted for the first time by Duncan Fletcher, who was due to take over as coach in the winter. Both sides had a chance of winning the series but England didn't help themselves by selecting a long tail of Caddick, Mullally, Tufnell and debutant Ed Giddins: effectively a rabbit and three bloodhounds. Alec Bedser would have undoubtedly fancied his chances of polishing them off, and he was eighty-one. It was arguably one of the worst batting orders England have ever fielded. And it was difficult to analyse any of them properly because, by the time I had found the appropriate TV pictures with which to explore the batsman's technique, he was out. Ian Smith, whose waspish humour and astute observations had given the commentary real bite, was positively gloating on the third morning, by which time New Zealand were well ahead in the game.

My abiding memory of the match was the sight of the muscular Chris Cairns advancing up the pitch to an apprehensive Tufnell, who visibly quaked as Cairns assaulted the ball past his right eardrum and into the stand. His whirlwind 80 set England the highest score of the match to win, and, as was so often the case with this side, once Atherton had gone, they folded. In the two innings England's last three wickets had managed a total of two runs. There was a message in there somewhere.

The defeat gave New Zealand the series, and Ian Smith the last (and longest) laugh when it was revealed that the result had consigned England to the bottom of the Test match rankings for the first time. Hussain was booed as he came up onto the balcony for the inevitable post-series interview. The headlines the next morning took a slightly sadistic pleasure in England's demise: 'WORLD CHUMPS!' said one; 'THE WORST TEAM IN THE WORLD!' declared another. As usual, the *Sun* went the whole hog and created a special souvenir edition fronted by a huge picture of burning bails headed by the announcement: 'RIP ENGLISH CRICKET WHICH DIED AT THE OVAL ON 22 AUGUST 1999'.

PART II

MISSION CONTROL
2000–05

CHAPTER 11 – 2000

NO-GO ZONE

I had bucked the trend. Like Mark Nicholas, I had managed to prove that you could commentate on Test cricket without being a player of international repute; or, in my case, much repute at all. It was all to do with starting your preparation early (i.e. aged ten). I don't know whether they were influenced by this, but the BBC announced they were dropping Fred Trueman and Trevor Bailey from their radio commentary team. Well, they did have a combined age of 144.

More importantly, I had proved you could commentate on Test cricket in total darkness without being able to see the pitch; not with the naked eye, anyway. In *The Times*, Simon Barnes attempted to orchestrate a campaign to get me into the commentary box: 'Why was Simon Hughes locked up in those bunkers beneath the Test match grounds?' he demanded. 'Poor man, incarcerated, cut off from the fresh air and merriment, doomed to watch television in the perpetual dark … I am against such inhumanity. Free the St John's Wood One!' It was kind of him to try, but I knew my place. Sky's David Gower and Ian Botham chuckled whenever they saw me around media centres. 'Get back to the lab, Professor!' they said good naturedly.

With no inclination of how long the Channel 4 posting would last, I still saw myself primarily as a sportswriter. I wanted to scale up my *Telegraph* contributions, believing my new TV profile would facilitate some big-name interviews. Top of the list was Michael Owen. He had the world at his feet (and usually at his door) and he was rumoured to be coming back from injury shortly. David Welch promised me a big spread if I could deliver him by the following Saturday.

I rang the Liverpool press office and spoke to the person who'd set up (or rather *failed* to set up) the Robbie Fowler interview two years earlier.

'Hi,' I said, 'it's Simon Hughes here.'

'Who?' said the girl.

'Simon Hughes: feature writer, TV presenter, the Analyst on Channel 4 cricket? I did the Sporting Relations piece with Robbie Fowler and Ian Rush, remember?'

'No, sorry, I don't,' she said.

'Well, anyway, I was wondering if I could have a few minutes with Michael Owen for a big Saturday morning piece. The whole country's interested in him and how his recovery's going.'

'All requests for interviews have to be in writing.'

'The thing is, it's Tuesday today and really I've only got tomorrow and Thursday if I'm to write it on Friday.'

'They've got a day off tomorrow.'

'Surely he'll be coming in for treatment?'

'No, they've got a day off.'

'Presumably he'll be in on Thursday, then?'

'I don't know what the manager's plans are, and I won't get to speak to him 'til Thursday.'

'OK,' I said, getting slightly exasperated. 'What about Friday morning? Can I talk to him then?'

'No, that's too close to the match on Saturday.'

'But he's injured; he won't be playing on Saturday.'

'We don't allow one-to-one player interviews the day before matches.'

'So when can I talk to him?'

'Well, I'm not sure about their schedule next week.'

'They're bound to be in on Monday.'

'I can't say definitely.'

'If they are, can I talk to him then?'

'All requests for interviews have to be in writing.'

I decided to explore more familiar avenues. I persuaded
Welch to let me travel to South Africa, where England were
due on tour in November and I hadn't been since the aboli-
tion of apartheid, to report on the progress of sporting integration. I'd heard it had become an extremely dangerous
country since I'd last visited and that crime in Johannesburg
especially was rife. But remembering my apprehension of visiting Northern Ireland in the eighties and never hearing so
much as a balloon pop, never mind a bomb explode, I took
that news with a pinch of salt. Within half an hour of arriving in Jo'burg, I'd seen an attempted car-jacking and had my
mobile phone nicked.

I felt safe within the confines of the Sandton Sun and
Towers, a concrete mini-town of interconnecting hotels,
shops and restaurants. But I had considerable reservations
about a proposed visit to Alexandra, Jo'burg's poorest township, where a good proportion of South Africa's sixty-five
murders a day were supposed to occur. But my taxi driver
said he knew the area well and would show me around.

It was an illuminating tour through a teeming mass of
primitive dwellings housing 400,000 blacks in an area roughly the size of Hyde Park. It's only ten minutes' drive from the
high-rise centre of Johannesburg, but it couldn't be more of
a contrast. We drove along streets cascading with people and
livestock, past lines of vegetable and fruit stalls and trestle
tables groaning under a thousand knick-knacks. Most of the
dwellings were mere shacks, but the people looked happy as
they went about their daily business. Egged on by the driver,
I plucked up the courage to get out and buy a pineapple from
a stall. It was twenty-five cents. I gave the lady a one-rand
note and waved away the change, but she wouldn't accept it,
pressing other fruit items on me instead.

We made our way to the township's cricket ground. Part of
a large recreation area, overrun by footballers, it had an arti-
ficial cricket pitch and a clubhouse built with British funds
channelled in by John Major. In the nets, one tiny African
boy was bowling half a tennis ball to another who hit it with

a shoe. On the pitch was a match between Parktown Boys High, a posh Johannesburg school, and Dinkwe, a development team drawn from surrounding impoverished areas. Half the high-school team were non-white, as were all their opponents. The standard was higher than you'd find among sixteen-year-olds in England. The fielding was exceptional.

When I had last played here fifteen years before, West Indies' Colin Croft was turfed out of second class on a train, Collis King's car was shot at, first-class cricket was all-white, and blacks had no status and only menial jobs. Now it felt as if sporting integration was genuinely starting to happen. Local cricket results in the Johannesburg *Star* regularly featured names like Elite Mabena, Abner Letsie and Sonnyboy Letshele. The captain and wicketkeeper of South Africa's Under-19 team was Thami Tsolekile, who had shared a two-room shack in Langa township with a dozen relatives until he was thirteen. Clearly he'd relish the opportunity cricket afforded. And wouldn't be inhibited by close fielders.

I discovered strong white resistance in the professional game to quotas – two players 'of colour' in each first-class team, five in regional junior sides. But it seemed the only way to redress the awful imbalances of the past. And some whites, like the former Springbok and Essex all-rounder Huw Page, were trying to help the process by acting as mentors to young black players. He was supervising the progress of Welcome Plessie, a teenager from Soweto, who a year earlier had witnessed his father murdering his mother.

I sat in the foyer of the Sandton Sun and Towers, enduring a muzak version of 'You'll Never Walk Alone', thinking we didn't know we were born in England and contemplating how South Africa had changed. Now they had reclaimed their country, were finding their niches, discovering their athletic prowess.

The England team had just arrived. I lay by the pool with Nasser Hussain for a few minutes and told him what I'd seen. 'There's lot of potential, but they're in turmoil,' I said. 'You'd better beat them now before they get really good.'

Hussain grimaced. 'I'm afraid we're probably going to get worse before we get better,' he said.

He was not wrong. Three weeks later, at the first Test, he was staring out from the Wanderers' dressing room at a scoreboard reading 2 for 4. England were annihilated. Gavin Hamilton, the guy I'd recommended to Hussain at Billericay three months earlier, made two ducks and had bowling figures of 0 for 63. What is known in the trade as a fresh-air game. He never played for England again.

There was a predictable clamour for youth to be given its head in the England side, and proper spending on 'grass roots', often by people at counties who'd just employed thirty-nine-year-old batsmen on three-year contracts (Kim Barnett to Gloucester, Alan Wells to Kent). But they were overlooking the tiny shoots of a revival that had sprouted in that game. Michael Vaughan, just turned twenty-five, made an assured 33 on his Test debut, and Andrew Flintoff, only twenty-one, showed signs of becoming a genuinely exciting all-rounder. What England needed was *less* chopping and changing, not more. I calculated that eighty-six different players had represented England in Tests during the 1990s. The equivalent figure for Australia was forty-one.

Anyway, 'grass roots' are only any good if there is bright light above (i.e. a successful national team). That's how France and Australia, two massively successful sporting nations, had worked it. They had invested hugely at the top end of sports, creating superb academies and, as a result, sporting icons for young people to idolise. Pour in resources at the bottom and it simply tends to dribble away.

KING MUHAMMAD

I spent the rest of the winter writing my next book. Having made something of a success covering the highs and lows of a county career at home, it seemed logical to chronicle my exploits overseas. I had, after all, played in or written from all nine Test-playing countries. My mother had given me the idea. 'You should make something out of all the letters you wrote home,' she said, bearing a box full of them that she'd thoughtfully saved. Little did she imagine that it would also feature lurid details of my post-divorce bedroom charades. Sexploits as well as exploits. Sorry, Mum.

Ostensibly it was a book about cricket and travel, and I wanted to call it *Playing Away*. The publishers were adamant, however, that we forged a link with my previous book, so they decided to call it *Yakking Around the World*. My friends thought 'Yakking' should be replaced by 'Shagging'. Or, bearing in mind my general scoring level, 'Not Shagging' ...

I had one exciting interlude from the isolated routine of sitting in an upstairs room writing my book and pressing 'word count' every half an hour. As their occasional commentator on the World Cup, the BBC invited me to the *Sports Review of the Century*. Unusually, it was held at TV Centre (the annual show was normally staged at an exhibition centre near Westminster Abbey). I was seated between the Olympic oarsmen Greg and Johnny Searle, a couple of 6-foot 4-inch colossi, making me, a 5-foot $9^{1}/_{2}$-inch runt, feel smaller than usual. The highlight of the evening was, of course, Muhammad Ali being crowned Sports Personality of the Century. He shuffled on stage, hands tremoring from his Parkinson's disease, to accept the award from Evander Holyfield. The standing ovation lasted over five minutes. The producers weren't sure if Ali was going to attempt to speak, but they had fitted him with a microphone on his lapel anyway. Finally, when the applause had died down, he summoned up all his strength and said, in a barely audible whisper, 'I enjoyed my time in boxing, and I may come back.'

David Beckham, wearing an extraordinary, oversized checked tie and matching shirt, asked to have a photograph with him. Afterwards they brandished fists and Ali muttered, 'You're so pretty.' That could not be said of the three guests I became variously immersed with later. First was England's hooker Brian Moore, bald headed and gap toothed, who told me he was planning to open a chain of 'nail' bars, enhancing female fingers, he explained, which was an intriguing development from the traditional use of fingernails in the scrum to impale opponents' testicles. Then there was Dickie Bird, waxing lyrical about sales of his new book, although I was unable to concentrate on anything other than his three-inch nostril hair. Finally, the white-haired David Steele – BBC Sports Personality of the Year in 1975 – bemoaned the lack of English batsmen with a 'defence'.

Mark Lawrenson, the BBC football pundit, also told me he was earning £30,000 a year talking for ten minutes a week to a football website. It was a polite way of saying that I had just spent the past thirty-five years in the wrong sport.

DANGER ZONES

The Millennium Bug, against which the world apparently spent £400 billion protecting itself, never happened. (Was this because of the prevention or because it was a figment of computer boffins' imagination?) The papers were printed as usual on 1 January 2000, and the *Telegraph* produced an impressive fourteen-page sports supplement, looking back at the last hundred years of sport. Ali got everyone's vote as Sports*man* of the Century, but Botham was a popular choice as Sports *Personality* of the Century.

It was amusing to compare that with the sports coverage in the *Daily Telegraph* (price 1*d*) from 1 January 1900. The weekend football matches were rounded up in one column, with the only comment on the 1–1 draw between Manchester City and Blackburn being, 'This score fairly indicates the value of the play, for there was little to choose between the two clubs, the attack and defence on both sides being of an even character.' No journalistic licence there, or in the other sports column, on horseracing, and no pictures either, of course. The rest of the page is dominated with items headed,

'EXCITING POLICE CAPTURE' (the arrest of some jewel thieves) and 'CHEVALIER RECITALS'.

Now practically every paper had weekly football pull-outs, and the *Sunday Times* devoted a minimum of twelve pages to it every weekend, which was an interesting development considering the same paper stated in 1985 that football was 'a slum sport for slum people'. In millennium week there were acres of coverage about Victoria Beckham's revelation that David liked wearing her G-strings. The *Sun* even had a page devoted to a cut-out-and-keep 'Beckham Thong Sheet':

(To the tune of 'Glory, Glory Hallelujah')
Glory, glory buns divided,
Glory, glory buns divided,
Glory, glory buns divided,
And the reds go mincing ON, ON, ON.

Or:

(To the tune of the Gap Band's 'Oops Upside Your Head')
Ooh, ah, pants and bra.
Say ooh-ah, pants and bra.

Motivated by all this nonsense, and by Tanya's advice to 'be in his face more', I went to see David Welch to discuss an improved deal. We had lunch at the Front Page in Canary Wharf. Having established myself on TV, I thought I'd easily swing a big contract: more money, staff perks, complimentary cases from the *Telegraph* Wine Society. I underestimated Welch, who seemed to have acquired reptilian characteristics. Instead of seeing the advantages of my new-found exposure, he saw problems: 'Are you still committed?' he asked. 'You seem to have lost your once-a-week regularity.' I whipped out a page of feature ideas I'd drafted that morning and assured him I was as committed as ever to anything and everything. He seemed pleased and agreed a contractual monthly retainer in return for sixty articles a year. 'Congratulations,' he said, clinking my glass. 'Nice to have you properly on board.'

It was a red-letter day. I'd been paid piecemeal for six years. Now I was at last on the *Telegraph*'s regular payroll, entitling me to an official business card, and to use the paper's headed notepaper to get 10 per cent off hotel rooms and try (and invariably fail) to get upgrades on aeroplanes. I visualised immediate engagements to do major stories and big-name interviews, and, sure enough, a fax arrived from Welch later that week saying, 'I thought this might suit you,' accompanied by an invitation from a major sporting charity. This is what it said:

> We are sponsoring Olympic decathlete Daley Thompson on a visit to Sierra Leone. He will conduct some basic coaching sessions with orphaned children in war-torn regions of the country. We will pay for you to accompany him. You will fly to the capital Freetown by scheduled airline then be transferred by United Nations helicopter into the war zone. Officially a truce has been agreed, but there is a slight risk of encountering fighting from rogue guerrilla elements.

I stared at the last sentence for a long time. Was Welch testing out my commitment, or trying to dispose of me? Either way, I didn't fancy it. I'd heard about those 'rogue guerrillas' from my friend Dirty at *Loaded* magazine, who'd been to Sierra Leone and described them as lunatics who came reeling out of the jungle in women's clothes, high on bush drugs, and sprayed Kalashnikov fire willy-nilly. I pleaded unavailability and sent fifty quid to UNICEF instead. Daley didn't go in the end, either.

There were guns involved in my next assignment from Welch, too, but the only danger was when *I* was in possession of one. I was to interview an ace clay-pigeon shooter, Richard Faulds, as part of the build-up to the Sydney Olympics. He was one of Britain's big medal hopes, and Welch was a big track-and-field man. I drove to Faulds's home in Longparish, Hampshire, and he took me out to his specially built range in a nearby field.

It was an interesting experience, sampling how someone in a lonely, precision sport spent his day (six hours' practice). His prowess in his specialist event – double-trap clay – was obvious. Not only was he able repeatedly to hit two clays flying out simultaneously at different trajectories with his own gun (he'd recently broken the world record, hitting 193 out of 200), but after my hopeless attempts he stood beside me at arm's length, guiding my gun turret, shouted 'fire' and still struck with unerring accuracy. He gave shooting from the hip a new meaning. As with the British rowers, his total dedication put professional cricketers to shame.

MATCH-MAKING

The England cricketers had returned from South Africa in February 2000 with their reputations slightly enhanced after a morale-boosting fifth Test win, enjoyed by the unprecedented forfeiture of two innings. But then came the bombshell that South Africa's captain Hansie Cronje had been match-fixing. There were accusations about others, too, including our unpronounceable friend Ajay Jadeja, and some from Chris Lewis relating to England players.

The Cronje allegations were shocking, though perhaps an inevitable consequence of a surfeit of one-day internationals scheduled by greedy administrators. But I must admit I didn't believe Lewis. Anyone who got sunstroke in the Caribbean having shaved their head, and who once said, 'The only people I listen to are Ken Higgs and God,' must be ever so slightly unreliable. Added to that, match-fixing was as old as Beethoven: in 1817 William Lambert, a very talented player, was said to have 'sold a match' and was banished from the game. But it was not rife in Test or English domestic cricket. Tests were too hard to fix (except in very specific circumstances), and county cricket didn't generally attract big punters. If *any* punters. To me, Richie Benaud's favoured motto – 'Don't bet on anything that can talk' – made even more sense.

On a positive note, two important changes were afoot. County cricket was now split into two divisions, and the central contracts idea had finally been given the go-ahead. At last, some thirteen years after the concept was first mooted, the leading England players would be under the jurisdiction of the ECB – basically the coach Duncan Fletcher – rather than their counties. Somerset's insistence that Andrew Caddick, for instance, must play in some one-day caper three days before (or after) a Test could be overruled. And it was. Most of the obvious candidates received the contracts – Hussain, Atherton, Stewart, Gough, Caddick and Thorpe. But eyebrows were raised when one was awarded to Chris Schofield, the young Lancashire leg-spinner.

Channel 4's cricket coverage won a Bafta at the annual awards ceremony in May. The figurine was on display a couple of days later at our pre-Test commentators' meeting. I arrived with my new tool, a pitch-moisture gauge, a slightly modified version of those things surveyors use to test walls for damp. It was immediately christened the 'Dampometer'. The idea had come from a viewer who'd written in suggesting it as a better alternative to poking car keys into the pitch. I thought it had the potential to be quite a big hit, with the product flying off the shelves once club players had seen it in action on the telly. 'It will sell all round the world,' I informed the supplier. Certainly the players were intrigued by it, and Nasser Hussain kept coming up to me before the toss at Test matches muttering, 'Wossit saying?' I gave guarded answers, partly because of the match-fixing scandal that seemed to be consuming anyone and everyone, but mainly because I didn't trust it. Sometimes when the pitch looked dry it said fairly wet; other times the digital display went haywire just as I was going to air and I had to abruptly fix its reading.

Still, the Dampometer had value, not least as a way of

ensuring I was always the one doing the pitch report since I
was the only one who understood how it worked. In time, it
will revolutionise pitch analysis, I thought. But it never
seemed to catch on, and in the end the only person who rang
up asking about it was a friend who was buying a house and
wanted to assess it for rising damp. I lent him the device. I
never saw him, or it, again.

As a result of the Bafta, Channel 4's coverage received
more encouraging support. Lots of people wrote that it was
bright and fresh and innovative. They seemed more interested in that than the mini-series between England and
Zimbabwe. Certainly the gadgets were good – though the
Snickometer was strangely inaccurate until someone discovered the stump mikes hadn't been plugged in. But I thought
the most distinctive aspect of Channel 4 cricket was the tone.
When a batsman got out because of a bad shot, you could
just say, 'That were roobish!' as Boycott would have done.
You could also look at it another way, and point out that the
bowler had, by delivering a superb over or making a clever
field change, forced the batsman into an indiscretion. It was
just as much good bowling as bad batting. In the main, the
Channel 4 commentary team stressed that there were usually two sides to every story.

There was mild criticism from some quarters that we
lacked authority, because, apart from Benaud, we didn't have
oodles of Test runs and wickets to our names. That's OK, we
replied, we rely on the visiting commentators for that. It was
then pointed out that Andy Whittall, our guest Zimbabwean
commentator, had a Test batting average of 7 and had taken
7 Test wickets, each at a cost of 103.

A real star came into our midst during the Lord's Test,
however. I had developed an acquaintance with Sam Mendes
through our mutual connections with theatre and cricket.
He'd done the decent thing and invited me to his Donmar
production of *The Blue Room* starring a naked Nicole
Kidman, so, a month after he'd won an Oscar for *American
Beauty*, I returned the favour and invited him into the VT

truck at the Zimbabwe Test. 'Now meet a real director,' I said to Rob Sheerlock, who was busy cutting the cameras on live play.

The real reason for Mendes's visit, though, was to meet an unexpected idol. You'd imagine the wunderkind of British theatre and the toast of Hollywood would most revere legendary figures like Franco Zeffirelli, David Lean or perhaps his 'mentor' Stephen Spielberg. Maybe some great actors – Brando, Hopkins, Streep. But no. The person he had most wanted to meet for the past twenty years was Mike Brearley. Up in the Lord's media centre, I introduced them.

It was a loaded first encounter. As a teenager, Mendes had imagined himself opening the batting for England and had a poster of the *éminence grise* on his bedroom wall. As a student he'd devoured Brearley's ground-breaking book, *The Art of Captaincy*, describing it as 'a masterpiece', and admitted to carrying it around on set. 'One of its underlying themes is "treat every person differently, don't come with a pre-methodology",' he said. 'That was a very important aspect of how I directed *American Beauty*. The fact is, some actors need encouraging, others need simplifying … Like cricketers.'

Brearley, England's most successful post-war captain, had followed Mendes's recent directing career with considerable interest, and, as a psychoanalyst who regularly treats dysfunctional people, found *American Beauty* – a bleak tale about the breakdown of a superficially normal American family – deeply stimulating.

'D'you know Mendes used your book as a sort of director-ial prompt,' I said.

'That,' said Brearley, 'is one of the best compliments I've ever been paid.'

As soon as they sat down together at Lord's they were at ease, as if they'd been friends for years. The conversation flowed animatedly through England's current fortunes, across the theatre world and into the deep recesses of psychology, pausing along the way to consider why Nasser

Hussain had not yet declared against poor Zimbabwe. In spite of his global achievements, Mendes couldn't detach himself from the trials and tribulations of English cricket. He was an excellent club player and it alternately captivated and infuriated him; he could hardly stop talking about it. 'This stuff about each county being allowed only one overseas player – what's that all about?' he asked me, apropos of nothing. 'It's like me making a big movie and being told "You can have Tom Cruise but you can't have Julia Roberts as well."'

'Would you rather have won the Oscar or an England cap?' I asked Mendes, rather provocatively.

'I'm happy with what I've got,' he said. 'That film was two years' intensive work. Look at all those one-Test wonders – people like Paul Parker, Mark Benson, John Stephenson. I wouldn't trade an Oscar to be one of them. But if you'd have given me the talent of a Richards or a Gower, I'd have probably taken it.'

Wouldn't we all?

THE FAST SHOW

The Zimbabwe series was entirely as expected: uneventful. That could not be said about the rest of the 2000 season. The West Indies had arrived and Channel 4 mounted an impressive promotional campaign. There were 'Caribbean Summer' posters everywhere and some interesting support programming featuring documentaries about Bob Marley and the like, as well as adverts proclaiming, 'Cricket Just Got Better'.

After two pulsating Tests, a more accurate description would have been 'Cricket Just Got Faster'. The first was won by the West Indies in three days. The second, at Lord's, was an absolute humdinger. The West Indies made 267 in their first innings. On the breathless second day England were bowled out for 134. Then, inspired by Darren Gough's brilliant diving catch at third man, they promptly routed the

West Indies for 54 in two hours of mayhem. The session caused panicked rewrites of England-from-bad-to-worse stories in the press box, and Richie Benaud to say, when the Windies were 39 for 8, 'Well, I've been fiddling around with this game for more than fifty years and I've never seen anything like it.' Watched by 5.3 million viewers (more than tuned in to see Tim Henman's match at Wimbledon), England stole victory in the Saturday evening shadows, a narrow two-wicket triumph with only the debutant Matthew Hoggard left to bat. Though we didn't know it at the time, it was the defining moment in the turnaround in England's fortunes.

The momentum was lost for a while during the one-day series, in which I broke a significant record. At The Oval, not only was my 'commentary' position (the VT truck) out of sight at the opposite end of the ground to the other commentators, but, because of the space taken up by Sky's trucks, it was *outside* the arena itself. This must be a first: I was broadcasting from a car park a good 200 yards up the road from the Vauxhall End. It was three bus stops back along the Harleyford Road to get to Richie and the boys in the pavilion. Even though we were only making a highlights programme, I didn't see them all day. My location did at least make it slightly easier to nip off at lunchtime to be on Radio 4's *Loose Ends*, with Ned Sherrin. BBC Broadcasting House at Oxford Circus was probably slightly nearer than the Oval pavilion.

The match marked the international debut of Marcus Trescothick, who made an assured 79. The selection was hailed as an excellent Duncan Fletcher hunch since Trescothick had a modest first-class average, though it was also to do with Nick Knight's unavailability with a broken finger. It would not be the last time that luck and opportunism played significant roles in England's ongoing development.

The fitness message hadn't yet kicked in, however. Andrew Flintoff's weight had ballooned to 17 stones 12 pounds – the same as Lennox Lewis – and there were lots of rather spiky puns about his 'weight of stroke' and 'hunger for runs'. He answered the accusations with a powerful demolition of Zimbabwe in England's first-ever day–night international at Old Trafford, and began his post-match interview with 'Not bad for a fat lad.' But the criticisms were valid, in spite of Ian Healy pointing out at the Malcolm Marshall memorial match (which drew an incredible array of great players) that 'Shane Warne's idea of a balanced diet is a cheeseburger in each hand.' The point was that Flintoff's game relied on power and velocity, and maximising his potential, whereas Warne's was more about control and subtlety; and anyway, the Australian had been there and done it. It wasn't enough that the England players now ate healthy lunches at the ground and energy bars at tea instead of iced fancies and sponge cake, and that Flintoff had secured a deal promoting slimming products. Their whole lifestyle had to change if they were to compete with the mainly sharply drilled Aussies. In that sense, the emergence of Trescothick, nicknamed 'Banger' for his love of sausages, didn't bode well.

Still, England won the one-day series final at Lord's with ease and the serious business of Test cricket resumed at Old Trafford in early August. The England batsmen narrowly avoided the West Indies' thunderbolts (Trescothick made a promising Test debut) and I narrowly avoided being run over by the roller when doing the pitch report. (I was stooped down on the grass and couldn't hear it approaching as the director rabbited away through my earpiece.)

Coincidentally, it was both Atherton's and Stewart's 100th Test, though you could hardly meet two more different personalities. Over the previous couple of years I had got to know Atherton quite well, largely through mutual friends he'd met at Cambridge University. He had a small, fairly close-knit group of mates he'd known a long time, and the circle wasn't breached easily. After a generally discordant relationship with the press, he was understandably guarded with media people he didn't know intimately, so I felt quite privileged to be let in to his inner sanctum. He invited me to stay at the spacious converted barn he shared with his Guyanese girlfriend Isabelle, in rolling countryside near Alderley Edge, full of modern art and cream sofas and polished wood staircases ... and no cricket memorabilia whatsoever. Later, he came to dinner at our place bearing salmon he'd caught in Scotland. We laughed a lot and, unusually for a Test cricketer, he took an interest in other people's lives and revealed a fascination for twentieth-century American novelists.

It was only from meeting him in these situations that I realised the extent of his debilitating back condition – he had to take strong pills three times a day to ward off the pain (Stewart called him the oldest thirty-two-year-old in England) – and the appalling nature of his dress sense. Away from cricket, he tended to wear plain baggy jumpers, loose-fitting linen trousers and a pair of battered deck shoes that were so old they were almost back in fashion. But, to him, outward appearance is irrelevant. It's what's inside that counts. And no one had devoted more thought and effort to the England cause over the previous decade than Michael Atherton. He was definitely a person of substance over style.

I grew up almost alongside Alec Stewart. I knew him and his brother from school cricket, where we were regular adversaries. He often sportingly used to say, 'Oh, here am I to be your bunny again,' before a match, even though he invariably tucked into my bowling as if it were a plate of chicken and chips. But though I must have played against him at least twenty-five times, and interviewed him almost as often, I never felt I got past his cheery, chatty façade. There was always a Labrador-like willingness about him, both on and off the field, an exemplary manner and a scrupulous appearance, which made me wonder if it concealed other traits. Certainly you could never doubt his commitment. He was usually the first in the nets (unless Hussain beat him to it) and invariably the last out; his attention to detail was fastidious and his stamina remarkable. You did sometimes wonder about the slight obsession with his batting average (he was determined to keep it over 40, the benchmark for a top liner), but, hey, 100 Tests is 100 Tests. And a total of 6838 runs at that point (he eventually finished with 8463, at the infuriating average of 39.54), having kept wicket most of the time as well, was a remarkable achievement.

CALYPSO COLLAPSO

Typically, Stewart made a hundred in his 100th Test. Equally typically, Atherton made 1 and 28, not being someone motivated by personal milestones, even on his home ground. Rain ruined the match, and our production crew became increasingly addicted to the new phenomenon of *Big Brother*, tuning the truck's monitors to it whenever the opportunity arose. During the odd sunny interlude when play was in progress, there was some tomfoolery among the ten VT replay operators as they made close examinations of various female spectators' chests courtesy of the cameramen's zooms. On one occasion all thirty-two screens in the truck were displaying the same voluptuous pair of breasts as I went to air with a piece of analysis. It was just as well our executive producer Gary Franses was none the wiser.

Sitting in the commentary box in front of a panel of buttons, Franses had a lot on his plate. Every insert – adverts, break bumpers, graphics, archive scorecards, highlights of batsmen's fifties, trailers, county-score 'crawlers' – came through him. In the truck, I had to press the appropriate button on my intercom if I had an idea for some analysis and he'd sequence it in if he liked it. He was like an air-traffic controller with several things permanently stacked up and waiting for his permission to 'land'. By the end of the day he looked like he'd just done an eighteen-hour stint at Heathrow. The blood had drained from his face and he was losing weight by the hour: he had become the Thin Controller. In view of the pressure he was under, I had to forgive him the odd bark of 'Wrap, Yoz!' when some explanation was in danger of overrunning into the next ball being delivered.

During the day I could click between any of our twenty-odd cameras (it was quite fun tuning in to the studio one after lunch, to see how long Mark Nicholas's post-prandial snooze lasted) but I tried to have one of my four monitors always on the wicket-to-wicket feed so I could tell when another over was about to start. Volume levels in the truck were intense. Whenever anything half interesting happened on the field, the VT replay operators – each monitoring a different camera angle – would all be touting their wares: 'Wicket's great on purple!'; 'Blue gets the whole thing!'; 'Black for the reaction!'; 'Good celeb on orange!' At least twice an over, the truck resounded like a dealing room. I began to understand why most TV people suffer premature deafness.

Two weeks of dampness under foot, alternating commentating on the rain-interrupted NatWest semi-finals with potty-training our two-year-old Callum, led rapidly to the Headingley Test, and equally rapidly away from it. The match was over by 5.15 on the second day as the West Indies were shot out in their second innings for 61. Caddick finished things off with four wickets in an over, but it was Gough who'd done the significant damage with a devastating early spell. Despite their misgivings about each other, they were a real-deal opening pair now – the first consistently potent one England had had for over a decade.

We caught up with some of the euphoric England players in the hotel bar that night. Nasser Hussain was buying copious rounds of drinks – such a rarity everyone had turned up. Hussain had imbued England with a new ruthlessness (the West Indians had twice been bounced out – a taste of their own medicine). And, though buoyed by the summer, he voiced concerns about both Caddick and Hick with the Ashes approaching. He felt they were too easily intimidated by aggressive opponents. It's the kind of pithy detail you're dying to divulge to the public, but dare not for fear of being

labelled an informer. Yet the Australian batsman Michael
Slater, part of our commentary team, soon became party to
this information, and on the train back to London promised
the Aussies would be gunning for England the following
summer, once they'd demolished the West Indies 5–0 at home
(which they did). But just as he was starting to salivate over
the prospect of tucking in to some juicy Caddick offerings in
twelve months' time, someone rang to say they had got him
a ticket for the Bon Jovi concert that night in Milton Keynes,
and he became like a kid in a bouncy castle.

Hussain was back in our midst again a few days later as a
guest commentator for the (last-ever) NatWest final. He
declared himself absolutely knackered and praised Duncan
Fletcher's much-denounced insistence that none of England's
winter tour party should play any county cricket once the
summer's Tests were over. 'I need a holiday,' he said, 'to get
away from a cricket ground.' It's funny how the hobby you
can't get enough of as a kid becomes something from which
you are desperate to escape as an adult.

Except, of course, in the case R. Benaud Esq. He had been
going to cricket grounds for six decades, had played in or
watched more than 400 Test matches, and still he was unsat-
ed. On this particular day, though, he was obliged to watch
the racing on the telly, since it was pouring with rain outside,
and Channel 4 switched to a meeting from Newmarket. He
got completely immersed in the proceedings, perusing his
Racing Post assiduously between races, and raising the
famous eyebrow with pleasure when his nap selection in his
regular private Saturday wager with Jack Bannister romped
home. No money changed hands, though: they bet a mythi-
cal ten pounds each way on a nominated runner every weekend throughout the year, and Bannister kept a tally of their
imaginary winnings. The loser at the six-month cut-off point
had to buy the winner a lavish dinner.

The rain fell all afternoon. When the racing had gone off
and Richie had filed his weekly column for the *News of the
World* – 'The Voice of Cricket' – I presented him with a copy

of my new book, *Yakking Around the World*, and said I had been toying with the idea of writing a novel.

'That's very good,' he said. 'Make sure when you send in the synopsis of a novel, or a film, that you post one copy to the publishers or the studios and another sealed and sent recorded delivery to yourself – and never opened – to prevent plagiarism.'

We'd primed Richie to announce the Premiership football results live during the second innings of the match, but the bad weather forcing us off air denied Channel 4 viewers the pleasure of hearing it. Perhaps it was just as well since, when he was practising by reading the half-time scores off our graphics monitor, he said, 'Fulham one, Blackburn Rovers nought.'

The NatWest final was eventually completed the next day – it was Gloucestershire's fourth cup final win in succession – and Graham Gooch, trying hard to impress as a guest commentator with his professional future in the balance, made some funny observations about Jack Russell. 'I remember when he put his sunhat in the oven to dry and it caught fire,' he said, guffawing. 'It's incredibly noisy out there when he's keeping and you're batting. He's always rabbiting, and saying, "Not convinced!" after you've played a shot, even if it goes to the boundary.' These and other anecdotes didn't prevent our boss from declaring that Gooch's voice was 'too whiny' to be a good commentator and crossing him off his list of possibles.

BOTTOMS UP

England were on the brink of their first series win over the West Indies for at least a generation. With the final Test interestingly poised by Saturday night, I assembled a table for dinner made up of Derek Pringle, Sam Mendes and his actress girlfriend Rachel Weisz, plus Atherton escorted by his girlfriend Izzy, and Tanya, who was eight and a half months pregnant. With Mendes's revelations about life in Hollywood, Pringle's intimate knowledge of dub reggae and Weisz's origins behind the Iron Curtain, the conversation was predictably eclectic.

The evening must have done Atherton (36 not out overnight) some good, because he defied Ambrose, Walsh and co. for most of the next day in an epic display of concentration, to give England a big lead. He must have played and missed fifty times (Walsh frequently howled in anguish) but he remained steadfast. The ovation went on for an age when he reached his hundred. It was just as well he did, too, because an obviously weary Hussain recorded a pair in the match and the next-highest score was 26.

Monday 4 September was a memorable day. Because it was the last day of a riveting series with the West Indies requiring an unlikely, but not impossible, 341 runs to level it at 2–2. Because, in glorious weather, the Oval authorities allowed everyone in for a tenner (except for kids, who got in for free), even making the hospitality boxes available, by 10.30 the queue snaked way down the Harleyford Road – almost as far as my VT truck – and the gates had to be locked before the start, shutting out several hundred people. Because Brian Lara, not out at lunch and determined that his team shouldn't sacrifice its proud record against England, went straight from the middle to the nets at the interval, and straight from there back to the middle afterwards. Because, when England finally took the last wicket to win a series against the West Indies for the first time in thirty-one years, and the players clasped each other happily, Hussain sank to his knees, as much with relief as in exaltation. Because I witnessed on camera preview the rush in the England dressing room afterwards to clear away all the porn mags before we could film live from in there.

But it was memorable perhaps most of all because of the public's response. A year earlier on this ground they had booed their captain on the balcony and English cricket had been declared dead and buried. Now here I was stood among thousands of happy faces, men and women and children of all ages and creeds, old curmudgeons nestling alongside teenage trendies, grasping the opportunity to witness the rebirth. Beneath football's ever-extending tentacles, this declaration of latent enthusiasm for cricket in England was intensely reassuring.

We sent some champagne and congratulations to the England team, and a few minutes later as we were having a celebratory drink from cardboard cups in the not especially salubrious environment of the outside-broadcast trucks, we received a verbal message relayed back from the coach Duncan Fletcher. 'Thanks, Channel 4,' he said, 'your coverage made us feel a bit better about ourselves.'

I was soon feeling very good about myself. Our second child, Nancy, arrived in mid-September. The early stages of the birth were quite a struggle, and Tanya, in complete agony, exclaimed at one point, 'Remind me never to have sex with you again!' I didn't help matters by asking for hush during one of her later contractions to listen to the result of the double-trap clay Olympic final in Sydney on the radio, featuring my interviewee Richard Faulds (he won gold). But Nancy was gorgeous, and as she was born on her maternal grandmother's birthday we were doubly happy.

Then the ICC announced that as a result of further match-fixing inquiries, Ajay Jadeja would be banned from all cricket for five years. It was a joyous moment. I probably wouldn't ever again have to lose sleep agonising about the pronunciation of his name during a live Test match.

HOME TRUTHS

Finally, I landed the dream job: commentating for Channel 4 on the Pakistan–England series in the autumn. Not only was this a relief from sitting goggle-eyed in a truck for seven hours a day; also, it didn't involve me going to Pakistan. It didn't even require me to leave the London borough of

Hammersmith. The hour-long highlights programmes were to be made in studios less than a mile from my house. Some poor editor would have to beaver away from 5 a.m. (Pakistan is five hours ahead), cutting the programme's pictures together. Dermot Reeve and I would roll up in mid-afternoon to add the commentary. If we made a mistake, we could stop the tape and redo it. It was a completely foolproof system. And I would be back home just too late to bath the kids.

We tried to get into the spirit of things a bit by watching some of the live Sky coverage in the morning and then, in my case, having a curry for lunch. We even had poppadoms in the studio on one occasion, and before we began Dermot often did brilliant Imran impersonations. We resisted the temptation to say things like 'Incredibly hot here in the com box today; must be terrible for the players,' or 'Going to the High Commissioner's do tonight, Derm?' and anyway there wasn't time. Deliveries were cut close together and it was action-packed.

It was fun, too. A voice would say in our ear, 'Two Thorpe boundaries, no replays ... Thorpe wicket, dodgy decision, three replays,' and we took it in turns to feign excitement/surprise/outrage as events unfolded. My theatrical background and Dermot's natural excitability came in handy. People who had watched the 7.30 p.m. programme and then encountered me an hour and a half later in a pub in Soho seemed initially baffled. 'But I thought you were in Lahore!' they exclaimed. The power of TV, eh?

As the series progressed we watched less and less of the play at home beforehand, so, we said, to increase our level of 'surprise' when it came to add the commentary. Though in my case it was due to the fact that Callum went doolally if I switched over from his *Bug's Life* video.

The biggest surprise of all, of course, was England winning the series in the Karachi twilight. This completely caught out Michael Henderson, now at the *Telegraph*, who rather harshly criticised Atherton's laborious first-innings century:

"It was mainly insufferable viewing. In 9hrs 35mins, in which time one could hear the whole of *Götterdämmerung* twice and still nip out to the pub for last orders, he failed to score off no fewer than 350 balls. It was, in its own way, admirable. It was also stultifying and, one could argue, counter-productive."

In the end it was the Pakistani delaying tactics on the last day that turned out to be counter-productive. It was their fielders, rather than England's batsmen, who couldn't see the ball. Luckily, Graham Thorpe could, and England won their first series in Pakistan for thirty-nine years.

Hussain, who was also in at the end, was overcome with emotion in the dressing room, but he roused himself afterwards for an excellent interview with Mark Nicholas, who actually *was* in Pakistan. He paid tribute to his team and pronounced this victory more important than the one over the West Indies. In truth, it was Hussain's burning desire and unstinting defiance that had instilled in the rest the commitment to see it through.

Duncan Fletcher's hamster-like face was captured fixed in a toothy grin in the post-match celebrations. The last few months had been a triumph for him, too. His care of the players, sheltering them from overwork, quietly nurturing their talents, focusing their minds, equipping them with little strategies like pinching singles against the miserly Walsh and Ambrose, or the 'forward press' against the Pakistani spinners to get batsmen's feet moving, had all been crucial. He looked impervious behind his sunglasses, but he was the master of attention to detail.

The FA followed the ECB's lead with Fletcher and recruited a foreign coach. The appointment of Sven-Göran Eriksson didn't buy favour with football aficionados, though. 'It's cheating, and a betrayal of our heritage. What are we trying to create? The Harlem Globetrotters?' berated Gordon Taylor, head of the players' union. The *Daily Mail* declared, 'We've sold our birthright down the fjord to a nation of seven million skiers who spend half their lives in darkness.'

No one seemed to understand that fervent huff and puff and a Union Jack tattooed on your chest weren't enough to win international sporting contests any more. The insular belief that nationalistic passion and pride would be enough to drag England out of the sidings belonged in a Thomas the Tank Engine story. Fletcher (and contemporaries like Arsène Wenger) had proved that coaching required science not tub-thumping. We needed outsiders to save us from ourselves. Whether we needed to pay them four million quid a year and give them a lavish mansion overlooking Regent's Park was another matter.

The *Telegraph* sports desk Christmas lunch took place a few days after England's Karachi triumph. The paper still had the reputation of being the best for sport, but, though I worked for it, I wasn't so sure. Instead of news and features, the sports pages were increasingly dominated by ghosted pieces from famous, and not-so-famous, performers – athletes (mainly injured ones), racehorse trainers, past-their-best footballers – who usually didn't have much to say. The impartial view was that *Telegraph Sport* had more columns than the Parthenon.

The Times, sensing an opportunity (or maybe just keen to promote their stablemate Sky Sports), had recently launched a compact football supplement which was packed with features and analysis. I thought it was the sort of thing the *Telegraph* ought to be doing – for football in the winter and cricket in the summer – and I asked David Welch, who'd been instrumental in launching the *Telegraph*'s sports supplement, what he thought of the *Times* offering.

'Like a leaflet from Dixons shoved through your door, and it went the same way,' he said.

I had been deposed from the sports editor's top table at the lunch, although I thought I'd had a reasonable year, journalistically – perhaps the equivalent of 950 runs, average 38 – and I half expected a mention in dispatches. But in Welch's annual address about the greatness of the sports pages, he highlighted only a few star names, notably James Cracknell and Alistair McGowan (!). Later, a slightly tipsy Michael Henderson accosted me with 'Crap article about Ramprakash, Hughes!'

At a less mature stage this would have provoked me into another tyre-deflating episode, but not this time (Henderson had come by tube). Anyway, I guessed he was probably still in a tizz, having apparently been close to getting the sack for various outbursts against Hick, Salisbury and Atherton's slow scoring in Karachi. I felt rather sorry for him: he had a rare talent for writing and an even rarer talent for unbalanced slander. So I let the comment pass and soon we were having a rollocking good chat about awful ghosted columns, until an elderly correspondent, who was definitely a bit the worse for wear, got me in an arm lock, jerked my head towards his and, veins bulging round his temples, loudly declared, 'I've been doing this job for forty-five years!' I extricated myself and left.

CHAPTER 12 – 2001

UNFAMILIAR TERRITORY

January 2001 was a month of challenges. In Sydney, Australia set down the Ashes gauntlet, having hammered the West Indies to win their fifteenth Test in a row, a world record. In Hammersmith, Tanya set down the oven gauntlet, having gone back to work, leaving me to look after two children under three. Admittedly, this was only on Tuesdays, and I had wanted to do it, but it was suddenly daunting to be solely responsible with no one to bail you out when one child's vehemently refusing to eat his lunch, the other's feeding spilled peas into the video-recorder and the *Telegraph* sports editor's on the blower. On one occasion I had both kids sitting quietly watching a (de-pea'd) video, while I did a phone interview on 5 Live about England's prospects in Sri Lanka. I was just getting into the issue of Colombo's suffocating heat weakening visiting players' resolve when Callum came up behind me with a desperate look on his face and said loudly, 'Dad, I need a poo!'

The ECB had launched *A Cricketing Future for All*, a programme aimed at putting England on top of the world rankings in 2007, and making cricket *the* sport, but football's dominance in the media was becoming overwhelming: *The Times* had their weekly football 'handbook', the Sundays often devoted ten pages to it, and Ian Wright even had a chat show on BBC1. 'Ian Wright doing interviews? Dear God, give us patience!' Michael Parkinson, an outspoken critic of

Wright's behaviour on and off the field, exclaimed at a *Telegraph* lunch.

However, in spite of our efforts on Channel 4 to popularise cricket, I realised that the force was with football and that this was a can't-beat-'em-so-join-'em moment. Having picked the brain of my mate Scally, who had just defected from the BBC to ITV to edit *The Premiership*, their new version of *Match of the Day*, I handed a page of football feature ideas to David Welch.

There was another good reason for wanting to write about English football: it ensured I stayed handy for the rest of the winter to commentate on the highlights of the Sri Lanka v. England series. Annoyingly, Channel 4 changed tack at the last moment, and elected not to make the programmes in the studio round the back of my house. The production had defected to an editing facility near Carnaby Street. I had to take public transport to go to work. What an imposition!

The great advantage of this work, though, apart from its vast reimbursement for short hours, was that it enabled you to do other things. I spent several mornings researching a big piece about the demise of Spurs, the club I used to support until a succession of useless managers ruined it. Then I got deeply embedded in the murky world of football agents, receiving a number of blatant threats on the phone to 'keep your nasty nose out of it ... or else' from well-known protagonists when they realised what I was doing, before publishing a fairly damning story. A couple of proposed writs from offended parties came to nothing.

Conscious that my TV profile could be short-lived, I was pushing hard to find interesting sporting angles for the *Telegraph*. I took this to extremes at the San Marino Grand Prix. This race is invariably one of the writers' favourites in spite of the stench from the media centre's toilets at the circuit (primitive holes in the floor). It is staged close to Imola, a charismatic old town of cobbled squares and church bells and men in flat caps loitering about drinking espresso, rather than in some dull, remote location populated exclusively by

Germans. The racing is better, too, with the track swooshing excitingly through parkland and plenty of overtaking potential.

Determined to witness some live action rather than staring through the nicotine-laced fug at the screens in the press room, I followed a throng of spectators along a road, over a bridge and up a hill until I came to a large stand overlooking the famous Aque Minerale turn. Lacking a ticket for this enclosure, I got on my hands and knees and wriggled underneath the security fence, then squatted next to it. This gave me a fantastic view of the cars coming down the hill and through the sharp right-hand turn, and an ear-shattering thrill as they sped towards the chicane.

Two world champions, Michael Schumacher and Mika Hakkinen, drove the corner in starkly different ways. Hakkinen was slicker, gliding neatly round the bend as his engine slipped smoothly through the gears. His performance was, like him, rather colourless. Schumacher, driving by the seat of his pants, was thrilling. He took a tighter line, slicing across the kerb, slewing his car out of the corner. The engine's deafening scream never relented, reinforcing the Schumacher adage that braking is for wimps. He has no fear, is never pricked by self-doubt. In sport, that separates the truly great from the rest.

SPORTING IMPOSTORS

Meanwhile, the *Telegraph* was trying to steal a lead on its competitors. At a specially arranged lunch I attended, there was an important announcement. Finally giving in to the persuasion of David Welch, the paper was launching a daily sports supplement to fill the gaps between the Monday and Saturday ones. The editor, Charles Moore, made a short speech saying how proud he was to be associated with such a dynamic sports department. The supplement would be introduced on 14 May, he said, killing off the challenge of the

Telegraph's main rival, *The Times*. 'With their separate business section and weekly football handbook,' he added, 'they will have no chance of immediate response.' In fact, *The Times* got wind of the development and brought out a daily sports supplement a week earlier, on 7 May, forcing the *Telegraph* to rush one out on the same day to avoid humiliation. It's a devious old world, this newspaper business.

Thinking it might provide useful copy for the supplement, I had accepted an invitation to play in a pro-celebrity golf tournament at the Belfry, preceding the Benson and Hedges Invitational. I hadn't played for so long I didn't have a handicap, but what the hell, I thought, it might be fun and offer an insight into how the other half lives.

It did, initially. I got to drive in to the course through the competitors' entrance, parking my mud-lashed VW Golf – with its two chocolate-smeared child seats, its sundry empty crisp packets, its spilled juice bottles and discarded dummies – not in a muddy field miles away but in a reserved space next to José María Olazábal's slinky BMW. I was greeted by a pretty PR girl who ushered me past the tented village to the locker rooms. There, people nodded and scraped and a man cleaned my golf shoes and dusted off my golf bag, which had lain in a dirty cellar for several months. Then a buggy ferried me to the practice range, where I was presented with buckets of complimentary balls.

Another buggy ferries you back through the throng to the first tee, where you receive your box of new balls, are introduced to your complimentary caddy and meet your playing partners. The official starter gets on the mike and says, 'On the tee, Bernhard Langer.' This immediately attracts clusters of spectators, who've been browsing in the tented village, to the viewing gallery. Then, after he's clattered his drive 280 yards down the middle, it's the turn of the 'celebrities', mercifully a few yards further down the fairway. That's when you get your come-uppance. After Scottish rugby's Gavin Hastings has swatted his three-wood up the right-hand side, the starter emits those fateful words, 'And on the tee, Simon

Hughes.'

'Who?' you can sense curious onlookers saying. Or 'What's an MP doing on the golf course?'

The nerves are jangling, the ball looks microscopic at your feet, every enormous tree and hazard seems to be beckoning your ball towards it, and you feel that all the eyes of the world are on you from clubhouse windows and walkways and stands. Stewards hold up signs saying, 'Quiet Please' when actually you want everyone to be doing anything but silently watching you and imposing on your private grief. Then, when you ladle a lame five-wood into the light rough 140 yards yonder, you are sure you can hear people sniggering and someone muttering what you already know – that you have no place here, since you're neither a celebrity nor a decent golfer. You want to be swallowed up by the nearest bunker until you meet the kind face of Langer, who says, 'Don't worry: it's in play, and your golf is a lot better than my cricket.'

By the end of the round there was some doubt about the accuracy of that statement, but no doubt about the quality of Langer, as a player and as a person. He bothers to wait as you make your third attempt to extricate yourself from a fairway bunker, where other pros just march on impatiently. He politely offers swing tips, when he could quite justifiably advise you to take up gardening. He asks you admiringly how you managed to get an eight-iron from deep rough to stop on the green. ('Mud on the club,' I replied.) He was, however, a bit flummoxed about the correct etiquette when my sliced second shot on the seventeenth bobbled up a bank and hopped inside the anorak of a spectator who was asleep. Looking at his considerable size, I elected to declare a lost ball and take a penalty drop.

Langer is a remarkable man. Amazingly resilient, he has conquered the yips twice, and in 2001 was leaving his famous contemporaries – men like Faldo, Woosnam and Ballesteros – standing. He finished eighth in that year's Masters – the highest-placed European – and hadn't missed the cut since his first appearance there in the early eighties. Amid all that, he is still a devoted family man, happily ferrying his four kids to their various sporting engagements. He sat with us at lunch, cordiality personified. Forget BMWs and frankfurters; Bernhard Langer is Germany's greatest export.

LETHAL WEAPON

I hadn't forgotten the day job. For the summer of 2001 we were all rather excited in the Channel 4 team as we were launching a new tool: Hawkeye. Paul Hawkins, a Minor Counties cricketer and missile-tracking expert, had developed it at a research centre in Hampshire. Using a system of CCTV cameras linked to a computer, Hawkeye could forecast if the ball would have hit the wicket after it had struck the batsman's pad. It was basically the world's first LBW predictor. We had tested and modified it all winter, and were confident of its accuracy, so the system was given quite a big pre-match billing.

Unfortunately, though, Hawkeye couldn't predict the weather, and the first day of the Pakistan series was one of freezing winds and lashing rain. Instead of being left alone in my nice, air-conditioned truck, I was dispatched outside onto the Lord's wastes at regular intervals to supply live weather updates. I think I was seen as the most likely person to bring a rain report to life (or the most foolhardy). This was proved right when a severe squall blew my umbrella inside out on air.

The weather eventually relented and we unveiled our new toy. I suggested, only half seriously, that one day Hawkeye might replace umpires, and received a postbag of ferocious replies. It gave me something different to work with anyway, and with all my little tools I was developing a bit of a niche. Spectators at the Nursery End hailed me, shouting, 'It's the Analyst!' as I passed them after doing the pitch report, and I received some favourable comments about my work. I was really just illustrating all the things I remembered thinking as a player. During my career I could always see batsmen's strengths and weaknesses, and therefore knew exactly how to get them out. The trouble was I wasn't usually good enough to put the theories into practice. As the Analyst, I didn't have to deliver the ball, just a few words. It's a million times easier.

The Pakistanis were cold and rusty in the first Test and lost by an innings. They were better in the second, at Old Trafford, marshalled by the simmering Waqar Younis, very much on trial as captain. He instigated some rather unsavoury tactics, eyeballing and verballing every England batsman, provoking his former Surrey colleague Graham Thorpe to retort, 'You can call me what you like *between* balls, but not when it's on the way down.' The Pakistanis leered, jeered and sneered at every opportunity and incited mass hysteria round the bat every time there was a sniff of a chance. Watching on TV, Scally sent me a text saying, 'What is the similarity between me and the Pakistani team? We're both incessantly appealing!'

They hustled England to defeat, and though their skills were impressive, their behaviour was irksome, and I wrote as much in a hurriedly penned piece after the game. I often looked sympathetically on the lives of Asian cricketers, admiring their triumphs in adversity and appreciating their precarious existence back home, especially their captains'. But I felt here the Pakistanis had gone too far (and several times they were ticked off by the usually benign umpire David Shepherd). In my piece I called Waqar's captaincy a 'disgrace, overstepping the fine line between aggression and intimidation'. I was quite proud of taking a strong line for once, rather than the usual flowery, fence-sitting columnism.

Three days later, a typewritten letter arrived through my letterbox via the *Telegraph*.

Dear Mr Hughes,
I suppose you realise that your employer the *DT* is a broadsheet and not a tabloid; your report of 5 June was one of the
most racist pieces of tabloid journalism that I have had the
misfortune of reading; rather like that Paki-bashing *Daily
Mirror* reporter who died suddenly and unexpectedly; a
friend had promised that he would put the 'khiijazi' curse on
him and we all know what happened! You are a young
father and naturally don't want fate to deal you such a blow,
do you? Your reporting was reminiscent of the
Botham–Lamb days of Paki-bashing; but at least both those
patriotic 'thickos' were reasonably good cricketers ...

Ouch! My first thought was to ring the *Telegraph*, who'd
published a couple of similar, though much milder, complaints. My second was to ring the police. In the end I did
neither, realising the writer would then be getting the wider
exposure he obviously craved. Anyway, his signature was
illegible and he hadn't enclosed his address, just 'London
SW5', so wasn't easily traceable. Most of these types are ultimately cowards.

There were a number of them around, though, often found
charging onto the field that summer. At the first one-day
international, featuring Pakistan, there was a pitch invasion,
and Nick Knight was hit by a flying plastic bugle. They probably thought better of it at the next, Pakistan v. Australia at
Cardiff, not least because the umpires, Peter Willey and Alan
Whitehead, were not men to be messed with. Willey and I
had always got on, though he was one of many slightly
piqued by my suggestion that Hawkeye meant doom for
umpires. We were inspecting the Sophia Gardens pitch when
Shane Warne approached us.

'Hey Warney, have you met Hughesy, the Analyst?' said
Willey. 'You've taken three hundred and sixty Test wickets,
but he'll tell you where you're going wrong.'

So began an interesting little relationship between Warne
and me that summer, during the Ashes. He knew what I did,

and how closely I watched. As a player fascinated by the intricacies of the game, he'd come up to me on many mornings as I was poring over the pitch, and ask, 'Did you see that different googly I bowled to Butcher yesterday?' or 'What did you think of that lower-arm slider to Stewart?' or 'Shit, it wasn't coming out so well yesterday, was it? Wasn't following through properly, was I?' At first I was a bit suspicious and thought it was a wind-up to inject even more mystery into his repertoire, but I soon realised he was being totally genuine and it was just his natural enthusiasm about his art bubbling over.

And what an art. Two dismissals in that series, both of Atherton, illustrated his unique control and his brilliant cricketing nous. At Lord's, in the second Test, Atherton took a middle-and-leg guard, a stance favoured by batsmen keen to get across to the ball on or outside the off-stump, where it is most often aimed. After a number of near misses, Warne bowled him round his legs as he attempted to sweep. It was his famous 'pickpocket' delivery. To prevent this happening again, Atherton changed his guard to leg-stump for the next Test at Trent Bridge. He was trying to ensure he had more of his body covering the stumps when Warne attempted to pick his pocket again. It was an almost imperceptible change, but Warne spotted it. He altered his line to Atherton, probing him more around off-stump, knowing the batsman had to reach slightly more for the ball there. Sure enough, he prodded at one such delivery which spun sharply and dismissed him caught behind. Though Atherton claimed afterwards that he didn't hit the ball, it was still a brilliant précis of Warne's subtle but lethal prowess.

HIDDEN AGENDAS

It was the most eagerly awaited Ashes series since ... well, the previous one. The hype was especially intense because both teams had had a victorious twelve months. More important-

ly as far as the media were concerned, the 2001 series marked
the twenty-year anniversary of 'Botham's Ashes'. To commemorate this, Channel 4 commissioned a documentary to
be shown the night before the first Test. It wasn't, however,
just a simple case of cutting together the BBC archive around
interviews with the famous participants. For a start, there
was no way of getting the archive without breaking into BBC
vaults: they wouldn't part with it for love or money. So
Channel 4 had to cobble together ITV news footage of the
1981 Tests and make the best of it. Simultaneously the interviewees played hard to get. For Dennis Lillee, Kim Hughes
and others, it was a financial matter.

Money wasn't the issue for Mike Brearley, the orchestrator
of England's amazing 1981 turnaround. It was just the business of appearing on TV in the first place. As a professional
psychoanalyst, he'd refused ever since the early eighties,
when a patient suffering from schizophrenia had noticed his
billing on a programme with John Arlott. Concocting all
sorts of illusions in her head of what he might be talking
about, she had become practically suicidal. As a former
team-mate and perennial admirer of Brearley, I offered to go
round and try to persuade him to be interviewed on camera.
Before going out for a curry, he showed me his consulting
rooms, in the basement of his house, with a real couch and
shelves stacked with Jung and other philosophy manuals,
and he told me he had been in therapy himself during that
1981 series (as part of his psychoanalysis training), and it
had helped hugely in managing his, and others', aggression.
His concerns about the TV documentary were gradually
allayed over dinner with his Indian wife Mana and me. He
was particularly encouraged when it was suggested that in
return for his contribution Channel 4 would republish his
seminal work, *The Art of Captaincy*, which had been out of
print for over a decade. The promise was kept and the programme, with Brearley as its centre point, was fabulous.

Sadly, the 2001 series was no contest. Brearley had said
England had a chance of winning the Ashes only if they were

'on top of their form, as shrewd as they can be'. (Usual story, huh?) But Gough's first over at Edgbaston, after England had been dismissed for under 300, set the tone. It contained a couple of no-balls and a couple of juicy half-volleys. Michael Slater, whom I had bowled into good nick a few days earlier in the Lord's nets while he was still a Channel 4 commentator, lashed it for 18.

The Australians never looked back and by Saturday night most of the Channel 4 production team had descended on Legs Eleven, a Birmingham lap-dancing bar, in an attempt to lift our spirits. Unprofessionally, as the match was unfinished, we were still enjoying table dances at 1 a.m., which was not a good time for the mobile in my pocket to autodial home. Bleary-eyed, Tanya answered, but could hear only the dull thud of house music interspersed with muffled requests to 'come over here, babe'. Thank God I had told her earlier where we were going, or it could have been divorce number two.

England were outgunned by probably the best Australian team ever. Each Test turned into a fraught experience for them and, with a number of early finishes, the equivalent of an elongated stag weekend for us. Friday and Saturday nights in Nottingham, Leeds, Manchester and Birmingham are unadulterated flesh fests.

Trying to inject a note of home optimism into Channel 4's pre-match chat on the pitch before the Lord's Test, I made the mistake of loosely comparing Australia's attack with England's. 'They've got three right-arm quicks – McGrath, Gillespie and Lee – not dissimilar to Gough, Caddick and Cork,' I said, 'and Giles spins the ball from leg to off, like Warne.'

'Giles like Warne? *Giles like Warne?*' Ian Smith guffawed, standing between me and Mark Nicholas. 'I think the sun's getting to the Analyst's bonce a bit. Better put him back in the dark, eh?' And he creased up with laughter and wouldn't let the issue go all day, barely able to contain himself as he handed to me between overs with 'And now down to the Analyst, who thinks Giles is as good as Warne!'

Trying to make amends with a slick pitch report the next day (the only opportunity to escape from the VT truck), I compiled a sequence of wickets on tape illustrating McGrath's skill at exploiting the Lord's slope. I set off in good time for the middle, as usual informing the director and the stage manager that I'd need a monitor by the pitch so I could talk over the pictures. Monitors are the bane of sports presenters' lives. If you're outside and the sun's shining, you can barely see anything on them; and they are notoriously unreliable, having a habit of working perfectly in rehearsal and then dying just as you go to air. This particular day was cloudy, which was good, but our usual monitor man had been replaced by a nervous-looking apprentice, which wasn't so good. He seemed to know what he was doing, though, and a senior man checked the battery twice and confirmed it was fine. As the programme came to me on the pitch, I glanced down at the monitor and saw myself in vision. So far so good. I led confidently into the first piece of McGrath footage, heard the director say, 'Cue Analyst VT,' and looked down at the monitor to talk through the action. It was now showing an episode of *Friends*. I tried to continue talking about McGrath's wickets while frantically wondering whether the viewers were, like me, watching Joey arguing with Monica, or if this was just a local fault and they were still seeing cricket. Despite the Thin Controller doing his best to help by describing the pictures through my earpiece, I made absolutely no sense at all, and at one point I said, 'A bit of extra bounce there did for Chandler ... I mean Butcher.'

I was a gibbering wreck for a long time afterwards: my commentary hopes, already dashed by Nasser Hussain's late availability for a domestic match we were covering, were in tatters. The experience did, however, imbue me with unmitigated respect for Mark Nicholas, Steve Rider and the other leading sports presenters who breeze through regular monitor failure, sound loss, set disintegration, sudden changes of running order and all sorts of other freak occurrences as if they've never happened.

IMMORTAL PRESENCE

Standing in the middle at Trent Bridge before the third Test made me remember how lucky I was. Out in the middle with me were the captains Atherton (deputising for the injured Hussain) and Steve Waugh, the other players and officials, and some greats of the game – Gower, Gooch, Willis, Botham (permanently on the phone), Border, Chappell, Thomson and Lillee. It was an immortal gathering. Botham was obliged to record his pitch report for Sky early so he could be out of the way (which he always dutifully was) for me and my Dampometer to be live on Channel 4. It was an immense privilege, untarnished by the genial former Australian captain Mark Taylor, who was commentating on Channel 4 that summer, saying mischievously after I'd finished, 'That Dampometer thing is just a load of bullshit.' As a qualified surveyor, he knew what he was talking about.

England were beaten again by an irresistible force and, having lost the first three Tests, surrendered the Ashes for the seventh time in succession. The *Sun* and the *News of the World* led the call for the ancient urn – which resided in the Lord's museum – to be transported to Australia forthwith, and you could see their point. The triumphant Australian coach, John Buchanan, was not the first (or last) to put the blame on the county system, calling it 'the true servant of mediocrity'; after his frustrating season with Middlesex in 1998, he was definitely an authority on the subject.

It was all a bit of an anticlimax as we rolled our vast production unit into Leicester for the Cheltenham and Gloucester semi-final against Lancashire. Rain fell all morning and the dreaded television word 'Fill!' resonated in our eardrums. I was dispatched to the middle to interview the umpires and the groundsman and then to the dressing room to chat to Phillip DeFreitas about his habit of visiting stately homes (yes, really) and Atherton on his love of fishing. ('You're a keen angler, aren't you, Athers?' 'Yes.' 'Caught anything much lately?' 'No, I've been playing cricket!')

Finally I was offered the Pakistani Shahid Afridi, whose English was fairly poor.

'Not like this back home in Karachi, is it, Shahid?' I said, unable to think of anything to talk about except the continuing downpour.

'Oh yes,' he replied. 'I rang my parents at home and they say heavy rain there, too.'

It was real award-losing TV.

When the match finally got under way, on an unsuitably damp pitch, the play was mediocre. Lancashire collapsed abjectly to the slow inswing of Scott Boswell, a short, thickset individual of the type more commonly found on the village green. It was Atherton's early dismissal to Boswell – rather than his constant hounding by Glenn McGrath in the Tests – that surely cemented his decision to retire. Especially when Boswell displayed an inability to hit the cut strip in the C&G final at Lord's and was summarily released.

The destination of the Ashes had been decided, but the series hadn't finished. First there was the Headingley Test, an extraordinary match, as many Headingley Tests seem to be. Extraordinary because of Mark Butcher's mercurial, match-winning 173 not out. Extraordinary for the determination of some of the younger Australian players to get off with female members of Channel 4's production crew, and extraordinary because it coincided with the first edition of ITV's *The Premiership*, produced by my friend Scally, which flatteringly featured a much better-looking version of me (Andy Townsend), doing analysis in the 'Tactics Truck'. It was also extraordinary for something Richie Benaud said. Well known as a man of succinct appraisals of a situation, we were increasingly using him to set the scene at the beginning of the day, after his familiar 'Morning everyone' welcome. On the third day of the Test he was ready as usual to kick off the commentary after the regular Saturday morning *Roadshow*. The ground was slowly filling up, and seasoned Benaud-watchers would have been anticipating his encouraging 'still

plenny of room if you wanna come along'. But what he actually said was: 'Morning everyone. No packed house here at
the moment, but there will be later on. Lot of shopping to be
done. Get all that back and stacked in the fridge and the shit
on the shelves [that's what it sounded like anyway] and then
they'll be down to the ground.' There were one or two raised
eyebrows in the commentary box (though not Benaud's, as
he began calmly describing play) and down in the truck we
looked at each other, wondering if we'd heard right. Had he
really said what we thought he'd said? We weren't entirely
sure, but we checked the tape at lunch, and, whatever he was
trying to say, that confirmed it. No one remarked on it afterwards or, to my knowledge, has ever mentioned it to Richie.
He, typically – because he is not the type to dwell on his own
words – has never mentioned it either. But in our eyes it made
him even more of a living legend than he was already.

Then there was the Oval Test, a time of mixed emotions.
Atherton, England's rock for a dozen years, retired with no
more than a sheepish little wave after being dismissed by his
nemesis Glenn McGrath for the last time. He was not a man
for emotional farewells and was happy to send up his final
day as an England player with a funny little episode at the
end of his excellent autobiography *Opening Up*. He's sitting
in the dressing room after England have lost and all the players are coming up to congratulate him on a fine career. A
recalled Phil Tufnell shuffles over last, fag lit, looking a little
careworn. Atherton accepts his handshake and, having loyally supported him during some difficult times, awaits his little
eulogy. 'Athers ... I bowled all right, didn't I?' says Tufnell.
'Jesus, I've gone for a hundred and seventy on a bunsen but
I bowled well ... didn't I?'

THE GOOD LIFE

England's loss was Channel 4's gain. Atherton had signed a
contract to commentate the following summer. Meanwhile,

the channel's strategic guru, David Brook, had done some crafty spadework and secured the Test match rights for the channel for a further four years, before they were officially up for renewal. There was a sudden and rather unseemly rush, metaphorically speaking, to the door of Channel 4's head of sport, Dave Kerr, to negotiate long-term deals.

I thought I had a good time as a county cricketer, but this was better. I had a beautiful, clever, prosperous wife, two gorgeous kids, a supportive family, decent health and financial stability. Dermot Reeve and I had also been booked to do our highlights-doddle for England's tour of India. I'd even had a letter from a regular correspondent, who usually defined my comments about pitch, weather, swing, etc. as 'utter bollocks', containing half a compliment: 'You're all right, but tell that Reeve to button it.'

We in the media like to think we're all powerful, of course. In sport there's a perennial debate about who needs whom most, with the sports reporters proclaiming that without them sport wouldn't receive any publicity, and the players retorting that without them the reporters would be out of a job. At the end of the season the cricket press had a chance to exercise their influence when some, including me, were invited to air their views at a 'Future of English Cricket' presentation at Lord's.

Proposed scheduling of Test, one-day and county cricket was set out by the ECB for the next four years. Much of the forum's reaction was negative, especially the arranging of thirteen one-day internationals each summer (far too many, we said: ten was more than enough) and the lack of provision for the establishment of a playing level between county and Test cricket (city or region based), which we argued was vital to straddle the vast difference in standard. All our suggestions were ignored, and the ECB stuck with the original plan. So much for the power of the press.

In October, I journeyed back in time. I went on a novel-writing course in deepest Devon. Organised by the Arvon Foundation, it was a week long, and held in an old, remote farmhouse ten miles from Okehampton. There was no telly, mobiles didn't work and the payphone didn't accept incoming calls. I told the *Telegraph* I'd enrolled to improve the quality of my writing, which was partly true, though it was as much to escape the imminent destruction of London after 11 September and my mother-in-law talking about 'Andrex' scares. I also did actually want to write a novel, and had signed a deal with my publishers to do so.

There were about twelve of us holed up in the house, more women than men, ranging in age from a dentist of twenty-eight to Sylvia, a well-presented woman in her late sixties who told a funny story about a famous cricket commentator clumsily attempting to kiss her at a posh dinner, 'sticking his tongue laced with cigars, red wine and misogyny into my mouth'. We shared rooms and took it in turns to cook using local produce and herbs from the garden. All very Felicity Kendal. There was a group seminar every morning on some aspect of novel-writing, then we all sat around and composed excruciatingly overwritten prose which we were obliged to read out. After each extract everyone clapped and cooed and proclaimed the author the next Jane Austen/Somerset Maugham. The afternoons were more one-to-one orientated, as tutors went round looking at people's work in progress. I didn't have any, so I thought I'd better get started. I began a story about a young football reporter who discovers a prominent team are using a bizarre concoction – calves' blood mixed with Red Bull – to gain advantage. This is what being trapped in isolation for a week with frustrated writers does to you.

It was a very relaxing week, and I did learn a few things. One. Was. To Keep. Sentences. Short. And avoid cluttering simple prose with overelaborately constructed adverbs. Another was that keeping boring details of everyday life (weather, food, conversations) in a diary might be useful later. The tutor was preaching to the converted there. I have kept a diary since I was eight, though for the first couple of years the entries were confined to the outside temperature in Fahrenheit and centigrade.

Enthused by the new descriptive techniques I'd acquired, I climbed a hill on the last day and rang the *Telegraph* from my mobile to enquire what was on the agenda. As I was in Devon, they had me pencilled in to go and watch one of England's lowliest football clubs, Plymouth Argyle, who were experiencing a resurgence. 'Great,' I said. 'I'll give it "Stonebridge grazed the peeling woodwork of the crossbar with a sublime volley as rain began to scratch its fingernails across the blackboard sky."'

'Heh, heh, very good,' grunted the football editor. 'You can put it in, but we'll cut it out.'

BACK TO THE FUTURE

I didn't do the Plymouth trip in the end. Instead I was sent to Sandhurst. This was not to knock some common sense into me after a pretentious week debating the literary techniques of Penelope Lively. It was to attend a pivotal moment in the development of English sport: the launch of the English Cricket Academy.

Sandhurst army base was chosen for one main reason: the ECB didn't have anywhere else suitable to go. (The intended permanent location for the academy hadn't yet been selected, so they were starting in Berkshire, then moving on to Adelaide.) The first intake included Andrew Strauss, Ian Bell, Stephen Harmison and Andrew Flintoff (who volunteered at the last minute). The facilities were superb, there were expert trainers in all sorts of disciplines and it was a perfect location for the players to become acquainted with the commitment of an Olympic gold medallist rower (James Cracknell), a mountaineer who had recently conquered Everest, a UN officer stationed in Cambodia and a round-the-world yachtsman.

I joined in their session on the army assault course, set around a large lake. It revealed who had the heart and mind to lead less able colleagues through the ordeal, or, as one commander put it, 'which ones are sheep and which ones are goats'. Flintoff and Bell were definite goats, while Strauss took everything in his stride and Harmison strove hard. Later I was allowed into the players' media-training session, for a presentation entitled 'The Media: An Opportunity Not a Threat'. Though here the ECB scored an own goal by inadvertently proving the opposite.

Later at dinner in the mess, the academy's director Rod Marsh enthused about all the coaches he had lined up for the players when they arrived in Adelaide in a few weeks' time. The list included Ian Chappell, Terry Jenner, Dennis Lillee and a range of other experts. 'They'll have the best of every-thing, these lads,' he said.

I was just bemoaning the lack of a cricket academy in my youth when a sergeant major barked, 'Right, lads, you've got a lie-in tomorrow.' A few smiles. 'Be downstairs in your gym kit at ten to seven.' A few groans. 'And don't forget your rucksacks and survival kits, because after training we're sending you out into the wilds of "Barossa" [dense wood-land] for the rest of the day and the night.' Several players slunk off to buy emergency supplies of jelly babies, and by 9.30 p.m. most were in bed.

It didn't prevent several from saying things like 'I'd run through a brick wall to play for England' and 'I'm just des-perate to play for my country.' In an era when gardeners were becoming national treasures just by going braless, and most teenagers were looking for the short cut to fame, it was an encouraging sign that some were still prepared to take the tougher route to potential stardom. Added to which, if Britain suddenly needed to strengthen the Home Guard against fanatical insurgents, here were sixteen freshly drilled reinforcements.

CHAPTER 13 – 2002

MORE POWER TO THE ELBOW

The world was in turmoil, but my year began with the following exclamations:

'What a tungsten-stackin' daddy!'

'He's whipped up an electro-magnetic storm!'

'Staying with him is like trying to hang on to the pants of Halley's Comet.'

They were just some of the eulogies lavished on Phil 'the Power' Taylor by Sid Waddell, Sky TV's irreverent darts commentator at the Circus Tavern in Purfleet. I had gone there to report on Taylor attempting to win his eighth World Darts Championship title in succession, and his tenth overall, confirming him, in Waddell's words, as 'the greatest arrows-thrower that ever drew breath'. He had to be regarded as Britain's greatest living sportsman.

Any cricket writer who in future complains about the conditions in the fabulous, futuristic media centre at Lord's (and believe me, some will) should be sent to Purfleet. It's a good hour drive's east of London along the A13, past Tower Hamlets and Canning Town and through the southern equivalent of ICI Billingham. I never realised such blighted areas existed in the city in which I've lived for forty-two years. The Circus Tavern, a twinkly lit nightclub and cabaret venue – sort of Essex-man's Ronnie Scott's – is on a desolate site near Dagenham's Ford works. The car park was jammed with coaches and stretch limos and souped-up Escorts. Inside you were met by gaudily dolled-up hostesses and shown into the heaving room.

Taylor, a stout chap from Stoke with Jesus tattooed on his left calf, was introduced as 'the Eighth Wonder of the World'. He entered the arena to strobe lighting and thumping dance music – 'I've got the Power ...' – and ecstatic cheering from a thousand adoring, universally white fans, sitting at long, red-clothed tables drinking beer and eating chips. Four black-tied heavies escorted him in, one bearing his darts pouch.

His first throw in the final against Peter 'One Dart' Manley was a treble 20, and it was soon clear why he's so invincible. Nothing moves when he throws except his right arm and an eyebrow. His eyes are lasered on the target. It's the same for cricket superstars: the most accurate fast bowlers – McGrath, Hadlee, Ambrose – keep their heads the stillest. Taylor's opponents jerk their back leg or twitch their head on delivery. His body and head are rock solid throughout. His darts land in precise little clusters, nestling inconceivably close together, rarely more than a centimetre outside the treble 20.

His crowning 'checkout', a three-dart 121 – treble 18, treble 17, double 8 – was the acme of his superhuman accuracy and impenetrable focus. 'We're walking in a Taylor wonderland,' sang a table of heavyweights from Bedford.

'He could pin a fly to "tops" by its eye,' Waddell crowed exultantly.

For enthusiasm, knowledge and turn of phrase, Waddell the sports commentator is a damn good blueprint.

This mission and a few sorties into football's nether regions (a visit to the bitterest local derby in Britain – Cardiff–Swansea – for instance, and watching Paul Gascoigne's debut for Burnley with my mate Scally) had the twin aims of pieces for the *Telegraph* and material for my novel. Assuming anything relating to football would sell, I'd structured my story around the life of a struggling football reporter. It should have been about the experiences of a struggling novelist, as I was finding the process incredibly hard. Writing non-fiction, you reach a fork in the road occasionally, and have to decide whether to veer right or left, but it generally doesn't have a huge bearing on the final destination. With fiction, you come to a veritable Spaghetti Junction of options several times a day. I'd agonise nightly about some plotline or other, which made me (even more) irritating to live with. A first novel is like profusely growing ivy, spreading through every crevice, taking you over.

The central problem was that I didn't want to write one of those ropy football thrillers featuring clubs with cheesy names – Lanchester United, Pork Vile Rovers – but a sort of whodunnit with real teams. I'd vaguely camouflage the players – Roy Clean, Ted Sheriman – but I thought the clubs themselves would be fair game. Tanya attempted to talk me out of this, but when it was obvious my mind was set, she dispatched me off to discuss it with a former *Sun* sports editor who knew football writing inside out. We met in a pub and I told him the plot.

'Hold on,' he said, 'let me get this straight. You're not talking about writing that players from the *real* Manchester United are taking a performance-enhancing drug, are you?'

'Yes,' I said.

'See you in court, then!' he said.

I should have seen the light then, abandoned ship and got back on terra firma. But I remained blind to the bleeding obvious.

REACHING MY GOAL

In late March I was summoned to Canary Wharf for lunch with David Welch. Initially, this was to ask gently if I was interested in becoming the *Telegraph*'s next cricket correspondent. (Michael Henderson had defected to the *Daily Mail*.) Five years earlier, I'd have jumped at the chance, but now, firmly embedded in TV which neatly avoided the obligation of following England abroad for at least three months a year, I politely declined the offer. In any case, the prospect of having to write about cricket practically every day, rather than once a week, filled me with dread. I wouldn't have had anything left to say after a fortnight. I don't know how the daily reporters do it.

The names of other prospective cricket correspondents were aired at the lunch, but the *Independent*'s Derek Pringle, my best friend in cricket, stood head and shoulders above the rest, and not just because he's 6 foot 6. He'd done the job well at the *Indy* for eight years and needed a new challenge (and better pay). He was promptly appointed.

The conversation then moved on to other matters, including Welch's concern about the imminence of the Queen Mother's death. 'If she dies before five it's OK because they have time upstairs to produce a separate commemorative supplement,' Welch said. 'But if it's after five they'll take over the sports supplement and we'll have one hell of a job fitting sport on to five pages in the main paper. Knowing our luck, she'll die about six o'clock.'

In the event she died on a Saturday, so the daily paper had ample time to get its act together. I was in Plymouth that particular day to do the story about the football club's promotion from the Third Division, and how they might be affected by the recent collapse of ITV Digital. The Plymouth ground had a pleasantly old-fashioned air, epitomised by the modest Seats and Toyotas in the players' car park, and Lou, the old press steward – clad immaculately in a commissionaire's outfit – ferrying the silver teapot and plate of custard creams to the grateful press at half time as he had done most winter Saturdays for the past forty-one years. Press and season-ticket holders assembled in the little bar under the stand at the end of the match to watch *Final Score*. But instead of Ray Stubbs, there was a glum-looking Peter Sissons on BBC1, in – shock, horror! – a burgundy tie, for which the BBC were inundated with complaints, to announce the

Queen Mum's passing. The reaction in the bar was unemotional. 'Oh, great, that'll be another bank holiday,' declared one bloke.

I wrote up my piece on Sunday, and bought the *Telegraph* on Monday, as usual, to read it. I was amazed to see the little box on the sports supplement's front page advertising the contents. It read:

INSIDE:
FOOTBALL   2&3
RESULTS   2&3
SIMON HUGHES   5
RACING   6&7
CRICKET   8

Added to that, I discovered that Channel 4 cricket had been nominated for another Bafta, and that I'd been shortlisted by the Royal Television Society – alongside Alan Hansen and John McEnroe – as Sports Pundit of the Year. My dad, used to life's vicissitudes as an actor, would have called it a 'Let's take a taxi down to Budgen's' day'.

I was having a quietly self-satisfied dinner at home with Tanya later when she said: 'I'd like a third.'

'Oh ... I was hoping to save it for lunch tomorrow,' I said.

'I meant child, not lamb chop,' she replied.

'*Really?*' I exclaimed.

'Really.'

'Are you *sure?*'

'Sure.'

Talk about taking the wind out of a man's sails. I was already in sole charge of Callum (four) and Nancy (two and a half) for one and a half days a week while Tanya was at work. The meal chaos, the perpetual noise, the endless toy clearance, the unmistakable 'Dad, could you wipe my bottom?' when I was discussing ideas with the features editor, the house always reeking of nappies and Sudocreme when Channel 4's Thin Controller was round for dinner. I couldn't bear the prospect of a third. *I couldn't take any more.*

'A third? OK,' I said quietly.

MICROSCOPIC ANALYSIS

The Bafta television awards were a week later. I'd been invited along with Mark Nicholas and our two key producers. I walked through Covent Garden Market to Drury Lane Theatre, where the event was being staged. All the surrounding streets were crammed with rubber-neckers held back behind temporary barriers. I flashed my tickets, the security cordon parted and I walked up the red carpet nodding in acknowledgement to the hundreds of onlookers' screams and cheers, though it was slightly off-putting that they were all calling me John. Then I looked over my shoulder: Joan Collins was immediately behind me.

Mark Nicholas and I sat at the back of the stalls, making small talk with Kirsty Gallacher, except when the Thin Controller and his able lieutenant 'Storming' Normington were called up to accept the Bafta for Best Sports Programme. 'Two Baftas in three years, incredible,' said Miss Gallacher, though unfortunately it wasn't incredible enough to secure anything else. Anyway, Mark had diverted his attentions to Joanna Lumley. I finished up in the bar with the Sky News presenters who were cradling a Bafta for their coverage of September 11. While their skill and integrity were not in doubt, it seemed a macabre subject for which to earn an award.

We were still in self-congratulatory mood ten days later at our first production meeting of the year. Before setting out the agenda, David Brook, Channel 4's garrulous strategist, was waxing lyrical about the coverage, and Mark Nicholas in turn complimented the channel on its wonderful vision and commitment. Michael Atherton, newly introduced as part of the team, added his own observations: 'Eee, why don't you just blow smoke up each other's arses?' he said.

After a brief bout of convulsive laughter round the table, the meeting came to order and a productive couple of hours ensued, focusing on how cricket might lure more viewers. A programme of ideas and events was drawn up on the theme of 'Indian summer' (the Indians were arriving in June for four Tests and ten one-dayers) and proposals to get the England players, who were becoming increasingly remote from the media, more onside. Atherton said afterwards that if he and other players had realised the level of detail and planning involved in the production, they'd probably have been a lot more forthcoming in interviews.

For detail, though, no one beats Benaud. At the commentators' get-together before the first Test against Sri Lanka, we were issued with a sheet featuring the mug shots and names of the Sri Lankan and Indian players. Richie was very keen to get their names phonetically correct, so we went through the pronunciations one by one. The former Indian all-rounder Ravi Shastri was there to help. 'Is it Sanat Jayasuriya or Sanath Jayasuriya?' Richie asked. 'Sanath Jayasuriya' was the answer. 'Tillekeratnay or Tillekeratna?' 'Tillekeratna.' 'Mahela Jayawardena?' Spot on. V. V. S. Laxman was a stumbling block (we were told to say 'Laxchman'), so you can imagine what it was like when we got to Muralitharan. Richie was used to saying 'Muralitharan', but I wondered whether the 'th' should be pronounced 't', and Mark Nicholas preferred Tony Greig's version – 'Muraleedooran'. So we debated that for some time before settling on Richie's version.

I spent the rest of the day looking at Pathé footage of old cricketers for a lunchtime series we were doing on how the game had changed. It was fascinating looking at shots of W. G. Grace with his enormous beard and jerky, upright batting style, of the bizarre hop-skip-and-a-jump bowling actions of some of the leading protagonists, of the huge crowds escorting the captains out for the toss and of the exceptionally nonchalant reactions of the 1953 England players strolling calmly off the field having regained the Ashes after an unprecedented nineteen-year gap. The overriding impression I formulated of the players of yesteryear, however, was the appalling condition of their teeth.

I didn't win the Sports Pundit award. Well, what chance did I have against two men (Hansen and McEnroe) with out-standing sporting talent, forthright opinions and full heads of hair? McEnroe was rightly crowned. And the Sri Lanka series was rather overshadowed by the football World Cup. As well as the blanket coverage of matches, *The Times* even ran a clever series analysing football pundits, and allowing readers to evict them, *Big Brother* style. 'Is Ron Atkinson's gold chain impeding the flow of blood to his brain?' asked one respondent. Another suggested Trevor Brooking was 'more neutral than Switzerland'. We were lucky cricket was too anonymous for there to be anything similar.

The third Test coincided with England's second-round tie with Denmark, and we joined in the spirit by staging our own penalty competition on the Saturday morning *Roadshow*. This featured Atherton, Slater, Reeve and me, though it nearly didn't happen because two minutes before we were due on air all the balls had been kicked onto the roof of the Old Trafford nets and the Thin Controller was doing his nut. One was retrieved at the last minute but I wish it hadn't been. I completely missed the target with my opening shot and threw myself to the ground in mock-shame (Slater scored – oh, the humiliation of losing to an Australian!). Covered in grass and mud, I suddenly realised that there was no time to change before the slightly more serious business of the pitch report. I was dirtier than all the groundstaff.

Old Trafford had become our favourite Test venue, not because of the ground, which was looking shabby, but because of where we stayed. We were booked in to the mag-nificent Lowry Hotel, a *Footballers' Wives*-type place on the south side of town with a huge white atrium, white leather banquettes and immaculate receptionists in black suits. The rooms were the dimensions of tennis courts, with emperor-sized beds and chaise longues. A bit style over substance, but very Primetime Television. Not at all Daily Rag: the press were mostly billeted in the Crown Plaza in town. (TV personnel are generally pampered, while the written media tend to travel cattle class, as Atherton and I discussed on the way home from Lord's in a smart people-carrier when we overtook Angus Fraser lugging his *Independent* laptop and briefcase to St John's Wood tube station. It's a parallel of batsmen – the fancy dans, favoured and fawned over – and bowlers, cricket's downtrodden labourers. As with bowlers' feelings towards batsmen, many pressmen harbour a latent resentment of commentators.)

You met interesting people in the Lowry bar, too. One night we ran into Jeremy Paxman, looking a bit harassed. I offered him a drink. 'Sorry,' he said, 'I'm at Granada doing four episodes of *University Challenge* in two days. Got to do my prep!' A keen cricket fan, he was nevertheless persuaded to stay, and before long was extolling, with Atherton, the virtues of various Scottish salmon beats. Paxman had even published a vast tome, *Fish, Fishing and the Meaning of Life*, about his favourite pastime. I don't know how people like him find the time to brush their hair, never mind write books.

CHOCOLATE HOBNOBBING

The combination of the Lowry's ambience and the regular embarrassment of parking my poky, juice-stained Golf next to all the 4x4s and Jags in the players and officials' car park at grounds persuaded me to get a better car. I negotiated a deal for a BMW X5. Apart from the annoyance of the bleeping sound whenever I was reversing into a parking spot (whatever's wrong with bump parking?), it was a revelation. You climbed rather than crept into it and emerged from a three-hour journey without spinal contractions. The England players, most of whom had treated me with slight suspicion ever since I'd evolved into the Analyst (it was one of those show-us-your-medals situations), were suddenly all my mates. 'Is that the three-litre version or the four-point-two?' 'That GPS is handy, isn't it?' 'They're paying you well these days, then!' Hanging about in the players' car park secured me an interview with Graham Thorpe and several invitations to dinner. Little did they know I had borrowed the car from a friend who was BMW's press officer. I had to give it back at the end of the week. Still, it was fun while it lasted.

England had evolved into an impressive outfit. Centrally contracted, expertly coached, scientifically trained, they were starting to resemble supreme athletes rather than the assortment of lumberers and featherweights of previous eras. They were always gazing at laptops in the dressing room, I noticed. While the material being viewed might occasionally have been a modern version of the *Knave* magazines players used to keep in their cricket cases, most often they were looking at themselves. The team now employed a computer analyst who input all the details of each delivery – type of ball, speed, length, direction, shot played, runs scored – into a database, enabling players to make specific CDs of their innings or bowling spells. As soon as he was out, a batsman could select all his front-foot shots, all his attempts to duck bouncers or any other isolated action, and look at them ad infinitum in the dressing room. It was all very sophisticated, and in stark contrast to my attempts fifteen years earlier to look at my bowling on my parents' recording of a Sunday League game. It took extensive trial and error to pause the video at the right point of my delivery and try to glean something from the shaky freeze before the machine inadvertently jerked forward several frames. And that was if *Celebrity Squares* hadn't accidentally been recorded instead.

Players' lifestyles had altered. They were all nutrition-conscious (eating pasta and cereal bars at lunch rather than steak, chips and spotted dick and custard), rarely socialised and were normally in bed by eleven (although Thorpe was up half the night during one game, pouring out his heart about his marriage). Generally it sounded professional, but not much fun. There was no Botham to take the opposition out and get them wrecked on red wine so they couldn't perform the next day. To underline how times had changed, I wrote in a column that – 'the Great Beefy is now a Doctor of Science (UMIST). Coming next, David Beckham gets an English PhD from Cambridge.' It was a cheap shot, and not remotely sensible given that Botham is not a good man to antagonise, and on the day it was published I was commentating on a one-day international in the Channel 4 box, next door to his Sky one. While I was chatting outside between stints, I felt a large hand on my collar. I swivelled round and was confronted by the considerable displeasure of the great man. 'I was given that honorary science doctorate because of my leukaemia charity work, you bald-headed pea brain!' he remarked coldly, and skulked off. I fluffed my lines on my next commentary stint and was in a state of some anxiety all day, not helped by Atherton mischievously brandishing a very large wooden spoon and constantly popping in to the Sky box to stir him up about it. I did print a profuse apology, which he accepted, but I avoided commentary for a few matches after that, preferring to tuck myself safely away in the VT truck instead.

England hammered India in the first Test at Lord's, enjoyed by Scally and a couple of his mates whom I got in as usual with a couple of Channel 4 passes. There was a buzz in the VT truck at one point as someone answered my mobile phone while I was briefly elsewhere and the caller identified herself as Kate Winslet. I had arranged to meet Sam Mendes for a drink after the game and he had asked, 'All right if I bring my bird?' He and Kate were now an item, and she was ringing to say they couldn't get a babysitter. All twelve video-tape editors immediately offered their services and I'm pretty sure the action replays were out of sync for a few minutes. News quickly leaked to the commentary box where Atherton and Ian Smith had a field day, referring to me as the 'Hollywood hobnobber who's been stood up' and suggesting in lieu I could invite Kate for a tour of the truck, which Atherton had now renamed the 'caravan'. Smith even dredged up my comparison of Giles and Warne the previous year, and hoped that I wasn't still getting too much sun. They were just jealous, really.

RITE OF PASSAGE

At a sponsors' dinner for players and TV personnel, I sat next to Michael Vaughan. He was excellent company, telling funny, slightly indiscreet stories about players – that Andrew Flintoff's party piece was to drink from three bottles of Stella at the same time, having bitten the tops off, for instance – and appearing interested in finding out what my Analyst job entailed. He wouldn't have to worry about a TV career for a while, though, because he was having a fabulous summer. The stuttery feet and uncertainty that I'd remembered from the A tour to India all those years ago had gone, to be replaced by flair and confidence, and he scored three majestic centuries against the Indians. After one of these, at Trent Bridge, Michael Henderson gave him a glowing write-up in the *Daily Mail*, drawing slightly unfavourable comparisons with Michael Atherton: 'Atherton never played – could never play – with the freedom and range of stroke that Vaughan displayed on Saturday, nor could he hit the ball so hard ... Too often Atherton, concerned mainly with protecting his wicket, ignored bad balls or stroked them to fielders.' I didn't think this was entirely fair: Atherton had been a very fluent player until his back, and the rest of the England team, began to let him down. Henderson then added more barbed remarks about Atherton's nascent television career, even though our new colleague had been insightful and occasionally humorous, and had taken to commentary with aplomb.

Atherton read the piece and was privately upset by it, particularly as it had been written by someone he considered a good friend. But, knowing that Henderson had called his pal Angus Fraser 'the highest-paid apprentice in history' after he'd abruptly retired from playing to become cricket correspondent of the *Independent*, he put a brave face on it. 'It's a sort of rite of passage,' he said.

We came to the conclusion that it was something of a privilege to be insulted by Henderson. Apart from me, he'd done the same to Derek Pringle, Vic Marks and Jonathan Agnew, among others, all of whom had subsequently earned exalted status in the sports media. A lambasting from Hendo had become an initiation which former players had to endure before they could emerge from their cricketing cocoon to enter the real world of early deadlines, running copy and readers' letters from Salford criticising the 'guff' about swing being induced by humidity.

At the Leeds Test various journalists, commentators and producers were sharing a nightcap in the Malmaison Hotel bar when several trendy-looking types accompanying a crazy-looking bloke with a wacky cockatoo haircut wandered in. 'That's Liam Howlett of the Prodigy,' whispered Derek Pringle, a veritable music encyclopedia. He broke into a riff of the punky anthem 'Firestarter'.

One of the trendies, ignoring Pringle, Atherton and the others, made a beeline for me. 'Hey, you're Simon Harris!' he exclaimed.

'Uh?' I said.

'No, no, I recognise you … You're Simon Harris … the chap who sits in that dungeon …'

'Caravan,' Atherton corrected.

'… and do all your fancy graphics and stuff. Hey, Liam, it's Simon Harris, that bloke on the cricket!'

Howlett, it transpired, was slightly out of it after performing with the Prodigy at the Leeds Festival. But it did emerge that the band, one of Britain's most outrageous, had a telly in the recording studio permanently tuned to the cricket and found it annoying that there was not a version of 'Desktop Richie' – the cartoon Test information service – for their studio Apple Macs. I said I'd see what I could do.

On air, Benaud was giving me encouragement, and I got slightly carried away illuminating bowling spells with brightly coloured patterns of balls we called beehives, and annotating triple-split screens of batsmen's stances. Trying to be too clever, I botched one attempt to scribble on Tendulkar's backlift and apologised for my cack-handedness as I was linking back to the commentary box. 'That was a very instructive piece of analysis,' replied Richie, 'and don't worry about the drawing, Simon. Picasso used to struggle on Sundays sometimes.'

One viewer had a starkly different view, however. Mr S. Wood of Hove wrote:

'Rubbish Hughes!! We can all do without your stupid diagrams, crosses and circles, all in Technicolor and cartoon fashions. One big bore. We would rather watch TV adverts than your silly rubbish. They want to lock that shed up where you sit and kick you out.'

There was no danger of getting too big for your boots in this outfit.

GIMME SHELTER

Generally, Benaud seemed energised by the move to Channel 4. He was fascinated by the innovations – the Snickometer was definitely his favourite – and enthused about each day as if it were his first. He was excellent at putting things in perspective and gave the programme bags of gravitas. When Harbhajan Singh took a five-wicket haul and his figures were included on a graphic of great off-spinning performances of all time, Richie said, 'Ah yes, J. C. Laker, best figures in Test history, ten for fifty-three at Old Trafford in 1956 ... [Pause for effect] ... and I was one of them.'

On another occasion he listened with interest as Michael Slater commentated on a wicket. Articulacy not being Slats's strength, he stumbled over the past tense of 'sneak'. 'Is it "sneaked" or "snuck"?' he asked those in the box. Benaud, sitting in his corner, perusing the *Racing Post*, thought for a moment. Then, only half looking up, he said with delicious poise, 'Well, I can think of quite a few "ucks", but "snuck" isn't one of them.'

Benaud would undoubtedly have raised the famous eyebrow at events in the press box during the Headingley Test. The cricket writers are an acceptable bunch superficially, but below the surface there are some prickly little cliques. One of these had been penetrated by a *Daily Mirror* journalist who had acquired a reputation for glancing at other hacks' screens and snaffling their stories. Everyone knew that he wasn't a cricket specialist, so a couple of the regular cricket writers lured him into a hoax. One left a bogus story on his screen reporting that Mick Jagger had pumped millions into a minor county to make them the nineteenth first-class team. It was headlined: 'JAGGER INVESTS £3M IN BERKSHIRE'. He somehow misconstrued the 'facts', and a piece appeared in the *Mirror* the next day claiming that old rubber lips was rescuing *Yorkshire*. Incredibly, the *Yorkshire Post* picked up the story and ran with it on the front page. Leeds city centre was thick with billboards declaring: 'JAGGER'S £3M BAILS OUT TYKES'. Journalists play a sort of modern version of Chinese whispers.

I couldn't claim exemption. Geoff Boycott had resurfaced at Headingley, commentating for an Indian channel, and his throat cancer hadn't dented his pride. I heard him outside the commentary box apparently complaining to an Indian producer that his number of first-class centuries was listed inaccurately. A little unscrupulously, I recounted this episode in a column, saying Geoffrey was back and in fine voice, 'and could be heard loudly discrediting some statistician who had him down as having made 149 hundreds. "It's 151, I tell you, fifth best ever ..."' I received a handwritten note from Boycott a week later. He was unhappy with my column, arguing that the discussion 'was not about me, but about Herbert Sutcliffe, whom the statistician had on screen equal with me on 151 centuries ... *Wisden* is the cricketer's bible and records the great batsman [Sutcliffe] as 149 centuries'. He continued: 'Why get it wrong and try to make out I was being boastful. It's not the first time you have tried to score a point off me or be "smart arse" about me. I don't know why – I don't know that I have ever done you any harm.' He hadn't, it was true, and I felt guilty for the inaccuracy and sent him an apology.

The last day of the Indian Test series at The Oval was a washout. Although the series was nicely poised at 1–1, the match was heading for a boring draw anyway. We used the morning airtime on Channel 4 to debate England's party for the winter tour to Australia, and Ian Smith ruffled a few feathers – notably Hussain's – by suggesting that he had lost it as captain and should be replaced by Mark Butcher. Then six commentators and Gary, our Thin Controller, repaired to the Ivy for a long and very enjoyable lunch.

It was around this point that Channel 4's enthusiasm for cricket began to cool. This wasn't solely because of the bill from the Ivy. Commitments to *Big Brother* and other 'reality shows' were commanding most of the channel's attention. The powers that be had also been underwhelmed by the Indian series, and had been losing heart with the early evening scheduling of the highlights programme, *Today at the Test*. By the following year it was on so late we thought it should be renamed *Yesterday at the Test*. The channel did at least agree to screen the winter highlights of the Ashes (it was live on Sky). But my hopes of commentating on England at last regaining the urn – broadcasting from Australia or in an airless booth in Soho, I didn't care which – were dashed. They went for the cheaper option and took Channel 9's commentary instead.

So instead of enjoying the opening day of the Ashes series from the commentary box in Brisbane, I watched it from a hotel lounge in Burnley. I was in the town with Scally and his dad, both ardent Clarets fans, to watch the re-enactment of a great sixties footballing encounter, Burnley v. Spurs. The two teams had been drawn together for an evening match in the Worthington Cup. Beforehand we lingered in the club's Centre Circle bar, with its swirly patterned carpet, flock wallpaper and the kind of red velvet curtains you only find at crematoriums. We'd come to listen to a famous man of both clubs, Ralph Coates, reminisce, and marvel at the survival of his iconic hairstyle, with its parting four millimetres above his left ear lobe.

After the bedlam surrounding Burnley's win had died down, we retired to the bar of a quaint hotel full of model ghosts and witches and watched the opening exchanges from the first Test at the Gabba. With bowling resources already depleted (Gough had already been sent home, Flintoff soon would be), Hussain, perhaps over-respectful of Australia, bewilderingly chose to field first. The Australian opening pair of Matthew Hayden and Justin Langer soon thrust out their chests and asserted themselves against nervous opening spells from Hoggard and Caddick. When Australia had rattled along to 67 for 0 in 14 overs, we went to bed in the hotel sensing the worst. The fears were confirmed when I woke up six hours later: Hayden was still batting, Australia were 350 for 2 and England's best bowler, Simon Jones, had seriously mangled his knee. England had dropped catches and bowled abysmally. They ultimately lost the match by 364 runs, prompting the Sydney *Daily Telegraph* to wheel out its now-customary full-page headline: 'IS THERE ANYBODY IN ENGLAND WHO CAN ACTUALLY PLAY CRICKET?'

It took Australia a mere eleven days of cricket to claim the Ashes for the eighth consecutive time, so it seemed the answer, depressingly, was 'no'.

CHAPTER 14 – 2003

LONDON CALLING

Matthew Hayden's imposing physique symbolised Australia's dominance in the 2002–03 Ashes. A bear of a man with a snarl to match, he ripped England's ravaged bowling resources to shreds with three pugnacious hundreds, and put the wind up various England batsmen with a sequence of provocative comments in the field. He was the muscle man of the moment. He even made it into the *Telegraph* sports editor's eulogy at the Christmas lunch. 'It's been a great year,' said David Welch. 'Our rowing columnist James Cracknell won the World Pairs Championship. Our running columnist Paula Radcliffe won the London Marathon. Our rugby columnist Matt Dawson starred in the victories over Australia and New Zealand. And our cricket columnist Matthew Hayden took three hundreds off England in the Ashes!'

Welch misconstrued his emphasis there, but he was the driving force behind a campaign to get London to bid for the 2012 Olympics. The government was lukewarm about the idea, but Welch drummed up support among the *Telegraph* sportswriters and sent them on various missions. I felt our lacklustre attitude to sport barely merited an Olympic Games, but I was dispatched to various events in the capital one Saturday to canvass opinion.

I began at a cross-country event at Alexandra Palace, which attracted more than 250 runners despite the icy January weather. I moved on to West Ham, near to the proposed Olympic village, to talk to Hammers fans congregating in a pub about the Olympics potentially coming to London. Judging by the unhealthy state of some of these fans, the Olympics were long overdue. One fat bloke was being ironic when he called his home suburb, Romford, a 'hotbed of athletics'. I asked him what he did for a living. 'Bodyguard,' came the reply. 'But he don't guard his own too well,' said his only marginally slimmer mate. Then I went south to Crystal Palace, where I chatted to swimmers and runners who were in somewhat better shape, and spectators at a London Towers basketball match.

All day only one person voiced any opposition to the idea. I drove back through the pitiful estates of south London realising I hadn't before appreciated the depth of sporting commitment in my own city, often in spite of woeful facilities, or the diversity of activity. It was an uplifting experience and I was immediately converted to supporting the bid. I was pretty sure it would be futile, though.

Billy, our third child, was born early in 2003. I worked at home in an upstairs bedroom for a few weeks, alternating columns with my novel. I was having real trouble with the latter, suffering serious writer's constipation, despite having read Stephen King's excellent book, *On Writing: A Memoir of the Craft*, which is packed with useful tips. I ploughed on, regardless, and at least came up with a title I liked – *Pipe Dreams* – apt in my mind because the book was about a young football reporter with unrealistic aspirations who also happened to be a part-time church organist ... natch. (And I thought it would sell!)

Meanwhile, I investigated selling the serial rights to a mass-market publication. Tanya, well connected in the tabloid world, arranged for us to have dinner with Andy Coulson, editor of the *News of the World*, and I told him about the project. He sounded interested, but cautioned by saying, 'Mind you, I don't think we've featured a work of fiction in our pages before.'

'What d'you mean?' I said. 'Your pages are *all* fiction.'

He took the slur quite well, but I paid the (very large) bill to compensate.

Paternity duties kept me from going to the Cricket World Cup. While England were competing in the group stages, and Tanya was heading to her office after six weeks off, I must have been the only cricket commentator in the land struggling to school several times a week with three kids and a double buggy. I frequently encountered a nice old lady walking her dog through the park who'd say, 'Shouldn't you be in South Africa, Simon?' But I didn't feel put out. In fact, Sky gave me the best of both worlds. While playing with Billy, I could follow the whole event from my sofa and write a weekly column on it. And I could call it 'work'.

England, still erratic in one-day cricket, paid the penalty for refusing to go to Zimbabwe (the ICC and the ECB staged a procrastination world championship over this issue, making me, and most of the country, want to shout, '*Oh, just make a decision, you blithering idiots!*') and had to beat Australia to progress. They had them reeling at 135 for 8, chasing 205, but were unable to finish them off. So England's fourteen-year humiliation by the old enemy continued. Hussain immediately resigned as England's one-day captain.

It was the right move, as one-day cricket was too pre-programmed and contained for his liking. As a one-day batsman, he was a terrier in kennels: the shots that allowed him to break out of the shackles in Tests realised only a single in one-dayers. As a one-day leader, he was an astute commander confined to square bashing. Hussain was an outstanding Test match captain because he was a manipulator who trusted his instincts, but one-day captains are chiefly hostages to fortune: there is little scope for a captain to express himself. Hunches occasionally work, but if they don't, there's no time for damage limitation. One over costing a dozen can be game, set and match, as happened when Hussain took the gamble of giving the forty-seventh over of the Australia match to the inexperienced James Anderson. Hussain was not a particularly lucky captain. You wouldn't say he had the

Midas touch. He was someone who needed time to work the oracle, motivating and reminding and reinforcing the message. He did not turn water into wine, but he did make sure the water was put to more effective use.

There was a lot of conjecture about whether the man to take over from Hussain would be Vaughan or Trescothick. If anyone had looked at the Christian names of previous England captains, they would have known the answer. Since 1980, alternate England captains have been called Michael (Brearley, Gatting, Atherton). So after Nasser Hussain it had to be (Michael) Vaughan. And it was.

With England's exit from the World Cup, interest in the tournament, which had never been close to fever pitch anyway, evaporated. So I reverted to writing columns about football. In one, I drew a comparison between Paul Gascoigne and the emerging Wayne Rooney. I introduced a story I'd heard about Gazza's first day working for ITV on the World Cup. It was a big career opportunity for him and the ITV chiefs had taken him into an anteroom for a serious pep talk. As they sat down, Gazza had asked if he could have a fag. It was a no-smoking building, but they agreed. Then he asked for a drink. A bottle of red wine was produced. At last, the big chief got his complete attention. He had just reiterated the seriousness of the role when Gazza's mobile rang. 'It's for you,' he said, handing over the phone, which promptly ignited, singeing the boss's hair. Everyone fell about laughing at the prank, but Gazza was a flop as a pundit, and he ended up being dispatched to canvass opinion on building sites while running up an astronomical bar bill.

This story had been told to me in confidence six months earlier by my best mate, Scally, now football editor at ITV. Arrogantly believing enough time had elapsed since it had happened – and wanting, like most journalists, to catch the reader's eye – I relayed it in full. It caught the reader's eye all right. One reader in particular: Scally. He was furious.

'Jesus fucking Christ!' he said. 'You've just ruined my career.'

'What?' I blustered. 'What's the matter?'

'What's the matter? *What's the fucking matter?* Everything's the fucking matter. You ... you ... you've just wrecked any trust people had in me, which ... I've been religiously building up for years. My ITV bosses won't trust me with their plans, thinking I'll leak them to the press. Guests won't trust me, thinking I'll divulge their secrets. We'll never get anyone decent on *The Premiership* again!'

Well, you've never had anyone decent on it before, I felt like saying, but held my tongue.

'And *I* can't trust *you*,' he continued. 'I told you it was not repeatable. Not only do you go off and use it anyway, but it gets blown up and distorted out of all proportion. Betrayed by my best mate. Well, that's fucking friendship for you. Now everything's ruined. They'll probably fire me.' And he hung up.

I experienced conflicting emotions: shock at his reaction, shame at the way I had blithely betrayed a confidence, and a slight sense that he'd overreacted. It is, unfortunately, the dilemma you often face as a journalist. You have a hot, or funny, piece of news; you're sworn to secrecy but are just dying to divulge it. Journalists, though, are by nature storytellers, and hopeless at keeping shtum. As a result, the best ones don't have many, if any, friends. Tanya was reassuring: 'He'll get over it,' she said.

LAWS OF THE JUNGLE

Two extraordinary events dominated April. Baghdad was claimed by the Allies, with the seminal moment being the toppling of a statue of Saddam Hussein in a Baghdad square. Meanwhile, in deepest Queensland, Phil Tufnell was crowed King of the Jungle in *I'm a Celebrity, Get Me Out of Here*. Mike Soper, deputy chairman of the ECB, suggested Tufnell 'has done more for English cricket in these last ten days than anyone I know'. Others, mainly Tufnell's former playing colleagues, were considerably less charitable, grunting that even after reaping £1 million in spin-offs, he still probably wouldn't buy a round. In truth, Tufnell may have been one of the weakest characters ever to spin a ball for a living, but he was still a good deal stronger and more interesting than a host of 'celebrities'. It didn't say much for the members of the *Hello!stocracy*. But it said a great deal for the time-killing skills developed by bored tail-enders, used to hours of watching their batting colleagues accumulating runs. When he wasn't asleep, Tufnell had always been an entertaining dressing-room companion, full of cheeky observations and funny gestures. Beneath the maverick exterior, he was a smart cookie.

After the three-day Lord's Test, allowing me to make my peace with Scally by getting to his wedding, Tufnell was the star attraction in Durham for Chester-le-Street's inaugural Test. 'Hello, Yoz,' he said when I encountered him perched on a red sofa by the sightscreen, and he shrugged as if he didn't understand what all the fuss was about. I knew, though, that he had perfected the nonchalant-chappie persona and was already making a good second living out of it. Naturally talented but a slightly reluctant competitor on the field, he had finally found his niche.

The Durham Test was slightly underwhelming – poorish crowd, even poorer opposition (Zimbabwe again) – and with all this reality-TV stuff around, and Channel 4 there only to do a highlights programme, we had time to spare. We came up with a formula to guarantee the future success of Test cricket in England, and possibly the world: create a programme called *I'm a Test Cricketer in the MCC House*! Twenty inmates cooped up in the Lord's pavilion, with no one allowed to enter or leave except with the permission of the stewards. In an item called 'You snooze, you lose' if the scoring rate drops and there are at least five asleep – indicated by five lights on the scoreboard – one of the batsmen in the middle is evicted. Mike Atherton rarely gets to face a whole over. If the team doesn't score 150 by lunch, they don't get any food. There'd be a bun-eating contest at tea.

I travelled back from Durham with Atherton and

Nicholas, who were both popping in chez Botham on the way back for a barbecue. Botham and I hadn't had a lot of contact since my faux pas about his honorary degree, but he had said it was fine if I came along. Still, I was a bit apprehensive, but he couldn't have been nicer, standing over the fire in a large apron and shorts nudging seven different types of sausage around the grill. All the Zimbabwe team were there, too – looking like university students, wide-eyed with awe at the fine house and its magnificent, sprawling grounds and the vast quantities of meat on offer.

I mentioned to His Beefiness that soon it would be exactly ten years since he'd retired from the game.

'Ten years? God, is it really?' he said. 'Better drink a toast to that on the day. When is it?'

'The final of the Twenty-20,' I said.

'Ah well, I've got the week off then,' he said gleefully. 'Saturday afternoon I'll probably be in the beach bar by the Desert Springs golf course, where I've got my Spanish villa. About thirty yards from the first tee, actually.'

I asked him if he'd picked up a bat since that day in 1993 when he'd bowled a few overs for Durham against the Australians and then kept wicket (in batting gloves and no pads) before waving goodbye.

'No, not once, like I said I wouldn't,' he replied. Botham had been, as ever, a man of his word.

We didn't leave Botham's barbecue until about 10.30 p.m. I drove through the night all the way back to London from North Yorkshire, relishing both my rehabilitation with Beefy and the luxury of driving a car (Nicholas's) that was fast, spacious and not strewn with spent juice bottles and empty crisp packets and that didn't have back-seat occupants demanding 'Little Bo Peep' on the CD every five minutes.

A month of one-day internationals sat like a dead weight in the middle of the summer. It was all right for Sky, since they had the live rights to every game, providing sustenance to their viewers in the brief interlude between football seasons. We at Channel 4 were obliged to cover the matches too, but, because we were only producing forty-minute high-lights shows, most of what was said hit the cutting-room floor. As a result, we went round with a skeleton crew, and Benaud was given the month off. He and his wife Daphne returned to their apartment near Nice. 'I'll be in Beaulieu sur Mer just opening the chilled Chardonnay when you're in mid-innings in the day–nighter at Old Trafford,' he said with that mischievous look. He kept a close eye on proceedings, though, watching all the matches on telly in France.

The rest of us were not always quite so professional. As the umpires emerged for the start of that Old Trafford day–nighter, the Channel 4 commentary box was practically deserted. Messrs Nicholas, Slater and Barry Richards had been taken to Atherton's golf club, Hoylake, for a morning round; and Atherton, in his home town, had got lost on Manchester's bewildering motorway system on the way back. Dermot Reeve had broken down driving up the M6, and my flight, which was due to arrive just an hour before the start, had been delayed. The only person to commentate on the opening exchanges was the England women's captain Clare Connor. Our Thin Controller often said that working on Channel 4 cricket was his dream job. On days like this, it was his worst nightmare.

A bunch of beered-up lads from Accrington accosted me in the toilet at that game. 'He's the Analyst!' one said. 'Well, analyse that,' said the bloke in the next urinal, pointing to his appendage. Another, overhearing, asked me to sign his ticket. 'Now I've got the autographs of Mike Gatting and I-don't-know-who-he-is,' he said.

THE SHORT KISS GOODBYE

The New Zealander Ian Smith arrived in mid-July to commentate on the South Africa series. 'The Americans have got two Husseins,' he said, referring to the assassination of Saddam's brothers, 'now I'm coming to get the third.' He had

never been a great fan of Nasser since he'd refused to bat
with an injured thumb in the second innings of the 1999
Lord's Test. New Zealand won that and went on to clinch the
series.

Smith soon got his wish. Before the match at Edgbaston,
Hussain had absent-mindedly confused the first name of the
young South African captain, calling him Greg Smith. He
certainly knew it well enough afterwards: Graeme Smith
scored 277 and South Africa rattled up 594 for 5. Hussain
looked a tired and forlorn figure during the game, and
despite it petering out into a draw, he resigned at the end of
it.

This match featured my most impressively written piece
ever. Not because of its style or content, but because I composed it while doing 90 m.p.h. on the M40, perched with a
laptop in the back of Atherton's jeep. There was the reassuring presence of his one-year-old son's toys in the car, and the
advantage of having Athers's and Ian Smith's brains to pick.
There was the disadvantage of feeling queasy every time I
looked at the computer screen (not, for once, because of
what was written on it). The three of us came to the conclusion that Hussain had made the right decision. He'd been
through two unsuccessful Ashes campaigns, endured the
draining shenanigans of the Zimbabwe business at the World
Cup, and done a full four-year cycle of all the other countries. A proud, impassioned street-fighter, he had captained
in an abrasive, treat-'em-mean-keep-'em-keen sort of way.
He worried himself sick about the team and took communal
failure as a personal affront. He wore his heart on his sleeve,
and his greatest conquests – Pakistan, West Indies, Sri Lanka
– were achieved in the company of similar hard-boiled types
– Stewart, Thorpe, Gough, Atherton – the great British bat-
tlers.

He had seen during the one-day series how Vaughan's
less demonstrative approach seemed to help a new set of
players gel. Where Hussain steamed, Vaughan smirked. An
expensive over that might have brought out Hussain's

famous double teapot left Vaughan looking merely quizzical. He sensed that these lads perhaps preferred the carrot to the stick. The nucleus of the England team had evolved: it was now made up of men like Vaughan, Trescothick (the unflustered south paw), Flintoff (the beaming man-mountain) and Anderson (the phlegmatic ball-bender). Hussain had been an excellent England captain: the right man for the moment, stiffening players' resolve, raising expectations and standing up to bullying administrators. He had achieved notable triumphs and established better routines, but the unstinting effort had taken its toll and his captaincy had become increasingly erratic. The reservoir of commitment had run dry. It was time for a change.

People were beginning to mutter that about the Channel 4 commentary team, too. Atherton had slotted seamlessly into the job, making smart, succinct observations (writing his own weekly column definitely helped). He was forthright and not afraid to speak his mind. He understood implicitly that in this new career he had to offer more than curt one-liners, and he soon became adept at elaborating in the studio if there was time to fill. He was conscientious, and his regular presence as a racing tipster on *The Morning Line* dovetailed well with the cricket. He had become very relaxed with the TV medium. Laconic Mike had become Loquacious Mike. Furthermore, as my unofficial chauffeur, he had become an essential part of the team. However, his shoes were still terrible.

By contrast, the word around the traps was that Dermot Reeve was becoming a weak link. His behaviour had become increasingly bemusing. The previous winter during the Ashes in Australia he had infiltrated the Barmy Army and got them to strike up a chorus of 'Channel 4, Channel 4, Channel 4!' whenever possible. This had further inflamed a tense relationship between Channel 4 and Sky (who were broadcasting that series), which had at its root the constant championing of Channel 4's coverage (from Bafta and others) and the frequent denigration of Sky's. This was unfair, really – we had just a few weeks on air every year while they were at the coalface virtually 24/7 – but because of the contrasting make-ups of the two teams, comparisons were inevitable. Sky's commentary box was full of greats of the game. (After one teatime chat we'd broadcast on bowling injuries, we – Atherton, Reeve, Hughes and Nicholas – calculated that we had a grand total of five Test wickets between us. The men in the Sky box – Botham, Willis, Holding and Allott – had 983.) Inevitably, there was a slight difference in tone: Sky's tended towards tabloid hyperbole; Channel 4's was a little more reflective. Who was better or worse was totally subjective. The main thing was that there was a choice.

Reeve, perhaps feeling the pressure of Atherton's emergence, was now airing an assortment of hare-brained ideas and picking perverse arguments on air (with Richie, about the difference between a groin injury and a hernia; and with Atherton, accusing him of being unpatriotic when he lauded an onslaught by India's batsmen). To cap it all, during a commercial break in the Lord's Test, he pulled up his shirt and revealed his torso to Benaud. A small silver ring had been inserted through his left nipple, from where it dangled. 'What d'you think, Richie?' he said, mischievously. Thirty seconds later, as Rob the director said, 'Back on air,' Reeve had achieved the unthinkable. For perhaps the only time in history, a slightly open-mouthed Benaud had been stumped for words.

It was certainly a commentary box full of unusual words. Atherton had once uttered, 'Oh, he's dropped a goober!' Benaud's favourites, apart from 'leg-cudder', were 'mully-grubber' (shooter) and 'Dorothy' (meaning six, a rhyming reference to the Australian agony aunt Dorothy Dix). But Ian Smith's were in a different league from everybody else's. He summed up the moment superbly and had a succession of apt turns of phrase: whenever the newspapers were delivered to the commentary box, he'd look at the great wodge of paper and say, 'There's another hectare of Amazon forest gone telling us what Beckham had for breakfast.' And, being a Kiwi, he was the only one who said 'skupper' and 'wuckit' and 'eighty-five Tist suxes'. But while it amused us, and entertained most viewers, it didn't endear him to everybody. We had an email one day from a bloke who said he loved the commentary and the coverage in general but was put off by Smith's 'irritable vowel syndrome'. The printout was pinned on the wall in the commentary box and we all mimicked him a bit. I handed back to him after one of my thirty-second pieces with 'and now back to Ian Smuth, who's just funushed hus double fush and chups'. It earned the usual retort: 'Wull, if you were away making tea whun the Analyst was on, you hivan't mussed anythung.' Owing to my frequent failure to nail first go little forty-second pieces for the highlights show, Smith then christened me 'Thirteen-take Hughes'.

As usual at Lord's, I was inundated with visitors wanting to see round the truck. A string of mostly portly gentlemen and their sons were fascinated by all the screens and technology as well as the dealing-room atmosphere. Nicholas brought in one shortish chap, wearing funny little round glasses. He was introduced as Mervyn-someone, and I thought he might have been an old school tutor.

'What d'you do?' I asked blithely.

'I'm the governor of the Bank of England,' he replied.

I was chained to the VT truck most days, but on the Saturday at Lord's I took the chance for a short break when Sam Mendes invited me to his box. I popped up just after lunch when Channel 4 had gone racing and the cricket was only on Film Four (an appropriate title, we thought, since we reckoned that's how many people watched it). Kate Winslet, newly pregnant, was there, too. I gave her a quick peck on the cheek. The moment was caught by camera nine, operated by the veteran Neil Richardson, a sardonic Aussie, and played out to much mirth when we were back on air. There was I, in glorious Technicolor, proudly kissing one of Hollywood's most bankable female stars … with my flies

undone. Atherton's booming guffaw and Smith's cackle resonated through the Lord's media centre for some time.

THE PENNY DROPS

We palpably failed to turn around Channel 4's dwindling
enthusiasm for Test cricket, however. The tail was already
wagging the dog, with match starting times brought forward
so that play wouldn't run in to the precious evening schedules, and the highlights were now transmitted so late at night
we asked if it was OK for us to swear during commentary.
Although Andrew Flintoff had provided rich entertainment
in a losing cause with a swashbuckling century on the Sunday
of the Lord's Test, the TV bosses were interested in nothing
but healthy ratings. These were not forthcoming; and, what's
more, England's defeat with over a day to spare left an
annoying hole in the TV schedules.

The Channel 4 bigwigs weren't too enamoured with
domestic cricket, either, and the commitment to the
Cheltenham and Gloucester Trophy (the old NatWest) had
lapsed to the extent that we now covered only the semi-finals
and the final. This definitely contributed to the decline in the
competition's allure. But for us, at least, covering the second
semi-final at Worcester, and dining in a quaint village pub the
night before, was a pleasant diversion.

There was a quiet little ceremony on the field before the
third South Africa Test at Trent Bridge. In it Benaud became
an important catalyst in the evolution of the England team.
Following a custom initiated by Duncan Fletcher, England
players who'd made centuries or taken five wickets in an
innings were now presented with silver mementoes of their
feats by a prominent cricketing personality. Richie had been
invited to perform the honours on the field at Trent Bridge.
As Andrew Flintoff, the Lord's centurion, came forward to
receive his award, Benaud stopped him in his tracks. With
boyish reverence, Flintoff returned to the ranks. 'Now,

Freddie,' Benaud said. 'It was a marvellous thing you did at Lord's, one of the best innings I've seen. You have a wonderful talent. What I want you to do now is always be there at the end of the innings. That way you can have the most influence on it.' It soon became apparent that Benaud's touching little piece of advice had imbued Flintoff with real self-belief. Not only did he make telling runs from that point on, but he produced the decisive bowling spell of the third Test, forcing Smith back and eventually on to his stumps for his first failure of the series. The South African captain's bubble was punctured and never reinflated.

England won that pulsating third Test and were in a superb position to take charge of the fourth despite a cameo from the South African number nine, owner of the best nickname in world cricket – 'All Hands' Zondeki. Butcher and Trescothick were rapidly clearing the arrears when a typical bank of mid-afternoon Headingley cloud wafted over and the two (overseas) umpires offered the batsmen the light. Inexplicably, with South Africa on the rack, they accepted it. Even more inexplicably, I was sent out to ask the officials what was going on. They edged away from me as I pursued them with the mike. I reported back that they 'didn't want to talk about such a controversial issue'. 'Well, it's clear they don't want to talk to you, anyway,' said Ian Smith, chuckling in the studio. The pundits batted the subject around for a while, with everyone ridiculing England's decision, except Reeve, who took the opposite line and kept justifying himself to such an extent that Richie eventually said, 'Can we please talk about something else?' As so often happens when play resumes, wickets immediately fell and England's advantage was nullified.

By Sunday night they were 165 for 5 chasing 401, and they knew they were dead. That was clear by the way the not-out batsmen – Butcher and Flintoff – sampled a lavish late dinner in our hotel. Though they were not drunk by any means, both batsmen were out within two overs of the start of play next morning, and the match was lost soon afterwards.

England undoubtedly had talent, but their lack of total ruthlessness was frustrating. Leaving something to chance – not wanting to be seen to be trying too hard – was still endemic throughout the English game, from the club bowlers who didn't loosen up properly to England players not in bed before midnight. There was still a residual fear of failure, epitomised by the lingering habit of going off for bad light. They hadn't worried about the light when they were nearing victory in the pitch dark in Karachi, I noted.

The Headingley Test was the scene of Geoff Boycott's re-habilitation on English TV. He was invited on as a lunchtime guest to talk about his courageous struggle against throat cancer. He looked slightly thinner, and he sounded a little hoarser, but otherwise he was much the same. He certainly hadn't lost his forthrightness. When asked by Mark Nicholas why he wasn't commentating now, he replied, 'Well, you lot at Channel 4 wouldn't give me a job.'

He didn't help his cause when he popped back into the commentary box to collect his things.

'Has anywoon seen ma photos?' he said.

Jeff Foulser, the big cheese of Sunset and Vine, our production company, stood up, aware he'd been sitting on something. 'Are these them?' he said politely.

'There's more brains in a pork pie!' Boycott retorted, taking them. 'Who are ya, anyway?'

'Er, that's Jeff, our boss,' Ian Smith cautioned.

'Noo, Gary's yer boss,' Boycott said, indicating the Thin Controller.

'Yes,' said Smith, 'and Jeff is Gary's boss.'

'Oh. Howdyado, Jeff,' said Boycott.

The fifth Test of the South Africa series, at The Oval, was the match when England at last shed their old clothes and became upwardly mobile. The foundations were laid by Marcus Trescothick and Graham Thorpe – the latter making a hundred on his emotional Test match return after a year's turmoil and a messy divorce. But Flintoff and Harmison were the real catalysts when the game was in the balance. They had become best mates, as you could see during their ninth-wicket partnership of 99, which gave England a big lead. The South Africans were calling Flintoff all the names under the sun, but he and Harmison just laughed about it together and then Flintoff smashed their bowling to smithereens. Harmison followed up his batting efforts with a menacing spell to remove South Africa's most obdurate players (Kirsten and Kallis), which was the start of his climb to become the top-ranked bowler in the world. In a dramatic climax to the summer, England levelled the series 2–2. Channel 4, delighted with this turn of events and the creation of new English heroes, regained its faith.

This didn't mean, however, that they were about to reactivate winter highlights programmes. My days of travelling eight stops on the tube to commentate on England in India for a vast sum were no more. Working on Channel 4 cricket had become a bit like living in Iceland: a short, glorious summer, then eight months of virtually permanent darkness.

BEHIND CLOSED DOORS

I reverted to winter mode: looking after the kids (which, 90 per cent of the time, I genuinely enjoyed), writing for the *Telegraph* on an assortment of subjects, and redrafting my novel, which had been returned with a number of criticisms ('it's rubbish'). I took delivery of a garden office (OK, it's a shed), which meant when Tanya or the nanny were in charge, I could escape the zoo in the kitchen and lock myself in my own personal Tardis.

As the autumn nights closed in, there were occasional reminders of my TV existence. I had a letter from a Vivienne someone saying she appreciated my analysis but, after considerable deliberation, she had decided she didn't like my shirts, 'especially the stripy one you wore on the first day at Lord's which looked like you were in jail'. She added that 'at least the plainer one you wore on the second day was better'.

I was also invited to give away the prizes at a Surrey Colts evening in Croydon. There were over 300 kids there, and most were more interested in having their photo taken with the Analyst than with either of the two Surrey and England stars present: Ian Salisbury and Alex Tudor. Television is indeed a persuasive beast.

The Rugby World Cup was on the horizon in Australia, and Tanya wangled me an interesting assignment associated with it. One of her PR clients, Lucozade, was sponsoring the England team and had spent some time adapting its product for performance in hotter climes. I was invited to do a training session with the England scrum-half Matt Dawson to test the drink's effectiveness. Sadly, this didn't involve flying over for a workout at Surfers' Paradise, but running on a treadmill in the SmithKline Beecham gym at Brentford, which had been specially heated to 30°C. Various wires and sensors were attached to me and I jogged for forty minutes, taking regular slugs of different Lucozade formulations, supervised by a sports scientist. Dawson, claiming it was his 'week off', just sat and watched. Lazy bastard. The sports scientist was astonished by the results at the end of the session. 'Your core temperature has hardly changed!' he said. 'Either your body's efficiency in hot conditions is exceptional, or this Lucozade is even better than I thought.' 'Wow ... impressive, Hughesy!' said Dawson. I was feeling rather pleased with myself, until the scientist discovered the core-temperature sensor that had been plugged into me had fallen off.

Having plunged both arms into deep buckets of iced water and got my breath back, I did a regulation interview with Dawson as he supped Lucozade (corporate sponsors are increasingly becoming the only route to leading sportsmen). Afterwards, making small talk, I asked what he was up to that afternoon.

'I'm doing a training session with James Cracknell at Twickenham, and I'm going to try and break him,' he said. 'Come along and join in if you want.'

This is a bit like being invited to spar with Lennox Lewis

and Mike Tyson simultaneously. Fascinated, I went anyway. All access-gates to the Twickenham pitch were locked, so I clambered over a fence and entered the West Enclosure. A surreal sight met my eyes. Here, in a completely deserted rugby amphitheatre, were two of Britain's supreme sportsmen driving each other to the point of exhaustion, relay-sprinting up and down the touchline. 'I'm getting rid of some anger,' panted a perspiring Cracknell, alluding to the loss of the coxless pairs world title three days earlier. They were taking it in turns to do a repetitive routine of short sprints and turns, specially tailored to Dawson's scrum-half requirements. After watching them for twenty minutes, I felt compelled to have a go, despite being completely inappropriately dressed. My thighs were burning after about the sixth rep, and my turns were already slowing. 'That makes me even more angry: being beaten by a bloke in jeans,' said Cracknell, modestly ignoring the fact that they had already been at it for forty-five minutes and were still maintaining a tremendous pace. I bailed out before they finished with several full-length sprints of the touchline. They had both pushed themselves to the maximum, and this was in supposed 'down time'.

I followed them under the stand, into the England dressing room. 'GREATNESS IS ACHIEVED BY THE DISCIPLINE OF ATTENTION TO DETAIL', proclaimed a sign inside the door, in letters so large they bored into your brain. From watching the build-up and talking to Dawson and others, it was clear this mantra had become embedded in the psyche of every member of the England squad. I had never seen such attention to detail and self-discipline in a team sport before. Alcohol free, diet meticulous and training obsessed, they were living the kind of ascetic lives you'd associate more with tough endurance sports like rowing, cycling and swimming. The England rugby team had left nothing to chance. They did not fear failure. To a man, they sensed this was their calling.

Six weeks later, after 100 minutes of nerve-tingling action in Sydney, they achieved their ultimate (drop) goal.

FRINGE BENEFITS

Vexed alternately by finishing my novel and the teatime din of three kids under six, I experienced my usual winter depression. It was dark and cold and the sentences wouldn't come, and I discovered that looking after three young children was like London traffic: it all runs just about OK until there is a minor hiccup (a slight shunt at a junction roughly equals a toilet emergency just as fish fingers are browning under the grill). Then everything seizes up (traffic chaos equals burned dinner and hungry kids), sadly underlining man's inability to multi-task. It never seemed to happen when Tanya was in charge.

England's Rugby World Cup win was a huge November pick-me-up. It was a riveting match with a fantasy ending, and being slightly acquainted with a couple of the protagonists gave it a vaguely personal touch (I helped get them fit!). Added to that, I was invited to attend Matt Dawson's benefit dinner four days after they returned home.

This wasn't your average tedious fund-raiser. Virtually the entire England team processed in, brandishing the World Cup itself, accompanied by a standing ovation which went on for over ten minutes. The players were overcome by the response. Later, after a series of cutting exchanges on stage between Dawson and Martin Johnson, there was an auction. A pair of Jonny Wilkinson's boots – never used – went for about £15,000. Lawrence Dallaglio had his picture taken with at least half the 700 guests. His face was virtually frozen in a satisfied smile. Others happily signed hundreds of autographs and proudly exhibited their medals. You hoped in thirty years' time they wouldn't be obliged to sell them, like some of the hard-up England heroes of 1966 have been.

The triumph showered everyone in range with happy dust. Still under the effects, I went out to buy the World Cup commemorative video. As I was browsing in the Virgin

Megastore, an attractive young girl in skinny jeans came up to me.

'What sort of music d'you like?' she asked.

'Oh, Moby, Eminem, Black Eyed Peas,' I said, trying to sound young and cool. 'Why?'

'Because it's my dad's birthday and I want to buy him a CD,' she said.

The England cricketers were galvanised by the rugby success, too. They had seen the ticker-tape ceremony and the reception at Number 10 and the Adidas advertising contracts and the countrywide impressions of Jonny's 'prayer' position, and they wanted a piece of it. They had also had a private evening with Martin Johnson, and absorbed the lessons about what it takes to reach the pinnacle of achievement (make a man who looks like the Terminator your captain). Within weeks, Michael Vaughan had instigated a tougher fitness regime, convincing players of the importance of getting super-fit in private so that team training sessions were largely cosmetic. Winning cricket had to become their vocation.

CHAPTER 15 – 2004

KNIFED IN THE FRONT

The rugby players came back down to earth with a bump in the New Year, when they put in a moderate performance in the Six Nations Championship. Previewing one round of matches, I was invited to Finsbury Circus to take part in a kicking clinic with Dave Alred, England's goal-kicking coach and the man who had first got Jonny Wilkinson to adopt his famous preparatory position, evoking a man on an imaginary toilet. It was all about 'stabilising your core', apparently. 'Think of the power in your navel,' Alred said as I looked up at a set of inflatable posts on a sopping bit of grass near Moorgate tube. 'Think of it as a burning glow. Try to channel all that power and energy into your foot.' This is why Wilkinson adopts his posture. His joined hands are directly in front of his navel. It is almost a meditative state.

It didn't do me a lot of good – I lost my footing as I was about to kick and the ball slewed sideways – but it was an interesting half-hour. I learned that when Wilkinson lines up a penalty he visualises a can of Coke in the hands of a spectator behind the posts. 'You must fix that specific target in your mind's eye,' said Alred. I wished I had known that twenty years ago, when I was running in to bowl, looking at some vague impression of the batsman (or trying not to look if that batsman was Viv Richards). I might have played forty Tests. Well, four, anyway.

I wrote an enthusiastic piece about the kicking session and received an approving call from Stephanie, the PR girl who'd

246

set it up on behalf of the sponsors. 'Great article, thanks,' she said. 'We're involved in other sports, too. D'you know anything about cricket at all?'

As the England cricket team set off for their all-conquering tour of the Caribbean, I was en route to Hammersmith Hospital for the fourth time in six years. The first three times had been to bring home wife and new baby. Now I was going to ensure that such an eventuality could never happen again. I had postponed my neutering twice (the 'v' word still brings me out in a cold sweat). I was traumatised by images of Johnny Bobbitt, as well as wondering if it was rash to eradicate for ever the chance of bringing more little people into the world. Then I noticed our weekly food bill of £198 and booked in immediately.

I arrived with various promises from people like Scally that I would in future be known to them as 'Eunuch' or 'Hermy' (short for 'Hermaphrodite') ringing in my ears. With usual NHS efficiency, I was left hanging about for hours. When it was at last time for the moment of truth, I was wheeled into theatre by a chatty Indian nurse and we got talking about cricket. She asked me who my favourite player was and I said Vaughan or Flintoff. I asked her the same question and I swear she said the Indian captain, 'Gongooly'.

I felt no pain during the vasectomy (there, I've said it) and left the hospital half an hour later with my manhood trussed up in a strange jockstrap-like contraption, creating a large lump in the front of my trousers. I got a few funny looks on the way home, but otherwise I was fine. However, I felt a sharp pain when I opened my mail. I had finally put the second draft of the novel – renamed *Spiked* – to bed a month earlier, and was feeling quite confident about the publisher's reaction to it. It was funny and risqué and dramatic, and I could see Dreamworks buying the film rights and putting Tom Hanks in the lead role of the movie (directed by Sam Mendes, of course). So I opened the publisher's letter in some anticipation. In précis, it said: 'It depicts a rather squalid view of the world.' (Uh?) 'There is a certain implausibility of plot.' (Really?) 'There are possible libel problems in naming a real Premiership team.' (Come off it.) 'Reviewers might have a real go at Simon for this, much as they have savaged that recent film *Sex Lives of the Potato Heads*.' (Eh?) 'We all have serious misgivings and we cannot recommend that this novel is published.' (Wince.)

Spiked had been well and truly spiked.

I reeled back in shock. It was a massive rejection after eighteen months of work. I felt a mixture of anger, resentment, resignation, disappointment, confusion and annoyance that I had wasted so much time for so little end product. It was a sensation like being kicked in the nuts. Then I remembered that three days earlier I more or less had been.

But I soon realised that the spiking of *Spiked* was for the best. The process had been a struggle, and it showed. Many of the criticisms were probably valid. Put simply, I just couldn't hack fiction. Why had I ever attempted to write a novel? First, it was a challenge. Second, Nick Hornby, Tony Parsons and Helen Fielding have become rich. Third, I intended to put into a fictional context all those stories and characters from my life that I hadn't had the guts to reveal before. Then I thought, Sod it, why don't I just reveal them anyway? This book is the result.

PARADISE FOUND

Anyway, how can you ever wallow in self-pity for too long in a job like this? On 22 March 2004, for example, I boarded a free flight to Grenada. Also on the plane were some of the most illustrious names from the last thirty years of English cricket: Derek Underwood, Derek Randall, Robin Smith, Graeme Hick, Phillip DeFreitas, Devon Malcolm. They were heading out for a week to play two one-day internationals against their West Indian conquerors of the 1980s. My sole duty was to write a piece on the event for the *Telegraph*. It was, basically, a free Caribbean holiday.

As we were met at Grenada airport by the event organisers, Allan Lamb and his former Northants team-mate Nigel Felton, some of the party wore a slightly haunted look. The memories of bruised pride and battered fingers had come flooding back. I myself could recall shell-shocked English batsmen arriving back from Caribbean tours to play county cricket with glazed eyes and leaden feet. They looked like war veterans. Having dodged the howitzer shells from Roberts, Holding, Garner and Marshall – with Croft supplying back-up bombing – to some extent they were. Lamb equated facing the fearsome Patrick Patterson on a corrugated pitch in Jamaica in 1986 to a sporting version of *The Killing Fields*. Robin Smith remembered the look in Curtly Ambrose's eyes, 'like a man possessed', as he mowed down England for 46 in Trinidad.

For them, this trip to the West Indies was a good deal less taxing. We stayed at a hotel on the beach and the first three days were spent lying under a shady palm with a rum punch, staring out at the glittering sea, totting up the various shades of blue. The only energy expended was Randall's jog along the sand every morning, until, with boyish enthusiasm, he initiated a practice session. But after he'd lost the only two balls we had in the undergrowth and advised everyone to 'mind the snakes' we all returned to the hotel. Randall himself fell asleep on the beach and the sea washed away his room key.

Beach parties with a large contingent of travelling supporters were aperitifs for the two matches against a daunting West Indies line-up, including Greenidge, Haynes, Richards, Richardson, King, Garner, Walsh and Ambrose. They all attended one pre-match barbecue, at a quayside restaurant. Desmond Haynes greeted me with, 'Hey, Yozzer, have you brought my money?!' He was still going on about the bonus I'd snatched away from him with my negligent last over in the 1989 NatWest final.

The benefit of the England players' leisurely build-up to the matches was somewhat eradicated by a madcap drive to the ground, during which the team's minibus wove and lurched about Grenada's narrow, winding roads as it attempted to keep pace with the police 'escort'. I, the honorary twelfth man, helped settle their stomachs with a few half-volleys on the outfield.

They were slightly taken aback by the seriousness of the West Indies' approach, however. In the first game, Greenidge and Haynes, piqued by the performances of the current West Indies team against England – when they surrendered all their hard-won former superiority without a fight – were clearly determined to reassert their authority. Greenidge, who'd put in several days' preparation, soon unleashed a trademark square cut which almost took Matthew Maynard's hand with it. Haynes nonchalantly flicked John Lever over midwicket for six. They could still play, they still cared passionately, and they compiled a rollicking opening stand of 110.

Their duel with Underwood, appearance and accuracy unaltered, rolled back the years. 'Deadly', still wearing his white clodhoppers and pudding-bowl floppy hat, floated the ball on to an area the size of a pound coin; Greenidge and Haynes stroked and swept without ever managing to take liberties. Viv Richards, swaggering to the wicket so slowly that the grass was beginning to grow over his shoes, tried something more adventurous and perished. 'Man,' he said, eyes glinting, 'my mind knew what I wanted to do, but my body wouldn't follow.'

The music boomed, drums rolled, and the 4000-strong crowd bellowed, as these Harlem Globetrotters of cricket exhibited glimpses of their magnificent skills: Richards's imperious straight drive (plonking a still-lively Malcolm into the pavilion); Richardson's colossal hitting; Collis King's outrageous shots after a gutful of rum; Garner's spearing yorker; Walsh's clever changes of pace; Ambrose's loping athleticism. The latter still took some playing, despite now spending most of his time strumming bass guitar in a reggae band with Richardson called Dread and the Baldhead. I asked him if his mother still rang that bell in the street like she used to whenever he took a wicket. 'No, man. The bell, like me, is retired,' Ambrose replied, beaming. 'Anyway, the way West Indies been playing lately, ain't been no reason to ring it.'

It was a blissful week of sun, sea, sand and sensational stroke-play – a reminder of what a loss the decline of West Indian flamboyance (Brian Lara excepted) is to the world cricket scene. Grenada is an idyllic spot with all the usual Caribbean assets and negligible crime. I canoed out to sea one afternoon, until the beach was a speck and it was just me and the warm, tranquil water. I'm being paid to do this, I thought. When Allan Lamb approached me to return for the same event in 2005, I almost bit his hand off. Six months later, Hurricane Ivan blew in and ruined everything.

500 NOT OUT

Steve Harmison was delivering a hurricane of his own elsewhere in the Caribbean, evoking shades of Ambrose, as he shattered the West Indies' batting to inspire England's first series win in those parts for thirty-six years. 'GRIEVOUS BODILY HARMISON', declared the *Daily Mirror*.

But England's success only partially alleviated the mood of apprehension lurking in a television production meeting regarding the summer of 2004. There was lots of talk about the new TV contract – Channel 4's current deal expired at the end of 2005, and bids for the next one were expected shortly. There was some speculation that the channel wouldn't renew. Mindful of the general vogue for hiring ex-England captains as commentators, I was also acutely aware, due to England's erratic performances in the last twenty years, how many recent ex-England captains were out there (fourteen, including stand-ins, since 1985) looking for work.

Boycott's name was back on the agenda as well. He'd been invited to commentate on the previous year's Cheltenham and Gloucester final, and his illness had definitely mellowed him. He still had a sharp eye, but his attitude and turn of phrase – "E couldn't 'ave 'it that with a frying pan!' – seemed a little old hat. We weren't lacking his vast cricketing knowledge now, either. Atherton was a modern Boycott – authoritative, astute and a team player. 'We don't need Boycott' was the general verdict. He was promptly hired on a two-year contract.

He attended the pre-Test commentators' meeting in May and sat quietly listening for a while. I was starting to believe he really had changed, but it didn't take long for something to perturb him. He stood up and said, 'With due respect ...' in a tone that intimated that unless you'd played a hundred Tests and scored a million runs you knew nothing. We all looked at each other, raised our eyebrows and prepared for a long summer.

Benaud, immaculate as usual in a cream jacket and striped tie, was altogether more demure. He absorbed the information about different graphics and nodded his enthusiasm at new Hawkeye tools. Then the Thin Controller mentioned that the summer's first Test (against New Zealand) was to be Richie's 500th as player or commentator. There was a chorus of congratulation. The great man blushed.

'When was your first?' I asked.

'SCG, 1951–52,' he said after a brief silence, smiling at the memory. 'First Test wicket: Alf Valentine. Bowled him through the gate. I notice he died the other day. He was probably still trying to get over it.'

He arrived early for the match, as usual, with his battered black holdalls, his books, his beloved laptop and his awareness of all the cricket news, often before it has happened. He reads everything and ferrets around in manuals and books or on the internet. He's a serial investigator. He should have been christened Research Benaud. As soon as he'd said, 'Morning everyone' for probably the 4000th time, and Mark Nicholas had asked him how he'd enjoyed the winter, he was declaring that the last twelve months had been as good a year as he'd ever had. He didn't mean because he'd spouted more bons mots than ever before or unearthed a new label of his favourite Sauvignon blanc or discovered the secret of eternal youth. He was referring to the cricket he'd watched: England against South Africa the previous summer; Australia against India Down Under; then the Australians' sequence of Houdini acts in Sri Lanka after that. He is the antidote to all those septuagenarian nostalgists. He doesn't have an in-my-day thought in his body. He is Mr Magnanimity, finding a smile and something gently encouraging to say about everything, from streaky shots to dodgy commentary. He arrives at work each day – even if it is the 2135th of his career – with infectious enthusiasm. He is alive and alert from the moment he sets off with Daphne from their habitual London base, the Montcalm Hotel, for their daily 6.15 a.m. walk ('takes between twenty-nine minutes and fifty-five seconds to thirty minutes and five seconds') to the moment he winds down with the latest Harry Potter before going to sleep. His eyebrows are fixed in an expression of permanent fascination.

Everyone's were during the Lord's Test, due to the increasingly bizarre behaviour of Dermot Reeve. On the first day, he disputed the unimpeachable credentials of Fred Trueman with a startled Boycott, who was admirably restrained, merely remarking later, 'Don't know why 'e wants to pick a fight wi' me.' On the second day, Reeve looked rather the worse for wear, with staring eyes and hair all over the place, and his manner veered wildly from confrontational to dopey. On the third day he had to be roused from his hotel bed at lunchtime. He blamed his lapse on sleeping pills, but there were rumours that he was taking cocaine. On the fourth day he appeared tired and distracted, and missed another commentary stint. He was yellow-carded for the fifth day and persuaded to go away and sort himself out.

He missed a momentous day in the chequered history of English cricket. Andrew Strauss, who had been drafted in to the match only two days before it had started when Michael Vaughan had twisted his knee in the nets, was on the verge of making two centuries on his Test debut. Then, on 83,

Nasser Hussain ran him out. Stirred by this calamity, Hussain, who had already had an influential match and was agonising about retirement, turned the clock back several years and surged to a scintillating hundred to pilot England to dramatic victory. Rarely has a cricketer had a more perfect opportunity to wave goodbye, and he took it. Through his Test career he had been like a bee trapped in an upturned glass, forever constrained by the rigours of time and place and England on 21 for 2. Now he was set free.

The match was also memorable because, due to Reeve's enforced absence, Atherton was pressed into service to host the post-match presentation ceremony. Ian Smith, chastened by New Zealand's defeat, joshed him about it beforehand, he looked pale and drawn on stage, and comically he forgot to offer the New Zealand captain Stephen Fleming the microphone, having asked him his first question.

Mark Nicholas, the mike-meister, managed rather better at the Royal Television Society awards ceremony that night, delivering a glowing – some said gushing – tribute to Benaud before he was presented with his Lifetime Achievement award. Richie, modest to a fault, responded on stage to the standing ovation in the only way he knew: 'The one thing I've learned in this business,' he said, 'is not to take yourself too seriously.' His remarks brought the house down.

NOISES OFF

I thought it might be hard adjusting from a winter indoors writing and looking after the kids to a summer in the full glare of the television cameras. It wasn't. For a start, I was still mostly indoors (and in the dark) in my Analyst's chair. There was an odd symmetry between domestic 'bliss' and life in the VT truck. The Hughes home tended to reek of full nappies. I'd often leave the house having wiped several bottoms, only to enter another environment where the vocabulary (as well as the atmosphere) had connotations of bowel movements. I'd arrive to find various VT operators 'dumping' (transferring their best replays from the previous day on to a 'dump' tape). Seeking a specific incident on tape from the previous day, I'd be advised to consult the 'logs' (sheets of A4 itemising each delivery, who bowled it, who faced it and what happened, documented by the 'logger', often a girl, who sat in a little booth intently watching the play and jotting down every detail; 'logging' was, I told various wannabes, a useful way into live TV). Rob, the Australian director, often said 'pan' when he wanted a camera to ease sideways or 'wipe' to activate a diagonal white line sweeping across the screen to distinguish a replay. He also liked referring to me as 'the Anal person'. It was a veritable bathroom cabinet of lavatorial terms.

The truck rumbled up to Headingley for the second Test against New Zealand. It rained on the first morning and as we were only doing highlights for this one, Dermot Reeve sat in and watched the tapes of the Lord's Test, admitting he could remember nothing about it. I went for a stroll up the road. The ersatz fashion sense of many urban Yorkshire women was underlined by a multitude of boutiques, tanning booths and hair salons. I popped into a barber's to have my hair trimmed.

There were a few hours' play, after which we watched the transmission of the highlights show. Atherton had had four half-hour stints behind the mike but not one of his commentary lines had made it into the programme. 'Nothing changes, Athers,' said Ian Smith. 'None of your batting ever got into the highlights, either.'

England dominated the game on the field, with the Australian-bred wicketkeeper Geraint Jones notching a stylish maiden hundred. Boycott, back on his home ground, was irrepressible off it, cheerfully hailing Francine, our young production coordinator, as 'Blondie!' whenever she was around, and constantly steering the conversation back to Yorkshire matters when Alastair Campbell popped by for a chat, thereby rather stymying Atherton's attempts to discuss the EU. (Campbell was there on behalf of *The Times* to interview Botham, who was clad in a Scunthorpe FC shirt, proudly proclaiming that 'the Iron have just survived relegation to the Vauxhall Conference'.)

By now it was clear that Boycott had definitely mellowed, and was even happy to accept the odd jibe. He brought the Yorkshire chairman in one day, who had read Atherton's rather critical piece about Headingley. 'Oh, don't you like our ground then, Michael?' asked the chairman.

Atherton, squirming slightly, replied that it was perfectly OK, but perhaps didn't portray enough of Yorkshire's history or great players.

'No, fair enough,' said the chairman.

'You could always have the Boycott Dot Ball Stand,' I said helpfully.

'All I can say is, look in *Wisden*,' Boycott retorted jovially.

I did. It says he made 48,426 first-class runs, the eighth most in history (and the most since the Second World War), at an average 56.83. Not bad.

CAUGHT IN THE CROSSFIRE

A youngish man in football shorts who never made a single first-class run stood beside me examining the Trent Bridge pitch for the next Test: the umpire, Simon Taufel, who'd never played top-flight cricket. He was the very antithesis of the traditional Test match umpire, the type who meandered through a fifteen-year county career, and now had the portly profile, the liquid diet and the yearning for uncovered pitches. Tall and slim, in his early thirties, Taufel had a dietician, a personal trainer and a life coach, attended team net practices before matches 'to get his eye in' and began every morning with a jog around the outfield. Hence the football shorts.

Mindful that the Test commentary team of Nicholas, Atherton, Boycott and Hughes, augmented by the print journalist Pringle, all belonged to the same *Telegraph* stable, and, as we all followed England around, were all milking the same cow, I tried to find something different to write about for my Saturday column. Taufel had just had an outstanding game at Headingley, and was regarded by the players as not only the best, but, as umpires go, completely sane. I asked if I could interview him that night. He was somewhat reluctant, but I talked him into it.

We met in the bar of his Nottingham hotel. I had started keeping a tally of right and wrong umpiring decisions as measured by our television technology. I was becoming an anorak.

'You're top of the class,' I said. 'By my calculations, you got ninety-two per cent of your decisions spot on at Headingley.'

'Actually, I make it ninety-six point two per cent,' he corrected me. 'I reckon I got one out of twenty-eight wrong.'

He elaborated on the process of making decisions, revealed how many would-be first-class umpires felt impeded by having been only moderate players, and told me he counted the balls in the over with a sheep counter that went all the way up to 9999. Quite a contrast to the pebbles or polished old pennies used by seasoned English umpires. He had an interesting story and I wrote it up for the Saturday *Telegraph*. Unfortunately, by then, he had made a number of uncharacteristic errors on the field. In fact, he had had a shocker. Commentators were calling him 'Awful' Taufel. His comments to me in the paper about his 96 per cent success rate, his decision-making and his castigation of the system of choosing English umpires were ridiculed.

This constituted a weird Trent Bridge hat-trick for me: letting down Michael Henderson's tyres, stitching up Merv Kitchen, and now Taufel. Henderson had written a forthright article himself during the Test about the Channel 4 commentary team. Mark Nicholas and Dermot Reeve were the main targets this time: he said Nicholas was too often 'Larky Mark' and not often enough 'Sparky Mark', and that Reeve seemed largely to be 'calling interplanetary craft'. Atherton and I escaped remarkably unscathed. It was quite a courageous piece in many ways, voicing the misgivings the press harboured for cosseted TV show-ponies. In English sport, there is a latent simmering in all media centres, with each group – the newspaper reporters, rival TV channels and radio stations – believing they are more important than the others. Then again, without the game, we would all be nothing.

It was a lively few days in Nottingham. Walking through the town centre, I noticed that every building that had once probably been a clothes shop or a jeweller's was now a heaving bar with a name like Dogma or Elbow Room (an ironic title, since there wasn't any). There was a noticeable absence of cricketers in any of these establishments. Where once you'd have encountered a Dominic Cork or a Darren Gough holding court, there were no England players to be found. They were back in their hotel 'warming down' or having room service or watching their batting/bowling on a laptop. Importantly, this dedication was beginning to show in their results.

For me, the incident with Taufel rather took the gloss off another England victory, and a handsome 3–0 drubbing of Ian Smith's Kiwis. 'Well, what can you expect if your team manager wanders out to the middle in Jesus sandals?' he said.

Smith got his own back at the one-day NatWest series final, his last day as a Channel 4 commentator. Apart from the Test victories, it had been a dispiriting month for English sport. England had lost to Portugal in a Euro 2004 penalty shootout, and to Australia and New Zealand at rugby; the cricketers had been eliminated from the NatWest series; and Tim Henman had been knocked out of Wimbledon. The *Sun* carried pictures of Beckham, Dallaglio, Vaughan and Henman below the headline: 'WANTED FOR CRIMES AGAINST ENGLISH SPORT'. Smith joined in, introducing the final with: 'Well, here we are at the headquarters of cricket, the scene set fair for a fantastic day. Two exciting teams, fast bowlers, dashing batsmen, bright sunshine, a full house expected later. There's only one thing missing ... England!' He chuckled maliciously, but he was indirectly making an important point. England, in spite of their major improvements in Test cricket, were still largely hopeless at the one-day version.

I explored why this was so in a large feature for *Wisden* magazine. I boiled it down to three factors: lack of imagination, lack of experience and lack of planning. Chiefly, one-day cricket is won by formula. As yet, England hadn't cracked the code.

Smith bid us farewell, saying he'd miss being in England because 'every time Andrew Strauss does well the cameras pan on to his wife ... and she's absolutely gorgeous'. He described Atherton as 'a thirty-five-year-old man trapped in a sixty-five-year-old body', and, at the news that Athers was trying for a second child, asked him how he felt about 'unveiling the unemployed'.

'At least I can see mine,' Atherton retorted.

ANCIENT AND MODERN

I took the opportunity of a day off to go to my first Twenty-20 match. It was also the first time Lord's had staged one, and 28,000 other people had the same idea. It was a balmy evening, and I sat in the Tavern Stand alongside gaggles of City blokes, women in bias-cut dresses, students, young couples sipping Chardonnay and eating M&S snacks, mums, dads, kids and extended Asian families (and even still the odd retired colonel) and lapped up the atmosphere. It defied the assertion of William Temple, the Archbishop of Canterbury, that 'Cricket is organised loafing.' This was three hours of jumping, jabbing, jerking and jiving. More like organised exhibitionism, and very much a sport for our style-over-substance times. Except that these exhibitionists have actually got some talent, too. As the crowd appreciated, humming along to the amplified strains of MC Hammer's 'U Can't Touch This', when they celebrated an extravagant Mark Ramprakash boundary through the lengthening shadows of the nineteenth-century pavilion, ancient and modern juxtaposed. Twenty-20 represents all that's good about cricket (drama, speed, skill, athleticism, bonhomie) while removing all that's bad about it (time-wasting, boring play, impenetrability, selfishness). It's a game for the public, boiling cricket down to its essence – runs and wickets – at a time when they can watch it. Like everyone else at Lord's that day, I loved it. Best of all, you can see an entire game in early evening, and still have time left to go out for dinner afterwards.

With practically all production funds being gobbled up by *Big Brother*, Channel 4's attitude to domestic cricket was becoming increasingly half-hearted. They took no interest in the Twenty-20, and at the one Cheltenham and Gloucester semi-final they agreed to cover, in Bristol, there was the bare minimum of cameras (eight), no Hawkeye, half the personnel. It was like the BBC coverage of old (well, OK, not *that* bad).

The match finished early and Atherton and I accepted a lift back to London in Benaud's 'taxi'. Meticulous about appointments, he was looking through his diary on the way, checking dates. He had already pencilled in the time of his flight from Australia to London the following April ('we land mid-morning, then get the flight to Nice about twelve'). Midway through the journey, he phoned the *News of the World* sports desk, having filed his 'Voice of Cricket' column earlier in the day. 'Any more needed from me?' he enquired. 'No. Excellent. OK. Goodbye.'

'How long have you been writing for them?' I asked.

'Started in 1960. I'm their longest-serving employee,' he replied, pride just detectable.

Quite a statistic. And quite a statement about his longevity. When he first began writing for *NotW* it was a well-respected broadsheet. It also pioneered the trend for having star players as columnists, with the difference being that back then they usually wrote their own stuff, and had something interesting to say.

SUMMER LOVIN'

The MCC hosted a dinner for the West Indies at Arundel Castle before their first Test of the summer. Players and officials were intermingled round the tables with MCC officials and other guests. John Barclay, the effervescent Old Etonian who'd captained Sussex and managed England, and was now in charge of the cricket academy at Arundel, was seated next to the West Indian opener Chris Gayle. With his usual effusiveness, Barclay tried to make polite cricket conversation ('I say, splendid pitch out there, isn't it? Your chaps were looking rather good on it') but Gayle, a raw, brooding Jamaican with gold earrings and substantial attitude, just stared into space. In desperation, Barclay enthused about his one trip to Jamaica, many moons ago, and how fascinated he had been by the city of Kingston. Gayle half turned towards him and said haughtily, 'Get much pussy, man?'

That comment epitomised the West Indian team's attitude during the series: they were cocky, unprofessional, lazy and apparently more interested in girls than cricket. Various players bombarded Channel 4's female producers with calls on the afternoon before Test matches, when they should have been practising, and couldn't handle rejection. The practice they did put in was mainly apathetic, and their fielding drills were so out of date they were almost prehistoric. When they rehearsed their slip catching, they stood in the wrong order, on the boundary (rather than close to where they'd be positioned in the match) and desultorily pouched a few edges at half speed. In the Tests, their batting was quixotic, their bowling was ordinary and they were butterfingered in the field. They were basically a rabble.

The tone was set at Lord's when Lara asked England to bat first. At the end of day one, the home side were 391 for 2. It was tough providing incisive analysis of the play, because any fool could see what was going on: the West Indians were serving up buffet bowling, and the England batsmen were helping themselves. Perhaps this odd reversal of fortunes confused Benaud, since several times he handed to me in the truck with, 'And now let's go down to Simon Jones.'

Undeterred, I used a bit of lateral thinking with Damien, my sidekick, to concoct some little features, using 'beehive' graphics and other paraphernalia, and I thought I'd had a good day. But towards the end of it, the Thin Controller received an email in the commentary box which said simply, 'Who *is* Simon Hughes?'

The one-sided nature of the match seemed to disorientate everyone. On the Sunday morning, Benaud, in vision, delivered his thoughts on the game, but initially talked into his glasses instead of his microphone (he made amusing reference to it afterwards); several times action replays froze; and at one point we lost all power and the picture went black. On the Monday, after we'd all rehearsed little pieces to camera in the middle about the previous four days' play, I was about to deliver mine live when drizzle began to fall. The groundstaff started the engine of the hover cover, and as I began speaking it was heading straight for the cameraman. I was trying to gesticulate to him while still talking but to no avail. The camera was knocked over and I fell out of picture while spouting absolute gibberish.

If that wasn't bad enough, I was then accosted by Andrew Flintoff, who, with feigned annoyance, said, 'I see you did that piece yesterday comparing me and Vaughany, saying I'm a slogger and he's a classical player!'

I was trying to protest that it hadn't been quite like that when Botham strode over.

'There he is: the world expert on batting,' he chortled. 'The bloke who used to fall asleep fielding at long leg. True, you know!' Well, sort of. 'Now then, Freddie, you and Harmy are coming out with me tomorrow night!'

I walked over to Vaughan, who was examining the pitch,

and congratulated him on his second century of the match. 'Thanks,' he said. 'Nice track, innit? D'you sit in that truck all day?'

'Yes,' I said.

'Wow,' he replied. An England player, never mind captain, who in the middle of a Test match takes genuine interest in the life of someone outside the team milieu is a rare bird. His ability to see beyond the envelope (not forgetting, of course, the considerable talent at his disposal) would make him, potentially, the most successful England captain of the lot.

'And you come up with all the ideas yourself?' he went on.

'Most of them.'

'Phew ...'

We chatted a bit more and he asked what Botham had been saying.

'Oh, he promised Harmy and Freddie he'd take them out tomorrow night,' I replied.

'Oh no he's not,' Vaughan said. 'They're not going out with Beefy!' He was acutely conscious there was another Test match in three days' time. The fun could wait. Vaughan's amenable exterior belies a tough inner core.

England scored a resounding victory at Lord's, and I have only one regret about it. When the rejuvenated Ashley Giles spun a vicious, very Warne-like delivery through Lara's gate, dramatically clean-bowling the West Indies' batting genius, Ian Smartarse Smith wasn't there to see it!

Few teams go from losing the first of two back-to-back Tests to winning the second, and the West Indies were duly hustled to defeat at Edgbaston by Giles with the ball and Trescothick and Flintoff with the bat. That gave England five Test victories in a row. One of Flintoff's seven sixes went straight to his dad in the crowd, who dropped it. 'He tells us all about the great catches for the club at the weekend, but that proves he's rubbish,' Freddie commented. Dedication and realisation had turned him into a serial assassin with bat and ball. But in an era of sporting sophistication and percentage plays, his uncomplicated hitting and jovial attitude provided a vivid union between the village green and the Test arena.

CONTRACTUALLY SPEAKING

The Test series moved on to Old Trafford. Driving into the ground, Atherton was uplifted by the survival of a large picture of him in action above the pavilion reception. 'It's still there,' he cooed. 'I thought they might have taken it down by now.' Though I couldn't imagine why anyone would: he's an Old Trafford legend and always will be, in spite of his well-publicised misgivings about the county game.

We parked at 8.30 a.m. just as Graham Thorpe's sporty Beamer drew up. Atherton nodded approvingly towards the car and expressed mock-envy at the wages centrally contracted players were on these days.

'I need all that to pay my ex-wife's maintenance. There's not much left afterwards,' said Thorpe ruefully.

It was a rainy first two days, so I grabbed the opportunity to show the Channel 4 'creative hub' (the trucks) to Somerset chairman Giles Clarke, a Jonathan Ross lookalike who was masterminding the new TV cricket deal. He was intrigued by all our bells and whistles, but made ominous noises about the next contract favouring satellite over terrestrial TV. It was going to be all about money, he implied, which wouldn't suit Channel 4.

In the press box, the talk was about the banality of Marcus Trescothick's column in the *Telegraph* (to be fair to him, he was never very keen on having a column and didn't want to upset anyone) and the finality of Henry Blofeld's fate at the *Independent*. His departure was imminent from the paper he'd first written for when it launched in 1986. He was prone to supplying hastily written material, which some thought contained little insight, between radio stints. His dismissal was perhaps a little harsh, but these were competitive times, and we were all watching our backs.

In little more than a decade the whole nature of sports-writing had changed. Reporting what happened on the field had become only a third of a newspaperman's job. After all, most readers had gleaned the basic facts from elsewhere – via radio, TV, the internet or increasingly on their mobile phones. As the media juggernaut rumbled onwards, journalists had to come up with something extra – an imaginative angle, sparky humour or some penetrating analysis that told you why, and what it all meant. Those who couldn't manage this were liable to be run over.

There was quite a clamour among students to get into the sports media. At Old Trafford, Michael Henderson, writing for *The Times*, had a young lad called Euan following him around on work experience. During one rain break, Hendo enquired about the boy's background: 'Where do you live?' he asked.

'Westminster,' was the reply.

'Oh, which bit?'

'Just off the Mall.'

'Oh, right. Which street?'

'Downing Street.'

He was about to ask him what number, but twigged just in time. It was, of course, the Prime Minister's son.

Flintoff, on his home ground, again played a key role in England's victory, hounding Lara with some explosive, well-directed bowling and escorting his mate 'Bobby' Key in a bruising and potentially awkward run chase. He was proving to be the best all-rounder in the world, while England were proving to be exceptional at wriggling out of tricky situations. The question was: would they, after this, their sixth Test victory in a row, become complacent?

The answer was an emphatic 'no'. England won their seventh Test on the bounce at The Oval by ten wickets, and made a clean sweep of the summer. Flintoff, the man of the season, hugged every team-mate individually when he came off. Asked why, he said, 'I felt ecstatic. I felt that we'd achieved something memorable together and I suddenly felt a great deal of affection for these guys.' That shows how the tenor of the game has changed: ten years ago, he would have been accused of being gay.

Afterwards, I chatted to some of the players about the primary reason for their success: central contracts.

'I feel so comfortable in the dressing room,' said Andrew Strauss, who'd won his first cap earlier that summer. 'We're all together, travelling, staying, playing through the summer. It really feels like *my* team. I can't imagine how hard it was for all our predecessors who had to go straight back to county cricket after a Test and felt more at home with their county than England.'

Ashley Giles, who'd sampled the previous era, said the same. Gone were the days when England players were constantly checking Ceefax in the dressing room for the county scores. England was their team, and that's where they belonged: all for one and one for all. The Three Musketeers' old adage had at last been realised.

Sitting next to Boycott in the studio after declaring our individual moments of the series, I asked him if he'd enjoyed the summer. 'Aye, I have,' he said. 'I can see the people here really work hard and like the game, and they deserve credit for their efforts.' He had certainly won me over: he had been worth having. Though, interestingly, he polarised viewers' opinions: they either loved him or loathed him.

England had had a flawless Test summer, equalled on air by Mark Nicholas. Frequently he'd be on the grass at the end of play interviewing a couple of players, with a countdown in his ear and a quick summation to do, and we were watching, expecting him to ask an inane question or miss the count or mangle his words, at least once, which would have been totally understandable. He never did. His composure is almost inhuman.

(WEST) INDIAN SUMMER

The season was still far from over. First there was the Cheltenham and Gloucester final, an event which, with the plethora of one-day internationals and the advent of Twenty-20, had become a rather sad sideshow, especially as it used to be such a highlight of the summer for county players.

The NatWest Challenge – three extra matches between England and India – was partly to blame. Driving up to the first of these, at Trent Bridge, Atherton and I were mainly intrigued by the revelations of expenses claimed by the Telegraph Group's former owners Conrad Black and his wife Barbara Amiel: $42,870 for a 'Happy Birthday Barbara Party', $3,530 for 'silverware for a corporate jet' and $90,000 for 'refurbishment of Rolls-Royce', among others. Outrageous. We reasoned it probably wasn't a good time to be applying for a pay rise.

Dermot Reeve was missing from our commentary team with a 'mystery virus', offering me an extended stay in the box. During the England innings, when I was on commentary, England's Vikram Solanki was hit painfully in the ribs. 'That's the problem with these super-fit cricketers,' I said. 'An absence of body fat means there's no padding.' 'Ah, yes,' said Benaud. 'The fittest players used to be skin and bone. Now they're just bone.'

England comfortably defeated India in that game, which meant it wasn't the best time for my *Wisden* magazine feature – written six weeks earlier, lamenting England's one-day failings and entitled 'Losing the Plot' – to hit the news-stands. Duncan Fletcher, whom I criticised only mildly in the piece, had obviously read it. He sidled over to me as I stood by the Oval pitch before the second game in the series.

'Well, I obviously did enough raa-raaing on Wednesday,' he said sneerily, piqued by my suggestion that his forte was more in enhancing individual skill and not necessarily in tub-thumping. 'And if you look it up, you'll find the Western

Province team I coached won the one-day stuff three years running.' Despite receiving almost universally glowing write-ups, Fletcher remained surprisingly touchy.

England won a high-scoring game, but because we were doing only highlights commentary, there was plenty of time to discuss the winter and what people would be doing. Atherton was working for Talksport in South Africa, and the Thin Controller had agreed to direct England's one-day series in Zimbabwe for a TV station. Girding myself for another long, Icelandic winter off the airwaves, I said, 'You're all just media prostitutes!'

'You're only saying that because Channel 4 are the only people who'll employ you,' the Thin Controller retorted.

But future employment was becoming a serious concern for all of us, with the bids for the new four-year TV contract in the throes of being negotiated. The issue had been hanging like a sword of Damocles for a while. Despite England's phenomenal summer, Channel 4 still seemed to be lukewarm about the business. In an eerie repetition of the BBC's apathy six years before, they didn't mount a charm offensive or plan a slick campaign. Three days before they were due to give a presentation to the ECB, the channel bigwigs finally rang, desperately casting around for a few innovations they could include in their last-minute proposal.

We came up with some ideas, and I tried to put the issue out of my mind. Instead, I attempted to develop another string to my bow with some travel writing. I wrote a glowing piece about Grenada after my week there in March. Just as I was about to send it in, news emerged that Hurricane Ivan was bearing down on the island. Two days later it had all but blown away everything. My piece went with it. Fascinated, in a morbid sort of way, I followed the storm's progress, and how the various islands dealt with it, for a few days. I loved the attitude of the Jamaicans: 'We'll be sitting it out and waiting to see if de waves break over de beach,' said Boom Donovan, a DJ smoking a big, fat reefer on the beach near Kingston. 'Then we'll be running up de hill as fast as we can.'

His attitude was symbolic of the demise of cricket in the West Indies. They had seen the Americanisation of their society coming a long way off – the materialism, the fast living, the fascination for basketball and athletics – but had just stood around and let it happen. There was no strategy, no investment. Now it was too late, and the formerly great team was being blown over at every turn.

THE SKY'S THE LIMIT

So to the most important game of the 2004 summer – the semi-final of the Champions Trophy, England versus Australia, at Edgbaston – perversely scheduled on a Tuesday near the end of September. At this time of year you're sweeping up the leaves and bringing the geraniums indoors and unpacking your winter woollies. Ticket sales were only modest, and it was merely the sixth item on 5 Live's 8.30 a.m. sports news, after Brian Clough's death (which had occurred two days earlier), Steven Gerrard's injury, David Beckham's remarks about Sven being 'tapped up' by Real Madrid and other peripherals.

It was still some match, though. Harmison's first ball was a bouncer at Adam Gilchrist that made him flinch and left a calling card. It was a prelude to the most intense England bowling and fielding performance I had ever seen. The self-belief was obvious. The plans were well executed. The fitness was exemplary.

When they batted, they were scratchy at first, but, fortified by Trescothick's and Vaughan's audacious stroke-play and a deft fifty from Andrew Strauss, they eventually cantered home. Australia had claimed before the match that they had about six plans for Andrew Flintoff. Most of these, it materialised, seemed to revolve around loud chirping. And they made the fatal mistake of neglecting to have a plan for anyone else. It was the first time they had lost a one-dayer to England for five and a half years.

Unaccountably, England lost the Champions Trophy final to the West Indies, but it didn't really matter. The ghost had been laid. Throughout England's inexorable summer progress, the question had always been whether they could live with Australia. Now we knew the answer was 'yes', if only for one day. England gave them a good old-fashioned thumping at Edgbaston, causing the Australians in the press box to wonder if maybe their bubble had finally burst, and the *Daily Mirror* correspondent, 'Machine Gun' Mike Walters, to exclaim, 'Come on, is there anyone in Australia who can play cricket?'

With the flourishing of English cricket and the Ashes in the offing, it seemed a good moment to go and see David Welch about a better pay deal. He said he was sorry but the uncertainties at the *Telegraph* – with a new editor, Martin Newland, and the title up for sale – meant a general pay freeze for the moment. He did, however, agree to me assisting Derek Pringle at England's first Test in South Africa in December, to see if they could secure an unprecedented eighth successive Test win.

With *The Times* having gone tabloid (their writers were instructed to refer to it as a 'compact') and pouring money into production, the *Telegraph* machine seemed rusty and sluggish by comparison. There was now great speculation about who would buy it. Also, in Fleet Street sports departments an ongoing game of musical chairs was taking place. Despite fifteen years at the *Telegraph*, Welch seemed particularly concerned about his own position (there had been rumours of a few run-ins with Newland over expenses, and the almost obsessive focus on London's Olympic bid). Welch admitted he didn't know what was going to happen next. Then he was sacked. Apparently, he had been resistant to Newland's 'back to basics' approach. (And it can't have helped that he was reputedly earning more than his new 'boss'.) The *Guardian* reported, 'Some believe that *Telegraph* sport has become overly reliant on big-name celebrity columns rather than the breaking news and analysis on which it built its reputation.' It was all rather sudden and brutal. But there is no such thing as a job for life these days.

Welch's loyal deputy Keith Perry took over. One of his first acts was to restore me to the top table at the Christmas lunch, with a seat next to John Motson. I seemed to be back at the top of the averages. But it turned out the move was only because I was booked to do a turn on the piano. (I'd written some new lyrics for the Animals' old hit 'The House of the Rising Sun', poking gentle fun at the sports department.)

Still, I was feeling quite pleased with myself. I roamed the room after my 'song', exchanging small talk with the great and the good and humouring my annual assailant with his story about my innocuous bowling. I was contemplating my imminent departure for South Africa and felt considerable sympathy for Michael Henderson, who was down on his luck after falling out with *The Times* and the *Mail*, and admitted he had even lost his fortnightly column in the *Spectator*. Someone like him is far too talented to be languishing on the sidelines. Unfortunately, in journalism as in life, it's less a question of being good, and more a question of being reliable and buttering up the right people. Henderson had a habit of antagonising them.

I boarded a flight that night from damp, dismal London and arrived in Cape Town the following day. I stood outside the airport terminal, I gazed at the mountains framed by bright blue skies, I drank in the warm air and I admired the slim-hipped women. Then I visualised Tanya at home, battling to get the kids to eat their breakfast. I caught a short flight to Port Elizabeth, arrived at my hotel and settled myself by the (admittedly minuscule) pool next to two women in (minuscule) bikinis. I couldn't help thinking, This is the life. In this blissful place, the Test match television rights, of which Channel 4 were now expected to get a reduced but reasonable share, were the last thing on my mind.

Then my phone rang. It was Scally, from back home.

'Are you sitting down?' he said.

'No, lying, actually,' I replied.

'Sky have just got the whole lot,' he said.

'What?'

'Sky have won the rights to all English cricket from 2006, with highlights on Channel 5. Channel 4 have got nothing. I'm so sorry for you.'

It was a sentiment voiced touchingly by a number of press-men and even the England captain Michael Vaughan. Initially it felt like a kick in the teeth. It seemed as if all the work to try to popularise the game – something of a vocation for people like Mark Nicholas and me – had gone up in ECB-generated smoke. More importantly, so had our profiles and handsome salaries.

After the initial shock, though, I tried to make a more rational assessment. It certainly looked like the game was taking a risk, potentially marginalising domestic cricket by putting it all on satellite TV, although it depended on who you listened to. Some, like Botham, said that without Sky's £200 million the game would die. I responded by saying that it had managed OK up to now, and there was a danger that the money would just line counties' pockets and be wasted on 'Kolpak' (non-English-qualified) players.

In the *Guardian*, David Hopps highlighted the real issue. By being confined to satellite TV, home Test matches would lose the kudos, that special place in the national conscious-ness, they shared with other auspicious events like Wimbledon, Royal Ascot and the Open. Test matches would, he argued, become just part of the endless wallpaper of Sky Sports. You couldn't blame Sky themselves. In a highly com-petitive, open market place, they are entitled to buy whatever they want.

Journalists kindly remarked that I needn't worry – 'You'll easily get a job with Sky!' I didn't share their optimism, par-ticularly when one paper, profiling the winners and losers of the issue, described my TV work as 'noting that deliveries are deviating at an average of one degree more than three Tests ago'. It reminded me that, overall, I'd been damn lucky to have been on any TV station for ten minutes, never mind swan around on Channel 4 for six years. And whereas I still had my writing to make a crust, the Thin Controller and his production staff relied on Channel 4 cricket for virtually their entire livelihoods.

There was a rather sombre atmosphere at a pre-Test dinner I shared with Atherton and Pringle in a Port Elizabeth restaurant. 'Sky are having a celebration, and we're having a wake,' Atherton commented ruefully. There was some consolation: we would become sport's version of *Fawlty Towers* or *The Office*, classic productions cut off in their prime, leaving people wanting more. It's always good to go out on a high.

The fateful news failed to dampen the exhilaration of watching England complete their eighth Test win in a row, an all-time record. Taking a leaf out of Australia's book, Matthew Hoggard got a wicket (the South African captain Graeme Smith's) in the first over of the first Test, an edge nonchalantly caught by Andrew Strauss. Though the game ebbed and flowed for a couple of days, it was a portent for the match and the series. Hoggard was the best bowler on either side; while Strauss batted in a faultless manner that confirmed God must be left-handed.

On the day of England's victory in Port Elizabeth, various members of the Fourth Estate joined with the players in celebrating their feat at a brasserie over the road from our hotel. Trescothick, Butcher and Collingwood were sitting round a table with Atherton, Pringle and Hughes, laughing about the fact that Angus Fraser, who seldom left the press box until it was pitch dark, was still upstairs, obviously tapping out another *War and Peace*, nine hours after the game had ended. Accepting every assignment, committee position and public appearance going, Fraser had now been nicknamed 'Martini' – any time, any place, anywhere.

Vaughan strode past, his dark mop looking a gelled mess. 'What happened to your hair?' I said.

'What happened to yours?' he retorted.

Touché. Or should that be toupee? He could say what he

liked. With a 65 per cent win ratio, he was, at that point, the most successful England captain in history. He led an impressive bunch of men, the best England team I had ever seen: dedicated, supremely fit, superbly coached, talented, confident and adept at turning precarious situations to their advantage. Perhaps, in my current situation of uncertainty, I could gain strength from that.

Two-day-old English papers materialised at breakfast the next day. My 'song' at the *Telegraph* Christmas lunch had received a mention in the *Independent*'s media diary. It was described as a cross between Noel Coward and Richard Stilgoe. I couldn't work out if that was flattering or derogatory. It certainly depicted me as old. Then I realised I was: it was my forty-fifth birthday.

CHAPTER 16 – 2005

NUTS ABOUT KP

After England's tenacious 2–1 series win in South Africa, 80 per cent of respondents to a national poll believed England would win the Ashes in the summer of 2005. There was a rising tide of optimism whipped into a froth by Kevin Pietersen's extraordinary performances in the one-day series in South Africa, where he scored three centuries in five innings.

Pietersen was in London in early March representing England at an awards ceremony. I was sent to do a *Telegraph* interview with him and the man loudly proclaiming his cause: one Ian Terence Botham. At first glance they made an odd couple: the dyed-in-the-wool Englishman and scourge of the Aussies, sitting next to the South African deserter who became English on a passage of convenience. The conflicting morality didn't stack up.

On closer inspection, though, there were similarities. They both had the same special talent, the buccaneering style (both with bat and tongue), the rebellious inclinations, the outlandish haircuts. Pietersen's blond cockatoo was only a little bit more alarming than the streaked mullet Botham had in his heyday. When Botham first met Pietersen he recognised a kindred spirit, and his management company, appropriately named Mission, was now looking after the young runmeister's affairs. He didn't approve of the hair though. 'First thing I'm doing when we're out of here is getting him to the barber's, get that dead mongoose off his head,' he said.

Pietersen elaborated on his story. Born to an Afrikaans

father and an English mother, he was, amazingly, overlooked by his home state of Natal, who regarded him as an off spinner who batted number eight. They argued they were hamstrung by the quota system (two blacks per team) and couldn't find a place for him in the provincial team. Clive Rice, the former South African captain, regarded this as 'reverse racism' and, as director of cricket at Nottinghamshire, found him a place at Trent Bridge instead.

That was in 2001, and four years later because of his mother, he was qualified for England. Traditionalists argued that Pietersen had secured a passport of convenience, like Greg Rusedski did, and he was liable to make equally gauche statements. The counter-argument is that, as we'd negligently allowed grass-roots cricket to wither, we beggars cannot be choosers. South Africa's loss was England's gain. Or should be. Botham was adamant. 'England have got to pick him for the Test side,' he said. 'If they don't, well, I can see the public hanging selectors from trees.'

Botham was in ebullient mood talking about England. 'When I first started commentating on them for Sky Sports we had to keep trying to make them sound good. That was tiring. It was hard work. We couldn't beat the Eskimos then. Now it's a pleasure to commentate on them because they're playing good cricket. They have the best chance they've had for about twenty years to beat the convicts. Whichever team's bowlers hunt in packs the best will win.'

The build-up to the Ashes had begun (it was March) and by the beginning of the cricket season on 8 April, anticipation was already reaching feverish levels. It was to be the biggest summer of cricket ever, the papers said, and several Sunday titles had begun previewing the Ashes with huge profiles of the protagonists, and Glenn McGrath had already declared that Vaughan and Strauss were in his sights and he expected to get his 500th Test wicket 'early on in the first Test at Lord's'. Weather forecasters were predicting a summer heatwave. Inevitably the first day of the season – MCC playing Warwickshire, the county champions, at Lord's – was sleeted off.

By the third day of the match, the weather cheered up and Lord's was looking a picture, reflecting the conversion of the MCC, once the domain of stuffiness and luddites, into a dynamic organisation. I explored the great old pavilion, which had been imaginatively renovated. I particularly liked the roof terrace on the top tier. Now you could actually watch the play in the afternoon sun rather than freezing to death (the pavilion was originally designed so the members were in the shade).

It made me think of all those times when, while the Middlesex batsmen strutted their stuff in the middle, we tailenders made the lengthy trek to the Nursery End to sit in the sun. Then, when there was a sudden crash of wickets, it was a breakneck dash from the other end of the ground to get ready. More than once I was hurrying out to bat breathless and sockless, trying desperately to strap all my protection into place before reaching the middle. It was not a state conducive to fending off Malcolm Marshall, Richard Hadlee and the like. If the roof terrace had been there then, I could have lolled in the sun watching Gatting & Co make hay, and it would have been just one flight of steps down to the dressing room to get padded up, allowing plenty of time for a nervous piss before going out to bat. Though admittedly, offering little more prospect of success.

Exiting the pavilion later, I discovered television screens had been installed in the downstairs toilets. Despite feeling a little disconcerted relieving myself under the gaze of an attractive female newscaster on Sky, I mentioned the innovation to Mark Nicholas. 'We can now broadcast to people while they're having a leak,' I said. 'Not for much longer!' he replied.

LORD TED

The 'relaunch' of English cricket took place at Featherston High School, Southall, on 20 April. Michael Vaughan and others attended and the ECB blurb proclaimed that 'three England cricket superstars will be recognised by 10 per cent of the population by 2009'. There were various columns in the following day's papers comparing the nation's unfamiliarity with individual cricketers to its instant recognition of footballers. Below a rallying piece in the *Telegraph* saying it was time English cricket shed its anonymity was a picture of a cricketer. It was captioned Andrew Strauss, England's left-handed batting star. The picture, however, was not only of a right hander, it was also of Robin Weston, a Middlesex player who wasn't even on the county's books any more.   I haven't made this up.

Comparisons were made with the amount the ECB were seeking to spend on grass roots (£5 million by 2009) with Rio Ferdinand's provisional salary for the forthcoming season (£6.24 million). It emphasised the massive gulf between the two sports. I was trying to do my bit for the imbalance by helping an Indian businessman friend revamp the marketing of Leicestershire, especially by trying to tap more imaginatively into Leicester's large Asian community. 'Leicester are a sleeping giant,' I wrote in a column. That week they lost to Durham by an innings and 216 runs. Clearly they were a bit slow coming out of hibernation.

I escaped the weather-beaten crawl of the first-class season for two days to visit the former England captain Ted Dexter in Italy. Dan Evans, the *Telegraph*'s deputy sports editor, had spotted that it was Dexter's seventieth birthday in May. Not only had he been an iconic English cricketing figure, a man of noble brow who dominated the best attacks in world cricket throughout the 1960s, and created one-day cricket in its modern form, but he also became a scratch golfer good enough to win a major open tournament. He was surely on a par with the legendary C. B. Fry (who played cricket and football for England) as the best all-round sportsman this country has ever produced. We hatched a plan for me to interview him in his birthplace, Milan.

Dexter himself was hugely enthused by the idea, and

immediately drew up an itinerary to document his childhood. It was quite a poignant assignment for me, since I'd known him and his wife Sue since my own boyhood, and it was seeing his panache on the field (and his stunning daughter off it) that had partly lured me into the cricketing fraternity in the first place. I knew a different side to the occasionally brash, impatient Dexter, one of commitment to his work and compassion for the game and great support to his family, one of whom, his younger brother David, was born with Down's syndrome.

We began on the steps of La Scala, where he recounted the story of his father, who'd been transferred from London to Milan to run an insurance business, taking Ted and his older brother Johnnie to the opera. 'Wagner's *Tannhauser* I think it was. After one act my father turned to us and we were looking very bored and he said, "Come on boys, that's enough of this" and we walked out. We were so relieved we jumped for joy and went whooping and hollering down the street.' He voluntarily re-enacted this scene for the *Telegraph* photographer in front of a mass of bemused tourists.

He did not have a deprived upbringing. He and his older brother grew up in a grand apartment with several staff close to the Jardini Publicci (a mini Hyde Park). During the Second World War, they returned to England and he and his brother were sent away to boarding school in Scotland. But after the war, the parents reinstated themselves in Italy and Ted remembers travelling back there in the holidays on the Orient Express. 'We lived in style then,' he said.

Much of his sporting pedigree is rooted on the banks of Lake Como, where the family had a summer house, and after lunch in Milan he drove us swiftly up there. Once alongside the lake I appreciated why Dexter was in a hurry. The glistening sheen of the water, the rugged mountains rising up from its surface set against the snow-capped Dolomites behind, the orange-tile villages clinging to the lakeside with their Renaissance bell towers, the blue sky and the rich blossom make this one of the most beautiful places on earth. You could see why film stars gravitate to it (George Clooney had recently purchased a villa here), why various popes had their summer retreats there, why Churchill was a regular visitor. It's a place to die for.

We made a brief pilgrimage to his old family house, Villa Lugarna, where Ted spent numerous school holidays. He had promised we'd be bowled over by it and he was right. The regal three-storey building with its huge shuttered windows and turreted roofs and surrounding lawn, stands back from the edge of a steep slope commanding unsurpassable views across the Lake Como to the mountains of Switzerland beyond. It is like a setting from a Scott Fitzgerald novel. You could imagine Dick and Nicole Diver owning it as a romantic getaway in *Tender is the Night*.

It was here where Ted first got the golf bug. A family friend dug out a few clubs and he and his brother had a go up the hill at the back. The catalyst for his addiction was half a mile up the road. The Menaggio golf club, impossibly constructed on a narrow mountain ledge by two Englishmen in 1902, had, at that point, fallen into disrepair. Ted, his brother and his father steadily reclaimed it after the war. 'We saw it evolve hole by hole,' he said as we took the winding lane up to the clubhouse. Tight, verdant and undulating, it enjoys wonderful panoramas of the lake and mountains from every point. It is the most spectacular golf course I've ever seen. If you were designing one in heaven, it would be the ideal blueprint. Having secured membership partly through Dexter's contacts, Clooney brought the entire cast of *Ocean's 12* down to play it.

After a quick tour of the course, we sat in the clubhouse library to chat. Not content with captaining England at cricket and winning golf tournaments, Dexter helped found Sunday League cricket in the sixties, owned horses, greyhounds and sports cars, got his pilot's licence, and, having become a journalist, flew his young family to Australia to cover an England tour. In the seventies his PR consultancy created the Deloitte's player ratings (now the standard way of assessing international cricketers) because, as he explained, 'I was pissed off with Boycott always being top of the averages.' In later years he became chairman of selectors, president of the MCC and captain of Sunningdale Golf Club. In fact, his CV makes exhausting reading. It has certainly been a life less ordinary.

COLOSSI INCORPORATED

Bearing in mind it was a quarter of a century since I first played at Lord's, I thought it was about time I took my family there to show the kids the place I called home for twelve years. Our visit happened to coincide with Andrew Flintoff's return to action for Lancashire after his winter surgery. We sat up in the top row of the Allen Stand and saw, in the space of seven overs, three wickets (including one where two stumps were uprooted), five fours, a six and several brilliant bits of fielding. I told the kids proudly that Daddy used to play out there, but still the general view was 'when can we go?' (and that was Tanya). Later when we were reviewing the events of the day, I asked Callum (seven) if he'd remembered the name of the ground we'd been at. He ummed and ahhed and then said, 'Was it Mould or something?'

A couple of days later I popped to Worcester to see Flintoff again. This time it was strictly business – I needed to discuss the DVD we were going to be making together after negotiating a deal with his manager Neil Fairbrother in the winter. But it was enjoyable sitting in front of the New Road pavilion and absorbing the sights and sounds of an afternoon's play in a county match, an all-too-rare experience for those of us on the international circuit.

As I watched the ball cannoning off the boundary boards in the evening shadows, I considered the ways the county game had changed in the twenty-five years I'd been connected with it. It seemed somehow more physical now: tall, galumphing seam bowlers banging it in short of a length egged on by vociferous fielders to clench-jawed, muscular batsmen. It felt more like business, less like pleasure (you certainly didn't do it for money in the eighties). But there was no business of playing for the close. Not so long ago, the Lancashire batsmen would have been nudging and nurdling their way through the last half-hour. Here every other ball seemed to be thrashed through the covers.

And yet, despite the presence of Flintoff, Muralitharan and Hick, there was only a sprinkling of spectators, of whom an elderly man with arthritis and a cravat was typical. I looked at the scene and pondered the future of four-day county cricket. I wondered whether ultimately it would go the same way as the village deli – a place to browse quietly for little luxuries that is eventually subsumed by a supermarket chain. The future is in multi-sport stadia like the Millennium Stadium in Cardiff. Grounds like Worcester will be preserved as relics of a bygone era, like the Old Curiosity Shop, staging exhibition matches, with a few extras in fancy dress, and the sound of Boycott on a loop over the PA saying 'That's joost bad techneek is that.'

After my meeting with Flintoff (which began with me asking, 'What do you want to see on a DVD?' and him joking 'Porn!'), I travelled back on the Paddington 'express'. I was the only person on it until Cheltenham, and was recognised by the middle-aged Welsh steward who plied me with cheap sandwiches and wangled me a seat in first class. Ah, what it is to be famous.

I went from one colossus of English sport straight to another. I was invited by the headmaster of a Buckinghamshire prep school to be a fly on the wall for a coaching session with the former England rugby captain Martin Johnson. He arrived promptly at eleven. He strode towards his greeting party, mainly eight-year-olds, like a giant in the land of Lilliput. He posed for photos outside the school, holding one young player in his arms. 'Did you see that, he lifted him up with one hand!' crowed another lad.

'Right,' he said to the first group, a bunch of seven-year-olds, 'we're going to start with a five-mile run. Happy with that?' Respectful silence. 'OK, we'll just do a quick warm-up once round the pitch.' Desperate to impress, they all set off, most in the wrong direction. He called them back. They arrived, breathless. 'Who was first? You. Good man. Two press-ups for being so quick.'

The mild 'punishment' for doing well is a common thread of his coaching ethos, and has the dual effect of containing egos and helping the best get better. You could see why he was such a successful captain. He won't tolerate complacency, likes to encourage and challenge at the same time.

Without delay another, slightly older, group was ferried in. He put them through a few exercises. 'Now,' he said, 'why do we do sit-ups? To get a six-pack and look good on the beach? Well, partially yes, but also it's really important to strengthen your core ... warm-up ... warm-down. Do that and you won't end up like me – stiff as a board.'

Johnson is a man without conceit. He talks down to no one. He treats everyone as equals. He had a race with them to finish. 'Breathe, relax, stay calm,' he said surrounded by panting ten-year-olds afterwards, in a manner that would have been invaluable during flashpoints in matches. He is a born leader. People do what he says. It does help, of course, if you're 6ft 7in and look like the Terminator.

Later, in a question-and-answer session, he provided the most pragmatic piece of advice for prospective captains I've ever heard. 'Captains always seem to believe they've got to be something different. You've got to be yourself. You've got to be honest. The best thing you can do as captain is play well.' Paradoxically, the best way to undermine a team is to inhibit their captain, as the 1980s West Indies and invariably these days Glenn McGrath have proved. In the summer, the issue of whether Michael Vaughan could wriggle out of his clutches would have a massive bearing on the destination of the Ashes.

CHANGING OF THE GUARD

In a diversion from the endless Ashes build-up, *Wisden Cricketer* magazine produced a feature entitled 'All Miked Up and Nowhere to Go' asking readers to vote for the six commentators who they'd prefer in Sky's team next year. All the runners and riders were profiled. Any remote chance I had was ruled out by my description as 'superficially relaxed but actually nerdy and intense' (written by Ian Smith, perchance?). Atherton was 'less dour than when he was playing but still not a bundle of laughs'. In fact his laugh is so loud at the back of the com box after one of Smith's wisecracks you could hear it on air and he has to be told to quieten down. Dermot Reeve is profiled as 'louche. Doesn't always turn up on time.'

Actually, he wasn't going to turn up at all. In mid-May it was announced that by mutual consent Dermot Reeve and Channel 4 had parted company. A day later the *Daily Mail* published a big story about him being addicted to cocaine (he admitted he was drug addled while commentating on the Lord's Test a year before) and how it had ruined his marriage and his career. He was taking a break to try to sort himself out. It was a worrying time for him and his family. Strangely, all but one of county cricket's recreational drug revelations has had a Warwickshire connection. Is Birmingham twinned with Bogota?

It all meant that when the Channel 4 cricket 'team' gathered for the annual pre-Test photo shoot at Lord's, Nicholas, Benaud and I were the only survivors of the first year. We'd all come from varying directions: Boycott from Cape Town where he has a house, Benaud from the south of France where he has an apartment, Nicholas from his second home at Sunningdale Golf Club, me from dropping the kids at school in Hammersmith. Benaud and I exchanged information about our books-in-progress. 'We've got the revised proofs in two days early,' he said. It was typical of him to be ahead of schedule and also to share the credit with his wife. He rarely uses the word I, except when talking about his cricketing exploits, and wanted to call his latest tome *Don't Leave Home Without Daphne*. It would have been a far more interesting and appropriate title than *My Spin on Cricket*, but he was overruled by the publishers.

After the usual commentators' meeting to go over the phonetics of the Bangladeshi players, we made our way to the England Player of the Year dinner, at the Saatchi Gallery. I sat between two members of the England women's team who were both taller than me. On the way to the loo, I bumped into Michael Vaughan. 'This'll be you soon,' I said, gesturing at the exhibition on the wall. 'Collecting fine art with all your money.' (He must be on at least £500,000 a year.)

'Aye,' he said, smirking. 'Now, Yozzer, have you got that job with Sky yet? Because if not you can be our nanny. We're expecting another one soon. I'll pay you three pounds an hour. We'll supply the nappies.' I said that, as I'd heard nothing from Sky, I'd let him know.

Old muckers Graham Thorpe and Nasser Hussain were sat together at the table next to mine, and I reflected on their contrasting prospects. While Hussain would be luxuriating in the Sky box all summer, Thorpe, scratchy and restricted in his strokeplay recently, faced an uncertain future. In fact, an unseemly hoo-ha arose the very next day when it was announced he would be heading for New South Wales in a coaching capacity at Christmas and therefore wouldn't be available for England's winter tours. Officials were miffed that they were not informed earlier and intimated they might hold it against him after his 100th Test a fortnight later.

This was preposterous. What he had decided to do in six months' time should in no way prejudice his selection for the Ashes. He had unfinished business against Australia, and would be utterly committed to it. What was of more relevance was his fading ability. Years of back-to-the-wall batting, eking out runs when England were in the mire, swaying the slings and arrows of the world's fastest bowlers, had taken their toll. Thorpe couldn't quite assert himself against the bowlers as he once had. A nagging back injury, and Ian Bell breathing down his neck, did not help.

He was experiencing that slow, almost imperceptible metamorphosis towards sporting middle age. His reactions weren't as sharp, his flexibility was reduced. It's a gradual development, as if, slowly but surely, your veins are filling up with lead shot. Still, the batting nous remained, and with the selectors already missing one trick – not including Kevin Pietersen in the first Bangladesh Test to get him used to the atmosphere and tempo of Test cricket – you felt they must not miss another. A feisty middle order of Thorpe and Pietersen – left hand, right hand, old warrior, young gun – was a must for the first Ashes Test.

As generally expected, the two Bangladesh Tests were a complete mismatch, enabling some almost gratuitous boot-filling in England batting ranks and a useful workout for the bowlers, nothing more. It was a battle finding anything interesting to analyse. The only uncertainty among the England batsmen (those that got in) was whether to hit the next ball for four or six. Bangladesh would struggle to give a minor county a decent game. The ICC, particularly Jagmohan Dalmiya, the Indian who was the Council's then chairman, deserve ridicule for allowing them to get Test status (the end result was to give the Asian block another vote at the table).

There were numerous voices calling for their immediate exclusion, though surprisingly Fred Trueman's was not one of them. 'You could have got some of them out, even now,' I said, when he rang up for a telephone number. 'Aye, shame isn't it?' he said, sympathetically. 'Good luck to 'em though. We called West Indies a bunch of beach cricketers in 1928 and they beat us in 1950!'

I wasn't knocking Bangladesh's inadequacies either. Well, as the world's seventh most populous country, they had a vital role in the future of Test cricket. More importantly, the three-day Lord's Test allowed me to join the rest of my family at a magnificent villa in Tuscany for the rest of the half-term week.

After the equally brief Durham Test, I found myself in the hotel bar among the BBC *Test Match Special* crew. The talk revolved around the cricket TV rights. Jonathan Agnew said that when the cricket was on Channel 4 the *TMS* post bag was full and emails were flying in. When it was on Sky there was an eerie silence, as if cricket was not on the radar. All the BBC people thought I already had a job with Sky. Nothing could be further from the truth. When I admitted as much, Agnew kindly said I should consider approaching them for work. Ironically, after all this time coveting the idea of being accommodated in the *TMS* box, I now couldn't imagine what I'd do.

GREAT EXPECTATIONS

The Australians arrived in early June, accompanied by a fanfare and their ex-players casting aspersions on England. Terry Alderman said Flintoff's technique was fallible and Rodney Hogg suggested Warne would sort him out. Ian Healy wrote off England's chances believing that they wouldn't win a single Test. He cited Australia's recent series against New Zealand, where all pre-series talk of hard-fought tussles were laid to rest by a rampaging unit.

Dangerous talk. Not because it could backfire and motivate England, but because criticising any sportsman was becoming increasingly risky. Gary Lineker was that week taken to court by Harry Kewell for comments he made about his transfer to Liverpool in 2003. Kewell was suing for defamation of character. Crikey. David Hopps, of the *Guardian*, who first called Ashley Giles a wheelie bin, could thank his lucky stars it was a couple of years ago (and that Giles was so forgiving – Hopps was now his ghostwriter).

But the way it's going we will all be in the dock before long for reporting that 'Jones got out to an iffy shot'.

There were plenty of those (and I think I'm safe from litigation here) on 13 June at the Rose Bowl for the first-ever Twenty-20 international between England and Australia. All of them were played by the Australians in the most intense England fielding performance ever witnessed. Darren Gough ran in like a man possessed, the other bowlers were equally irresistible and every shot in the air went to hand and, even more miraculously, was caught. After six overs the Aussies were 31 for 7! You had to pinch yourself to believe it. It was a double pleasure for me, since I was watching it at home lounging on the sofa, and, despite the pandemonium of five kids having tea in the next room, I was untouchable because this constituted 'work'. This job was the bee's knees.

The result created national euphoria, but the *Telegraph*'s headline the next day contained a note of caution: 'Australia 79 all out (Warning: Readers are advised to enjoy this headline to the full since it is unlikely to be repeated this summer).' The *Sun* said simply 'THRASHES'.

The tabloids had run out of hyperbole by the end of the following week. The Australians lurched to defeat by Somerset, prompting the *Daily Mail* to bump off its back page any number of football transfer speculation stories, and *The Times* to print a little cut-out-and-keep caption for the Australians, with a picture of a bat 'used to hit ball' and a ball 'for aiming at stumps'. Not satisfied with the embarrassment of that, the Aussies were then rumbled by Bangladesh, the equivalent of Brazil losing to Liechtenstein at football. The Australian bowlers – Gillespie in particular – looked like county dobbers. So after the first round of NatWest Series matches, the table had England on top, and Bangladesh second, with Australia bringing up the rear. Who would credit it?

The day after, the Australians arrived at Bristol an hour late (the coach driver got lost), reeling from their failures.

Adding to their woes, a key member of their one-day team, Andrew Symonds, had broken the team curfew and been discovered in a bar the night before at 3.30 a.m. He had been suspended for two matches. And there was a kiss-and-tell story in the *Sunday Mirror* about a female student's night with Shane Warne. She declared in the article that he wasn't very well endowed or long lasting, and that he soon fell asleep snoring. It caused some childish sniggering in our commentary box, as did the account of her mate's experience in bed with Kevin Pietersen, which she said included him instructing her to pant his name when she was climaxing.

Amusement turned to elation after Pietersen produced one of the most astonishing pieces of sustained hitting ever seen. England were struggling on 160 for 6 with 12 overs to go, chasing 252, when he suddenly took control. He picked up Kasprowicz way over square leg, as if he was wielding a tennis racket, then treated Brad Hogg like a schoolboy bowler. He hit everything, regardless of length, line or reputation. Long levers and a huge follow-through powered a good-length ball from the long-haired Gillespie, looking like someone who'd strayed onto the field from the Glastonbury rock festival, miles over long on. McGrath was flat-batted over cover. Gillespie launched for six again. Even if the ball was inch perfect he still managed to get it for a single. He batted like Javed Miandad and Viv Richards rolled into one. His barnstorming 91 not out enabled England to win with 15 balls to spare. It was an incredible innings. Michael Vaughan called it 'genius'. It wasn't an exaggeration. We were all panting Pietersen's name after that.

We were muttering darkly about Channel 4 though, because the highlights for such a titanic match were on at 1.05 a.m. The first big encounter of the summer between the oldest cricketing enemies at insomniacs' hour, regarded inferior to a repeat of *Whicker's War* (8 p.m.), *Big Brother 6* (9 p.m.), a new two-part drama (10 p.m.–midnight) and the *Download Festival* (music performances from Motorhead,

Slipknot and Papa Roach). It was cast-iron proof that the Channel 4 schedulers had completely lost the plot. The channel had recently declared a two-year extension of the *Big Brother* contract, costing the £30 million they could have used for the cricket. It was a fairly blunt statement.

To complete a miserable seven days, the Australians woke up on the Monday morning to a *Sun* back page depicting their four fast bowlers carrying handbags. Above was the headline, 'Is that all you've got, Sheilas?'

It was frustrating doing these matches only for highlights, but at least it allowed me time to watch the play with the naked eye, and everyone to turn up in casual dress (we were rarely seen on the programmes). It gave Atherton the opportunity to wear his favourite old deck shoes, which were so tatty I said if he left them on his front step the tramps round his way in Notting Hill would probably ignore them. 'Actually,' he said, 'I had one of them knocking at the door the other day asking if I had any clothes I didn't want. I went upstairs and dug out a pair of old blue cords. The tramp took one look and said, "I'm not wearing those!" and toddled off.' Atherton was not remotely embarrassed by this. Secretly I think he was rather proud of it.

All that and the Reuters news agency's departure from Fleet Street to Canary Wharf, leaving the great old thoroughfare totally bereft of news organisations for the first time in two centuries. The only national title left in the street was the *Beano*. It was truly an extraordinary week.

That, of course, was a mere aperitif. Then there were the hors d'oeuvres. Matthew Hayden and Simon Jones had a heated exchange at Edgbaston, Hayden continuing the handbags theme by squaring up to Jones when his attempted throw at the stumps, after he'd intercepted a firm drive, reared up into Hayden's chest. Paul Collingwood, all 5ft 8in of him, stood up for his team-mate and the umpires intervened just before Collingwood was laid out. Hayden, the Incredible Hulk, flounced off like a child. Jones walked away shrugging, muttering 'tart' to himself, then trapped his man LBW a few balls later. The papers latched on to the incident declaring it 'not cricket'. That old chestnut, which considering cricket's origins in the murky world of gambling, and regular acts of skulduggery in all forms of cricket since time immemorial, should have been buried with Guy Fawkes. The concept of the 'noble game' is a myth.

This was re-emphasised by the ECB circulating a story that Hayden had also sworn at and barged a kid in the guard of honour as he came out to bat. I checked the videotape and it was clear the allegations were total hogwash. Some papers ran the story, but it was unsubstantiated and the Aussies were livid, banning the *Sun* and the *Mirror* from their subsequent press conference.

Then Adam Gilchrist 'walked' against Bangladesh although replays proved he hadn't hit the ball. Were the Aussies going soft? We discussed this incident at the NatWest Series final, contested, contrary to early indications, by England and Australia. Benaud, back in the com box after his sojourn in the south of France, said, 'I did that once on a pair. Thought I'd nicked the ball and started to walk, then realised I probably hadn't hit it, but by then I'd gone too far so I kept going.' Before lunch he initiated his annual custom of unfolding fifty white cotton handkerchiefs, one by one, and spreading them out neatly for the commentators to sign. 'I get so many requests for these – from viewers, charities, clubs,' he says. The Benauds post them to the recipients themselves.

The Lord's final was perhaps the first real sign that the Aussies were starting to get their act together. They manoeuvred their way to a moderate 197, but then bowled and fielded like dervishes to reduce England to 33 for 5. It was the Rose Bowl in reverse. That England eventually scraped a nail-biting tie was down to their improved mettle, built up over the preceding sixteen months, and the normally indefatigable McGrath faltering in the final over with a no-ball and two full tosses. Somehow Giles scraped two

leg byes from the last ball to bring the scores level. It had
been the perfect appetiser for the Test series. If only it
had been the Test series that followed, instead of three more
starters. The ECB schedulers were clearly infiltrated by Mr
Creosote.

The first of these 'wa-ferrr theen mints' was at Headingley.
We'd been cordially invited for a party at Geoff Boycott's
house on the way up. I nearly fell off my chair in shock when
he rang up and announced it. But this is G. Boycott mark II.
Complimentary, generous, reasonable, modest (well, OK,
less boastful).

Atherton, Nicholas and I caught the train up to Wakefield,
everyone abuzz with the stunning news of London's 2012
Olympic triumph. Also there were *TMS* commentators and
producers, Yorkshire's chief executive, various other local
dignitaries and Mr Harold Denis (Dickie) Bird, who'd driven
the couple of miles from home in his Jaguar, which he'd
bought seven years ago with the proceeds of his books. He
admitted he had done barely 20,000 miles in it and had still
not fathomed how to open the boot. He is a creature of
habit.

Boycott's house had been transformed from the time I'd
been there before. Gone was the dark little shrine of a sitting
room full of England caps and portraits and other cricketing
memorabilia, to be replaced by a light airy kitchen, warm
colours and bonhomie. Rachael, Boycott's wife, was a viva-
cious hostess and there was a lavish spread of salmon, and
home-made cottage pies and mountains of veg.

I talked for a time to Boycott's brother Tony, an ex-miner
turned handyman who vividly described his former life down
the local pit – getting up at 4 a.m. to crawl about fixing
machinery 500ft down in a three-foot high tunnel six days a
week. It sounded like one of those 'I licked road clean before
I got up' lives, but he declared he enjoyed every minute of it,
that the camaraderie among the men was second to none and
that he would not have preferred to exchange his life for his
brother's. He said the word 'crickeet' exactly like Geoffrey. It

must be the local dialect.

The match at Headingley was utterly eclipsed by the London bombs. It was hard to focus properly on the play as news filtered through of the carnage. But England managed to commit themselves to the task, and disposed of Australia by nine wickets. Australia's demise prompted, in my mind, parallels with the collapse, a few days before, of one of the Twelve Apostles, giant limestone stacks that had protruded from the sea off the Victorian coast for more than 20 million years. The relentlessness of the Southern Ocean and the blasting winds that had gradually eroded the formation were a metaphor for the steady dismantling of Australia's imposing structure, first by the Indians and, this summer, by the English, to the point where now the edifice was looking extremely vulnerable. Cracks were appearing in the batting and bowling which a confident England were systematically widening. I sensed the end could be swift.

Come the Ashes, this situation, I felt, placed a big responsibility on Shane Warne's shoulders. He remained a mercurial figure – a brilliant confidence trickster – who would be stirred by the challenge. Three years in Hampshire's colours had, however, made him a less daunting, more familiar opponent. I spoke to Middlesex's Ed Smith, who had scored two fifties against him, one the previous weekend, and who agreed that while his cricketing brain was still above par, he bowled more loose balls now and wasn't able to build up the same pressure. You just sat on him and waited for the four ball. You usually didn't have to wait too long.

Here we go, I wrote. The Australian superstructure is about to crumble before our eyes.

Consequently the Aussies scored crunching victories in the subsequent two one-dayers, by seven and eight wickets respectively. The letter I received from my previous correspondent, a Mr S. Wood from Hove, was therefore not surprising.

Rubbish Hughes!!

'Fancy getting paid for boring 98 per cent of the Test

match viewers with your silly lines, circles, cartoons, etc. You and the others next to you should be booted out!
Rubbish!'

CHAPTER 17 – The Ashes

FREDDIE'S NIGHTMARE

After the one-day series, the general verdict on the Ashes was pessimistic from England's point of view. Most pundits predicted a 3–1 win to Australia, though Ian Botham said 3–2, and Mike Brearley and Dickie Bird preferred 2–1. Glenn McGrath inevitably predicted 5–0. A few wayward optimists – Gary Lineker, Phil Tufnell and Dominic Cork among them – had England to win. And so did I. Man for man, the Australians were more talented, but their bowlers were ageing and I felt they'd particularly struggle in the second and third Tests (Edgbaston and Old Trafford), which were back to back, with no recovery time.

Overall, I just had a feeling in my water about England. I had that feeling after mingling with Matt Dawson and Lawrence Dallaglio before the Rugby World Cup and I had it again now, having watched the cricketers at close quarters for some time, and having dinner with one or two of them. I had seen their collective drive and sensed that they really did believe that winning the Ashes was their destiny. I might, just might, be there when England at last regained the stupid receptacle. I bought a replica one from the Lord's shop to display in the truck as a good-luck charm.

Just prior to the first Test, I spent a whole day with Freddie Flintoff. We were shooting links for a DVD entitled *Freddie's Cricket Nightmares*, a compilation of great action and comic moments aimed at the Christmas market. It was a week before his first Ashes Test, a matter of days until he took his place in a contest he'd been striving for ten years to enter. He intended to treat it like any other Test, preparing as usual with a pre-match dinner with the missus and his usual low-key warm-up in the morning. He said he wasn't placing too much expectation on himself. I guessed that in reality he didn't quite know what to expect.

During our shoot Freddie was the opposite of a prima donna. He completed six hours of filming, repeating all manner of skills and stunts and short soliloquies in stifling heat without once complaining. His lunch break was taken up with a magazine photoshoot. He instantly charmed the crew. If only real actors were that cooperative. It mirrored his attitude on the field. Revelling in hard work, he is stirred by responsibility. With an indomitable spirit, he was thriving as England's dynamo in the field, the team's spark with the ball. Michael Vaughan would increasingly turn to him as soon as the opponents' best player arrived at the crease (Brian Lara and Jacques Kallis in recent series) or when he needed a few controlling overs.

In that sense Flintoff's duel with Adam Gilchrist was going to be vital to the outcome of the Ashes Tests. Gilchrist was the samurai sword of the Aussies' flashing blades, arriving in mid-battle to apply the mortal strikes to an already wounded opponent. An hour of him and the beast that you thought you had safely lassoed suddenly broke free and gored you. His average against England was a daunting 61. But against Flintoff in the one-day series, bowling round the wicket, Gilchrist struggled. He found the pace discomforting, the angle awkward and the persistence unwavering. It was clear England's strategy would be to try to save some Flintoff huff and puff for when the wicket-keeper swaggered in.

Flintoff's bowling had become truly world class. He delivered what we knew in the trade as a 'heavy' ball. I experienced that first hand when he bowled me a couple during our filming. One, barely above half pace, was just short of a length and hammered into the splice as I was still bringing the bat down, and scooted off to the third-man boundary before I'd finished the shot. He's invariably right on the mark from ball one, and has added shock deliveries – bouncers, yorkers and slower balls – to his accurate stock. He was bound to cause all the Aussie batsmen headaches. And yet more Test wickets would just deepen his own inner struggle, because what he really wanted to be was a batsman who bowled. 'My worst fears might be happening: I'm turning into a bowler,' he said, supping a Guinness after the day's work was done.

He reflected on the camaraderie that had developed of late in the England dressing room. 'We're all mates, we get on great. We've grown up at the Academy together – we're like a county team really. We're like eleven lads turning up to play cricket. The captain's really made a difference, encouraging us to enjoy ourselves, express ourselves. We respect the Aussies, but there's no fear. I think we can win the Ashes. I just can't wait for the contest to start.'

I went to the teams' net sessions the day before the Test. Fuelled by the hype, the tension in the two camps was tangible. Justin Langer, the boxing-training fanatic, was jigging around like a cat on a hot tin roof, and predicting that his first twenty minutes at the crease could be frenetic. Warne wheeled away in the nets for two hours. Ian Bell had been preferred to the struggling Graham Thorpe and he and other England batsmen later practised against Merlyn, a new-fangled spinning machine.

Among the acreage of pre-match coverage, Matthew Hoggard was quoted as saying the Aussies were 'getting on a little bit and it will be interesting to see if they can put in consistent performances for twenty-five days'. This was immediately translated as they are 'over the hill'. Michael Vaughan was asked what he made of his bowler being so outspoken. 'Ah'm right behind 'im,' he replied, smiling. He had refused to cede to Ponting's request that, in the case of dubious catches, the batsman should accept the fieldsman's word. Interesting …

And so, finally, to the event that had had just about the

biggest build-up since the Normandy landings. There'd been a public countdown from the day England beat Australia at Edgbaston in the Champions Trophy semi-final ten months before. There'd been six weeks of posturing and score-settling on the field and verbal fusillades in the press. There'd been Ashes supplements and previews and promotions, W. G. Grace rising from the dead on Channel 4 and Shane Warne being escorted away in chains on Sky vowing, 'I'll be back.' Billboards of Warne and Pietersen – one playing in his 124th Test, the other in his first – were everywhere. Tickets had been changing hands for £1000 a pair. MCC members, those guardians of morality, had been hawking their tickets for a profit (and were duly rumbled by the club).

I stood in the middle as the teams went through their final limbering up, bowlers marking out their run-ups with tape measures and tins of paint, Matthew Hayden standing on the pitch in his socks as if it were a precious ornament, visualising his innings. The air was pregnant with expectation.

The weather was overcast as the captains emerged, and the pitch, after hot recent weather, had hairline cracks. Mick Hunt, the groundsman, had admitted it was a little ahead of schedule, and as I lingered on the square with Mike Gatting, we said it was an important toss. Whoever won it would have to bat first. Ponting called correctly and declared that intention. Vaughan seemed unconcerned as he chatted kindly to the seven-year-old mascot while waiting to be interviewed.

It was a very different Vaughan who commanded the team huddle on the field twenty minutes later: his eyes blazed, his neck was taut, his voice was insistent as he led a call to arms. In a clear statement of aggressive intent, he handed the ball to Steve Harmison to bowl the opening over (it had always been Hoggard in the past), and Harmison immediately delivered. His second ball rammed into Justin Langer's unprotected elbow before he'd so much as flinched. Play was held up as soon as it had started, and Langer wasn't the only one who needed treatment in that first hour. Harmison also crusted Hayden and Ponting in his first spell, leaving the Australian captain with a cut cheekbone. There was a noticeable lack of English sympathy as Ponting stood, dazed, near the wicket, waiting for the physio. This England were clearly taking no prisoners.

Fortified by fervour, their four-pronged pace attack had the Aussies five down for 97 at lunch in what must have been one of the most intense sessions of Test cricket between these two adversaries. Bouncers flew past noses, helmets were clattered, throws whistled in from all angles, just missing the batsmen's heads; it was Bodyline II. The Australians responded with jabs, uppercuts and hooks. It was as if two heavyweights had finally been let out of their corners and were releasing weeks of pent-up energy. We were ducking and flinching in the VT truck, and that was 150 yards from the middle, hidden behind the MCC indoor school.

By tea, the Australians had been polished off for 190. Harmison had taken five wickets and the team were charging off like demented warriors. The MCC members were out of their seats with elation, some clearly risking a thrombosis, to give the team a rapturous reception as they returned through the Long Room.

In the media centre, the response was more muted (a journalist clapping is as rare as a solar eclipse), but at least those papers who had each sent five or six writers to cover this momentous event would have their worries about duplication soothed. There was enough material in that four hours of carnage to write a book. Tabloid columnists revelled in it. 'If they can't send over a better team than this, there's not much point in the Ashes,' one wrote. Another said, 'Maybe their women's team would like a game.'

Unfortunately, anything the England bowlers could do, Glenn McGrath could do better. With ruthless sangfroid, he burst England's bubble. A brilliant exponent of the Lord's slope, his relentless accuracy allied to a smidgen of movement cut England in half. They were soon 21 for 5. Vaughan, Bell and Flintoff were all bowled; the latter, walking rather uncertainly to the crease, out for a duck. 'Huh, I've waited seven years for that!' he grunted as he unstrapped his pads. Only Pietersen, batting as if he'd played Test cricket all his life, rather than for all of five hours, conjured a response. Having nudged and nurdled his way to 20, he slog-swept Warne and pulled Lee and got to 50 untroubled.

The following morning, with only the tail for company, he had the audacity to smite McGrath for a straight six onto the balcony of the pavilion, a shot as brilliantly shocking to the traditionalists within as Pietersen's ghastly streaked coif. He smeared Warne gloriously through the covers, then did the same to McGrath. England conceded the lead, but Pietersen had sounded the timpani.

Unfortunately, he brought his cymbals out onto the field, shelling a relatively simple chance from Michael Clarke when he was on 21 (one of seven chances England inexplicably put down). Clarke went on to make a match-transforming 91. In the hospitality area after play, the mood was morose. Those not inebriated were looking dejectedly at each other, imagining the usual nightmare unfolding. Dickie Bird roamed about declaring, 'Kevin Pietersen's just dropped the Ashes!' It was hard to disagree.

England, set a nominal 420 to win, folded after a promising start. Vaughan was bowled; Bell, advancing down the pitch to Warne accompanied by derisory hoots of 'Where's he going, on his holidays?' from round the bat, was soon suckered into shouldering arms; and a forlorn-looking Flintoff was duped by Warne's slider. He had made three runs in the match, to go with his four expensive wickets and one dropped catch. 'There were too many thoughts going on in my head and I just put myself under too much pressure,' he said later. 'I just wasn't myself.'

Pietersen again stood alone on the burning deck as the beautiful simplicity of Warne's art caused England's demise. They hung on until the fourth day, but then capitulated in a morass of hopelessness. None of the bottom four got off the mark and England were hammered by 234 runs.

'Here we go again' was the mournful cry, and those papers who'd been trumpeting England on the first day were quick to turn on them. 'Over the Hill ... and Far Away' was the *Daily Mail* headline, alluding to the Hoggard quotes. The *Sun* had 'Vaughan Again Losers'. In the *Daily Mirror*, Mike Walters wrote, 'You bunch of drips. England didn't just fluff their lines; they blew their screen test by succumbing with all the passion of eunuchs.' It was pretty savage.

The blunt truth was that, a dozen years since he had first come here, the man whose deliveries barely exceeded the speed of a milk float was still baffling us all. At Lord's Shane Warne confounded predictions, confounded expectations, occasionally even confounded the laws of geometry. Most significantly, he confounded the England batsmen. In most previous Ashes series he had arrived with a bag full of different deliveries: leg-breaks, top-spinners, googlies, flippers, zooters and sliders, one that was called the 'pickpocket' (it spun behind your legs) and another that nicked the off bail, whistled 'Waltzing Matilda' and then bobbled off to light the barbecue. Now, after careful monitoring, I decided his armoury had been distilled to a two-card trick: the big-turning leg-break and the straight-on slider. The problem was that none of the England batsmen, apart from Kevin Pietersen, appeared to be able to distinguish between them. And they only got the chance to try if they'd first managed to see off Glenn McGrath. Oh dear.

THE GREAT TURNAROUND

Mercifully, there was a ten-day break after Lord's. From England's point of view, a rethink was clearly needed. In the first Test the bowlers had done their job, but the batsmen, Pietersen excepted, had looked utterly overawed. The choice of a middle order, none of whom had ever played a Test against Australia – Bell, Pietersen, Flintoff and Jones – was seriously questioned. Encouragingly, though, the selectors held their nerve, echoing the famous order from captains of yesteryear: 'Same order; different batting!'

Undoubtedly, Pietersen had provided a ray of hope. His two displays of bravado had demonstrated that these great Australian bowlers could be tamed. Somehow, the other batsmen had to mirror his approach, if not his unorthodox technique. Pietersen himself was otherwise engaged, trapped between the sheets by *Big Brother*'s Vanessa, who then spilt the beans. 'He flashed around his middle stump, scored a duck in bed, then dropped me like a slip catch,' she was 'quoted' as saying. Flintoff, meanwhile, had escaped with his family to Bovey Castle, Devon, to do some hard thinking.

Inevitably, the Australians tried to intimidate England in the papers, with both McGrath and Ponting again predicting a whitewash. A raft of England players' columns appeared in reaction, mostly somewhat whiny, ye-of-little-faith type pieces. The Aussies must have been chuckling into their isotonic drinks. As usual, they had lit the blue touchpaper in the press and retreated a safe distance as the explosions went off in the England camp.

I watched England practise at Edgbaston on the Tuesday. There did seem to be a noticeable difference in their approach: they were giving Merlyn a bit of tap, and Flintoff was very positive. But having watched McGrath's metronomic accuracy in the Australian nets, and the energy and quality of their fielding drills (all fizzing throws and hollered encouragement), I was pessimistic. I could see the tourists going 2–0 up and then the runaway train would surge out of sight, as it usually did.

We all reckoned without Michael Vaughan's iron will and the freakish events on the first morning of the match. At 9.15 a.m. McGrath trod on a ball in fielding practice and was carted off to hospital. Forty-five minutes later, Ricky Ponting won the toss and put England in. It was a little overcast but the pitch was flat, and he had just lost his crackerjack fast bowler. His decision made no sense whatsoever. It was on a par with Tony Greig promising to 'make them grovel' ('them' being the 1976 West Indies of Holding, Roberts, *et al.*) as one of the most craven decisions in cricket history. Ponting's rationale must have been that this was the same old England, and that they'd lie down and die, whichever Okker was bowling.

That was an enormous miscalculation. Trescothick took 12 off Brett Lee's second over, which set the tone for the innings. Strauss was quickly up the pitch and belting Warne back over his head. They both laid into Jason Gillespie. Spared the law and order of McGrath, England batted as if on speed, frolicking in the middle, feasting on a liberal sprinkling of friendly deliveries. Bowling at Pietersen was like delivering at a revolving door; and Flintoff, having looked like a foal on roller-skates against Warne initially, eventually biffed an uncomplicated half-century with hooks off his nose. In the commentary box Greig loved it, crowing, 'Oh, Flintoff's hit that for another six ... and he's not even looking!'

If you live by the sword, you might die by it, and England lost wickets at regular intervals. Still, it was infinitely preferable to subsiding in a welter of pokes and prods as they had at Lord's, and 407 all out at five an over is pretty handy for a day's work. (Not so long ago, the average first-day Test match score was a soporific 240 for 4.) This followed the general trend for soaring run rates in Test cricket. Australia have rattled along at four an over for a decade or more, and other teams have followed suit. It parallels the general pace of life: faster, shorter, more concentrated. It's what people want: domination. These are the intimidatory batting years.

Australia tried their own brand of it when they batted, but it didn't come off. Vaughan's captaincy was clever – he set men on the cover boundary, for instance, to cut off fours and arrest the Australian bully-boy tactics – and the England attack was too persistent. The bowlers would not be cowed into submission and worked their way through the batting. Giles, who'd been clinically exposed at Lord's, had the satisfaction of trapping Ponting and Warne, going for a slog, and England engineered a precious lead of 99.

For England's second innings, Warne, still piqued by Ponting's decision to field first, reacted by urging on the quicks (the skipper stood about mainly looking nonplussed) and then producing a wonder ball out of the rough to bowl Strauss in the day's last over. It floated down innocently, pitching so wide it was barely on the cut strip, then spun wickedly almost at right angles to wave bye-bye to Strauss as he strolled unsuspectingly across his crease, intending to watch it pass harmlessly in front of him. Michael Slater laughed uproariously on commentary. The ball had turned so much it was almost comical. Hawkeye couldn't replicate it, pompously declaring that no ball could possibly spin to that extent. People were calling the delivery a 'double Gatt', although, as Gatting himself was now twice his former size, this was unnecessary.

I went up and congratulated Warne in our hotel bar later. 'That was incredible,' I said. 'You certainly keep my job interesting.'

He received my handshake in his big, strong mitt, and said, 'Thanks, Simon. I felt after the way we'd played, I had to make a statement and really turn a couple as much as I could.'

He thrives on people's appreciation – which is perhaps why he was in the bar, surrounded by admirers, rather than having an early night like the rest of the Aussies. He's also something of a stray, often conspicuous by his absence at team fielding sessions (partly because of being unable to throw). He was rather scathing about the team's batting, but reckoned they could chase 300 in the last innings.

In the end, England managed to set them a target of 282, largely thanks to the rejuvenated Flintoff, who clubbed four more sixes (making nine in the match). It was a phenomenal display of power that at one point featured all nine fielders on the rope, 'their mouths open like crocodiles at feeding time', wrote Michael Henderson, happily restored to press box action for *The Times*.

Australia set off confidently in pursuit, but Flintoff turned the tables with one of the most outstanding first overs ever in Test cricket. The first ball to Langer demanded a stroke; the second cannoned into the stumps via his forearm. The next two swung sharply into Ponting and rapped him on the pad; the fifth he edged to slip along the ground; the sixth, a no-ball, he left; the seventh swung away just enough to take the edge. Ambrose, McGrath nor Walsh could have bettered it.

England were held up by Michael Clarke, but Harmison produced a peach of a slower ball to bowl him with the last delivery of Saturday's play. Which left the position overnight as Australia needing 107, but England only needing two wickets. The result looked a foregone conclusion.

So how was it for you? The nerve-jangling, stomach-churning, breath-quickening, mouth-drying ninety-nine min-utes of Sunday's play? Nearly five million tuned in, so there's a good chance you were one of them. Behind the sofa for some of it? Couldn't watch? It was the same for me, sitting in Channel 4's VT truck. Except there was no sofa, and I had to watch every ball. There are eighty-odd screens in there, all showing the same damn thing.

We were distressed when Warne kept flaying wide balls through the covers or waltzing across his stumps to flick balls to midwicket. We were dismayed when Harmison seemed unable to find his rhythm. We were depressed when balls flew between Vaughan's carefully staggered slips. We were exultant when Warne finally trod on his wicket. We bayed at Flintoff when he bowled that yorker down the legside that went for four byes. We bawled at Harmison when he did the same. 'Don't let Geraint Jones anywhere near it!' someone said, alluding to his general fallibility.

But we still believed (or I did, anyway). Even when Australia required only 6 to win, I was blindly backing England, knowing that the summer – the England team's last on terrestrial telly – was over if they didn't. The Premiership was due to return the following weekend and take over the world. English cricket's obit writers had their pens poised.

Then it was 5 to win, then 4, and we could barely watch as Steve Harmison ran in and bowled a wide, juicy full toss to Brett Lee, who carved it through the covers. At that precise moment the match, the Ashes, and English cricket, that sideshow we'd endeavoured to save from obscurity these past seven years, had gone. Evaporated before our eyes. *Puff!* The urn was heading for Australia, probably for ever, and we were faced with an endless diet of Wayne Rooney and José Mourinho and three-in-a-bed 'roastings' from then on. But somehow Vaughan had managed to leave a man out for Lee's drive and the ball went straight to him. We breathed again, though we knew it was just a stay of execution.

But then, oh joy, Harmison speared one in towards Kasprowicz's throat, and Jones took the sprawling catch. The dismissal was a reprise of the Jonny Wilkinson drop goal in Sydney, stealing victory from the jaws of defeat. England had won on willpower; the Ashes were alive again. Cricket had been given a lifeline and so had we on Channel 4 after one of the greatest Test matches of all time.

The sensation I felt afterwards was like that feeling you get when you go over a hump-backed bridge, multiplied by ten. Sickness and euphoria combined. The enduring image, though, was of Flintoff consoling Lee moments after England had won: two prize heavyweights who had been grappling with each other for four days in a tender embrace. Flintoff's England had won ... just; Lee's Australia had lost. But victor and vanquished lingered as one at the end – Flintoff misty-eyed, Lee distraught – in a classic vision of sporting solidarity. Flintoff did not do this for show. He recognised in Lee a kindred spirit, someone who gives his absolute all but whose quest for success does not override his respect for his fellow man. In that instant, Flintoff became cast-iron favourite for BBC Sports Personality of the Year ... and a good man to be making a DVD with.

'INFREDIBLE!' screamed the back page of the *Sun* on the Monday. Inside it was 'Salvation Harmy'. The punning subs were having a field day. The following day the same paper devoted its front page (as well as pages six and seven) to Flintoff, 'Beero to Hero', declaring that he had given up the sauce in an attempt to help England regain the Ashes. An editorial said, 'Is Flintoff the new Botham? No. And for one good reason. You'd never have caught Beefy on a diet and having a quiet night in.'

The *Guardian* printed a huge picture of Flintoff celebrating in front of the crowd, over which was inscribed, in 'Affectionate Celebration of English Cricket which was reborn at Edgbaston on 7 August 2005'.

When he went to his local supermarket in Knutsford that night, Britain's new sporting hero was mobbed by his neighbours.

ONE SHORT

There was little time to draw breath. Three days later, the Old Trafford Test began. On the way up to Manchester a Channel 4 commentary eleven, augmented by the England manager Phil Neale, the ex-Aussie quick Geoff Lawson and various pals of Mark Nicholas, played a match in Shropshire in aid of sufferers of cystic fibrosis. A large crowd turned up to see Atherton caught at slip for 8, Neale taken at cover for a duck, Slater and Nicholas help themselves off some buffet bowling, and me dish up some friendly fare to a rather good young Pakistani. Atherton, loitering at slip, wondered aloud if I was Jason Gillespie in disguise.

Back to the real melodrama at Old Trafford, there was a shock even before the start of play. McGrath, whom I'd last seen hobbling about on Sunday in the team hotel looking for his Zimmer frame, had been declared fit. Australian cricketers were like cockroaches: you could damage their legs or cuff them on the head, but you couldn't crush them. Their spirit was unbreakable. Still, there was a hint of desperation in the way they'd rushed their half-fit main man back so soon.

The decision backfired as Australia lost the toss and were asked to field. Although McGrath's first over was immaculate, and he was unlucky with dropped catches, he finished the day weary and wicketless. Before the game there had been question marks over Vaughan's batting, largely because he'd been clean-bowled three times out of four. Some queried his method. A man of exceptional self-confidence, he had no such doubts, and on the higher-bouncing, almost Australian-style Old Trafford pitch, he made a masterful hundred. 'Technique's a load of bollocks!' he quipped to me later, more evidence that England had completely shed their cumbersome baggage of old-fashioned correctness.

Vaughan was aided by Ponting's strange reluctance to bring on Warne until the England skipper had rattled past 50. Rumours of a row between the two Aussies at Edgbaston after the toss saga were gaining credence. Dissent towards the captain? It all just added to the leg-spinner's mystique. But his attitude to his team-mates has never been straightforward: for instance, it's common knowledge that he's never seen eye to eye with Adam Gilchrist, even though they stand next to each in the field all day and bat together in most matches.

The England bowlers, with the ball roughed up on Old Trafford's abrasive surface and swinging beautifully, worked their way through the uncertain Australians. Flintoff and Jones were running up to bowl covering the ball with one hand so the batsmen couldn't tell which way it might move. Shades of Waqar and Wasim in their heyday. I got a bit overexcited illustrating swing in the VT truck, resulting in some botched drawing on the screen for which I apologised. Benaud came to my rescue with another of his 'Even Picasso used to struggle at weekends' lines. I always tended to be at my most enthusiastic when Benaud was commentating, hunting for comparisons or technical stuff, knowing he would be interested. He'd always been a massive inspiration that way.

Strauss and Trescothick took toll of the ravaged Australian bowlers and England built a massive lead, watched by both

Roy Keane and Alex Ferguson. The latter confessed cricket was 'upstaging the Premiership' and was underlining his mantra that 'youth does not know any fear'.

There were unprecedented scenes outside the ground at 8.30 on the morning of the fifth day. The queue for the £10 tickets stretched halfway back to the city centre. The traffic was gridlocked. Flintoff, travelling from home, had to drive down a cordoned-off street to get to the ground in time, incurring the wrath of a local traffic cop. 'Look, just give me a ticket, anything, I don't care, just let me get to the ground,' Freddie pleaded.

I was in a car with Tony Greig, stuck a stone's throw from Old Trafford. 'We've got to get in to do the telecarst!' Greig told the bobby on duty. We were waved back into the jam like everybody else. We got in eventually, but the masses weren't so lucky. The gates were locked at 9.30 a.m., leaving 17,000 people to make their way home. 'I haven't seen this since the 1970s when Lancashire were in their pomp,' crooned an elderly steward. 'Nowadays we have to lock 'em in!'

The England team were given a standing ovation when they emerged for their warm-up. There was a smaller one for Ian Botham when he came out to do his pitch report. Warne was whistled at, and there were loud calls of 'Where's your caravan?' to the long-haired, hirsute Gillespie as he made his way to the nets.

It was another day of unremitting tension. Everyone was gripped. The England bowlers executed their plans, but Ponting defied everything they threw at him with determination hewn from granite. It was a monolith of an innings as wickets tumbled around him. When eventually he gloved a lifter from Harmison, umpire Billy Bowden briefly looked on in sympathy before giving him the crooked finger of doom.

That gave England four overs to take the last wicket and go 2–1 up in the series. Despite the will of the 21,000 people in the ground and an extraordinary 7.7 million watching on TV (including my not-cricket-mad mother-in-law), they couldn't do it. Flintoff, immense all day, was exhausted; Jones went off with cramp; and Harmison just could not find the spark to make lightning strike twice in eight days. "E's joost not bowling in the corridor of uncertainty,' lamented Boycott. 'My whole life's a corridor of uncertainty!' remarked Tiny, the colossal figure in the VT truck manning one of the replay angles. When Lee successfully negotiated the final delivery, the Aussies rose as one on the balcony in a collective sigh of relief. Vaughan, a keen observer of body language, drew his team into a huddle, and, indicating this clear reduction in Australian ambition – celebrating a draw – pronounced that they were there for the taking.

The match finished just before 7 p.m., giving me an hour to write something vaguely intelligible for the *Telegraph*. The VT truck was being dismantled as I sat, monitors being unplugged on one side, wires pulled out on the other, people and props moving in all directions, so concentration was hard. It was like sitting in a large sandcastle being systematically destroyed by the incoming tide. The tension of the match was almost replicated by the pressure of meeting my deadline.

Journeying back from the match with Atherton, we encountered two families at an M6 service station who had also attended it. One had driven up in the early hours from the Sussex coast just to see the final day; the other from some remote part of Essex. They had been among the 40,000 who had queued up from before dawn to get tickets.

Many, we noticed, had been in the 18–30 age group; people who, we are assured by the marketers, are only interested in football, electronic gimmicks and reality TV. That they, and the seven-million-plus viewers who tuned in to the play on Channel 4, were attracted by an event which lasts for hours, and doesn't feature loud music, cheerleaders, gaudy coloured strips or groping in a Jacuzzi, was an interesting development in our instant-gratification era.

There were all sorts of reasons why: the advent of Twenty-20 cricket, a new generation of super-dominant batsmen, the creation of genuine, accessible stars – Flintoff and Vaughan, who both combine fabulous talent with earthy humour, the freak show which is Kevin Pietersen, and Steve Harmison, the reluctant hero. They live relatively normal lives, share the childcare, are not prone to wife-beating or fighting in night-clubs, drive smart but everyday cars rather than pretentious Hummers or Ferraris, and don't earn 245 times the national wage (as, for instance, does Rio Ferdinand).

But most of all, cricket's rejuvenation was due to England at last having a realistic expectation of winning the Ashes. This competition is special: England versus Australia over a five-Test series, a summer-long dispute between intransigent fathers and impudent sons that has prevailed for 130 years. Since 1989, the impudent sons had prevailed, and all home Ashes series had been decided by mid-August or earlier. Interest had waned. But with eighteen months of English success, a storming start to the summer, and oppo-nents whose impudence was turning into intransigence, this had had top billing all the way. Rarely can a show have exceeded such outrageous hype. And there was more to come ...

ASHLEY'S ASHES?

First, though, a much more important matter: the announce-ment of the commentary dream team by the *Wisden Cricketer* magazine. They'd had 12,000 respondents (reports that 3000 of them were from Mark Nicholas's mum were dismissed) and the lines were now closed. Richie Benaud coasted home with an incredible 10,128 votes, followed by Michael Holding, Geoff Boycott, David Gower, Mark Nicholas and Ian Botham.

Rumours were circulating that a Murdoch big cheese was trying to persuade Sky to hire Richie for 2006, but the great man rebuffed them, declaring he was a 'free-to-air man'. He added, 'All I'm interested in is making this Channel 4's best ever year. I might drop off the tweak tomorrow, so next year might not matter.'

I contented myself with the thought that people didn't really regard me as a commentator, but I got a few votes in the poll and finished ninth. 'Release him from his tin box into the light of day!' wrote one Nicola Flintham, though I wasn't sure if this was encouraging someone to hire me as a commentator or as a landscape gardener.

A couple of columns suggested Sky should snap me up, which was kind. Frankly, I had no idea what the future held. I enjoyed the whole business of explaining the game on TV. I particularly relished showing a batsman's growing neurosis during a series as he continued to get out in a similar way or to the same bowler. The beauty of a five-Test series is in the way it contorts the players' minds. Time reveals the man. But whether Sky, or whoever produced Channel 5's highlights, wanted someone as a sort of sieve, to refine all the material generated by the VT truck, I did not know.

I had pitched a programme idea to Channel 4 based on a village team that I would try to nurture through a season, uncovering the soap opera of village life along the way. But the channel said it would only work if the team contained a coke addict and/or a sexual deviant that redefined the term reverse swing.

There was a ten-day break before the fourth Test. All the England players were given the week off, which, unbelievably, was criticised by some county chairmen who had hoped to have their stars available for the Cheltenham and Gloucester semi-finals. These, of course, were the same stars whose unstinting efforts against Australia were captivating the whole country, and vitally raising the game's profile. These blazered killjoys are a walking definition of 'tunnel vision'.

At the Test, the Channel 4 team were billeted in the same Nottingham hotel as the Australians, and it was quite revealing observing them at breakfast. This team was a changed beast. No more were these men chomping on raw beefsteak while salivating over the prospect of dismembering England again. Now, after their humbling experiences, they were meeker, milder, eating fruit and yoghurt – a survival diet. The hunters had become the hunted.

You could see that in their approach on the first day. Deprived of the services of McGrath (elbow injury) and Gillespie (dropped), they were sitting back and waiting for England to make mistakes, rather than pursuing them aggressively. Ponting himself had a trundle, trying to tempt the batsmen into an indiscretion. To underline the fantasy of this Ashes contest, their two great spearheads of series past, McGrath and Gillespie – now twelfth and thirteenth men – emerged from the pavilion at 6 p.m. bearing tea and crumpets for the weary players. (Australians rarely say no to a bit of crumpet, although it was noticeable that on this occasion Shane Warne abstained.) Imagine what the odds would have been on that sight two months earlier.

To cap a bizarre day, two England fans in replica shirts fell out of the top deck of a moving bus and toppled onto the road outside the Nottingham restaurant where I was eating with Derek Pringle and assorted producers. Dazed and confused, they looked about them, at our astonished faces, at the shattered remains of the bus window, then picked themselves up and wandered off into the night. Like the team, these England supporters, who'd lived through years of thin and thinner, were made of strong stuff.

In the morning Flintoff, resuming on 8 not out and fortified by his dressing-room rendition of 'Rocket Man' and 'Maggie May', played his most responsible and best-thought-out innings in an England shirt. He defended stoutly, but missed no opportunities to score, employing the straightest of blades to bunt balls back past the bowler along the ground with wincing power. A proud, contented smile broke out across his face as he reached three figures against Australia for the first time, a poignant contrast to his exultant, vein-bulging celebration after taking an important wicket. He and the busy, but equally measured, Geraint Jones fashioned a partnership of 177, the highest for either side in the series.

Buoyed by the total of 477 and some old-fashioned swing, the England bowlers ran in with gusto, and for the Australian batsmen it was only a matter of time before they made a fatal mistake or were undone by a dubious decision. They were under siege from the England pace attack, the umpires, the press, the public. It's uncanny in sport how, once the tide has turned, misfortune descends in torrents.

Channel 4's Friday lunchtime contribution to the entertainment was a batting 'masterclass' featuring Michael Slater and Geoff Boycott. Wearing his golf spikes, Boycott gave a monologue about uncovered pitches and the intricacies of defence which inadvertently illustrated how the game has moved on. Slater managed to butt in occasionally and demonstrate the attacking priorities of modern batsmen who look, first and foremost, to dominate.

A veil was drawn over the session until Tony Greig, commentating with Boycott later, revisited it. 'You looked as if you were taking part in a bowls competition, Fiery,' he said mischievously. 'Noo, those were my cricket whites,' Boycott replied, 'and at least I can still get into my old gear, Greigy!' Their good-natured little spats had spiced up the commentary this summer, but while Boycott continued to be perceptive with a slick turn of phrase, he did still have an I-problem. As in, 'Well, I always used to be good in these situations' or 'I'd play Warne fine: joost block 'im out and get me roons the other end.' He seems incapable of not referring everything back to himself.

There were lots of interesting deliveries and overs to analyse, and I had a field day in the VT truck, magnifying images of contentious LBW decisions, or illustrating Matthew Hayden's inflexible footwork. At one point Atherton handed to me, chuckling: 'And now down to Simon Hughes for another interruption.'

On Saturday England, largely through Simon Jones, ran through the last five Australian wickets, and asked them to bat again. Repeat: to bat again. When England last enforced the follow-on against Australia, a seventeen-year-old Boris Becker had just won Wimbledon, Dennis Taylor had beaten Steve Davis to become world snooker champion (watched by 18.5 million on TV) and Jim Davidson was probably attending the birth of his third wife. Ian Bell had just completed his potty training.

Tempers frayed when Jones then limped off with an ankle injury and Ponting was run out by the substitute fielder Gary Pratt. England had frequently used subs during the series when bowlers, having taken on a lot of fluid during their spells, nipped off to the toilet at the end of one. The Australians had privately taken exception to this, declaring it was 'against the spirit of the game'. Ponting was positively steaming, letting fly a stream of invective at the England balcony as he returned to the pavilion. It was a symptom of the pressure he was under, invoked by England's relentless provocation. Anyway, what were the bowlers supposed to do? Have Portaloos installed on the long-leg boundary?

Sunday was a gut-wrenching experience. Bogus stories about Flintoff ball-tampering were circulating in the press first thing. 'How could I with these?!' he exclaimed, illustrating his fingernails bitten to the quick. He would have struggled to tamper with a fur ball with them.

He was bowling when a beleaguered Gilchrist emerged on the stroke of lunch. Australia had just nosed in front, but five wickets were down. It was a brief, scene-stealing duel, as the wounded cowboy stormed out all guns blazing for freedom, trying to give every ball some tap. Having partially succeeded, he walked in front of a Hoggard delivery soon after lunch. At that point, Australia, 277 for 6, led by only 18. Largely through Warne, they eventually left England 129 to take a 2–1 lead into the fifth Test.

It was a situation of unimaginable potential prominence, given the events of Lord's only four weeks previously, and one or two England batsmen suffered an attack of stage fright. Not Trescothick or Strauss, but certainly Bell (caught hooking) and probably Pietersen, though all his innings are so frenetic it's hard to tell. Never was there a more unsuitable person to be sponsored by Red Bull. Before he goes out to bat he'd be far better off drinking Night Nurse.

Warne, belatedly introduced after five overs (by which time the score was 32 for 0), stood between England and victory. It is a measure of his extraordinary prowess that he almost pulled off an outlandish upset. Australia had been outplayed for most of the past three weeks, and yet with England tottering at 116 for 7, the dressing room in upheaval and the nation chewing its collective knuckles, the Ashes were within his grasp. If Warne took the last three wickets and Australia won, England could only level the series, and the urn would (metaphorically) remain Down Under. All those weeks of English travail potentially nullified by three spinning lobs.

So it was that Ashley Giles, a useful batsman but previously utterly clueless against Warne, was joined in the middle by Matthew Hoggard, whose range of strokes could be written on a postage stamp ... with room to spare. Thirteen were needed. Warne twirled the ball from hand to hand, the fielders hovered around the bat like vultures, Gilchrist was in full voice through my earpiece via the stump mikes: 'Come on, Shane! We're owed one dodgy decision here. Come on, lads.' 'Not exactly in the spirit of cricket, that,' Duncan Fletcher later observed dryly.

Oddly, tail-enders experience a kind of serenity out in the middle in such crises. You have the potential for control at the crease which is denied the nervous wrecks in the dressing room. It imbues certain types with a powerful self-belief. And the great thing about this England side is that, over the last eighteen months, someone always comes up trumps. Giles suddenly handled Warne with aplomb. Hoggard dredged a cover drive out of his teenage memory bank with 8 to win, jabbing Lee's wide full toss to the boundary. If Lee had done the same with 4 to win at Edgbaston, the Ashes would now be Australia's. That was the magic of this series: the outcome hanging on two balls. When Giles, who'd gone visibly greyer in the last few weeks, stroked Warne towards the midwicket boundary, England had done it. They'd exorcised their Lord's demons, come back from the dead and won two out of the last three. The Ashes were within their grasp.

Yet, as Benaud pointed out, the Australians could still retain them, despite being outplayed in each of the last three Tests, if they won at The Oval. Über-resilience courses through their veins. Their body might be dangling over the edge of the cliff, but you still had to prise every last fingernail from the rock before it would fall. For the last sixteen years they'd had an octopus-like grip on the Ashes. There was still much tentacle-pulling to be done.

CHAPTER 18 – The Final Test

'Phew! What a Torture' declared the front page of the *Sun* the next morning. The result of the fourth Test took over the back page as well – 'Ash 'n' Grab' – and five pages inside, booting the weekend's football into the unread hinterland. The *Mirror*'s back page declared, 'The Ashes Are Coming Home'. Four weeks earlier, in the same paper, you might remember, England had been denounced as 'a bunch of drips'.

It was announced that 8.4 million people had watched the conclusion of the Trent Bridge match. This was wondrous news. It was ultimate fulfilment for those of us who'd maintained, in the face of mounting resistance over the years, that cricket, and in particular Test cricket, was the greatest game. The nation was at last savouring its unique ingredients and the special nature of the Ashes. The final Test was billed as the most important sporting event in England since the 1966 World Cup final. For the first time in a generation, the country was gripped by cricket fever.

I kept a diary of the days leading up to the grand finale.

Tuesday 30 August

Main issue seems to be getting Simon Jones fit so that England can field an unchanged side all summer for the first time since about 1066. He is being placed in an oxygen chamber several times a day in an attempt to get him fit. Everyone has a suggestion as to who might replace him. Tremlett, Anderson, Collingwood, Gough, even Caddick are all mentioned.

Reflecting on the series so far, I've come to the conclusion that the Australians totally underestimated England. Here's the evidence:

Channel 9, long-time home of Australian cricket, not bothering to bid for the home rights to this series, not perceiving it as a decent contest;

current and ex-Australian players dismissing England's chances out of hand (Ponting and McGrath talked of a 5–0 whitewash after Lord's);

Australia arriving without specialist batting or bowling coaches (John Buchanan was more of a strategist). Perhaps that's why they weren't able to accept the obvious decline in Hayden's batting or Gillespie's bowling ('They'll come right, mate') or to recognise the option of playing five bowlers ('Four have always been ample in the past');

Australia having virtually a week off before Edgbaston and then putting England in, assuming they would just lie down. There was no sense in their camp at that point that the Ashes was going to be anything other than a routine extermination of English endeavour. England had lasered in expertly on their general inflexibility, continually getting various batsmen out the same way, for instance. The Australians had Plan A, but no Plan B. Generally, they had been taken aback by an unexpectedly ruthless, confrontational England, and didn't know how to respond.

We staged our own mini-Test in the afternoon in my parents' garden – the very place I first staged my imaginary Ashes Tests aged ten. My eighty-three-year-old dad still coaches the Ealing Under-17s up the road (when not tending his nasturtiums). Fantastic. Augmenting our three kids were my sister Bettany's two girls, and three-year-old Josh Atherton. Despite the mysteries of my underarms, and the efforts of our youngest Billy (2½) with an action vaguely reminiscent of Muralitharan (a chuck that turns a bit), none of us could dismiss Atherton (Jnr). *Plus ça change*.

Wednesday 31 August

Ashes mania. Cricket is all over the papers and the airwaves, with countdowns to 'the biggest cricket match in history', long-range weather predictions for The Oval and huge Flintoff spreads everywhere. The state of Simon Jones's ankle has become a matter of national concern, like Beckham and his metatarsal a couple of years ago. There's a girl's guide to cricket in *Sun Woman*, and four columns of anti-Aussie jokes on the comment page, including one – 'Why don't the Australians need vaccinations before going on tour?' 'Because they're never likely to catch anything' – which traditionally was used after England's hapless efforts Down Under.

The *Independent* had a big piece entitled 'Is Cricket the New Football?' Hope not. We don't want our sport invaded by mercenaries, crooks and morons, and Alan Green exclaiming patronisingly on the radio: 'Stone the crows, what *was* he thinking?'

Thursday 1 September

Got a call from the *Telegraph* features desk asking about the England players' wives. Who were they, what were they like? They're certainly a more conspicuous group now, confident and independent (Rachael Flintoff runs her own marketing company, Ruth Strauss is an actress). They're much better looked after, too. They are given seats and properly catered for and a nanny is provided to help look after the kids. Contrast that with a decade ago when administrators regarded them as an encumbrance, players had to pay for their flights abroad and arrange their accommodation, and Ray

Illingworth virtually blamed England's loss of a series in South Africa on the arrival of the players' families for Christmas.

Friday 2 September

To our production company, Sunset and Vine, in Piccadilly, to plan my last Jargonbuster slots for lunchtimes in the fifth Test. All the match tapes of previous Tests are stored here, but most are being used, either for the Saturday *Cricket Show* or for any of five DVDs the company have been suddenly asked to cobble together to commemorate the series. One is the official ECB version, another is to be given away free with the *Telegraph* and another is for the *News of the World*, on which, it is suggested, the action could be interspersed with girls frolicking topless on a beach.

Pop into the Benauds' London hotel, the Montcalm, set back from the road in an elegant Georgian terrace a stone's throw from Marble Arch. They've been coming here for years and always stay in the same room. They've even had extra phone points installed so that both he and Daphne can be online when they're in residence. It's not a lavish place, but it's comfily furnished with chintzy armchairs and highly polished mahogany furniture. Like its famous occupants, it exudes calm and dignity. It's from here that the Benauds set off for their daily half-hour walk every morning at 6 a.m. prompt.

At the Cricket Writers' Club's annual dinner at the Intercontinental hotel that evening, the former *Telegraph* man Brian Oliver, now sports editor of the *Observer*, is one of several offering some kind words about Channel 4's cricket coverage, and asking what my future plans are (I'm still in the dark). He says if Australia crumble at The Oval, next Sunday's headline will be: 'Can't Bat, Can't Bowl, Can't Field'.

Saturday 3 September

The Cheltenham and Gloucester final at Lord's between Hampshire and Warwickshire. Standing in the middle, I'm savouring the atmosphere as the ground fills up, and it suddenly dawns on me that it is twenty-five years since my first major match here, the Gillette Cup final between Middlesex and Surrey. I, a twenty-year-old novice, pitched in among eighteen internationals, including such luminaries as Mike Brearley, Mike Gatting, the giant South African Vincent van der Bijl as well as the two fearsome West Indians Sylvester Clarke and Wayne Daniel. Not bad value for a £7 ticket (now it's about £40).

Nic Pothas, born in Johannesburg but a non-overseas player by virtue of his Greek passport, was opening the batting for Hampshire. I got a camera to follow his movements at the non-striker's end, knowing he had a strange affectation for stepping over the creases between balls. 'His superstitions also extend,' I said on air, 'to wearing different coloured underpants according to what he's doing. Green when he's batting, red when he's keeping and yellow when he's training.'

'And if he's about to face Frank Tyson or a fast bowler of that nature,' Benaud replied, 'they'll be a lighter shade of brown.'

It was Richie's last day of commentary at Lord's, and he enthusiastically read out some emails from viewers recounting their experiences of the Test series. Two were from church organists who had been playing at evensong. One received a text message informing him of the Trent Bridge result – 'A text in church!' Richie exclaimed – and reported cheering in the congregation. The other was listening to the match through an earpiece, and, when England won, he began playing the 'Hallelujah' chorus. One email was from Stephen Fry who declared that the trauma of watching the Edgbaston Test had taken seven years off his life – 'Do I sue the ECB or the ICC?' – and that he would be at The Oval, as long as 'a cardiac defibrillator and oxygen are provided'.

Sunday 4 September

The *Observer* reports that a ticket for The Oval has been sold on eBay for £1200, and that the *Sun* has rented a penthouse overlooking the ground for a week at £20,000. At Chelmsford Essex had hammered the Australians for 500, who replied in kind with 561 for 6. Matthew Hayden made 150. Asked afterwards whether he had been examining tapes of his dismissals in the Tests, he said matter-of-factly, 'No, I leave that to Simon Hughes.'

Monday 5 September

The news on Simon Jones is promising. Atherton has been on the phone to Duncan Fletcher, who thinks he'll play. Meanwhile, the ECB have booked Trafalgar Square for the day after the Test if England win the Ashes. They have stuck two fingers up to their current TV partners Channel 4 and Sky and sold the coverage of the parade to the BBC. They are cold-hearted mercenaries.

Monday afternoon finds me at my old club Ealing with Kevin Pietersen. His sponsors Red Bull have some PR time with him and asked me if I wanted to use it for a *Telegraph* article. With my masochistic head on I have suggested bowling at him. I had never conceded more than 16 runs off an over (I was lucky to retire before the advent of Twenty-20) and now it was time to join the real world. I set him a target of 24, fully expecting him to get it.

He is some sight at the crease, six foot four inches tall with a cut torso and arms to his knees. With a huge backlift and extravagant follow-through he assaults the ball like Tiger Woods. It had been said for some time before this summer that the way to play these Australian bowlers was to take them on. Pietersen, the 114th player to be tried by England since the Ashes triumphs of 1987, had been the man who put it into practice and proved it could work. More or less ever since, English batsmen have drunk from that vat of encouragement.

As it happened, he failed my challenge miserably (the pitch was a bit mischievous and his bat was rubbish), managing only one straight six and a solitary edged boundary. He did promise, however, to be ultra-aggressive against his mate Warne in the Test match. 'I know I'm going to try to score off every ball against him,' I quoted him saying in the piece. 'He thrives on trying to build up pressure and I won't let him do that to me.'

'Go for it, Kev,' I said.

Tuesday 6 September

Simon Jones is ruled out. At England practice Pietersen is knocking balls over The Oval's new OCS Stand and my phone is ringing incessantly with people wanting to interview me about the game. There's even a call from a South African TV station who had been taking Channel 4's feed, including me doodling in the van, and were declaring that I had cult status. Guess I'm cricket's version of David Bellamy, popping out from the 'shwubberwy' (a nest of TV screens) to pronounce on some strange new discovery.

Stood next to the nets with Atherton and his son Josh. Freddie wandered over after his net and had a chat. A doting father, he took genuine interest in Josh, going out of his way to fetch a ball so they could bowl to each other. He said he'd been followed by paparazzi the last few days (as had Rachael), and they were camped outside his door when he got home after Trent Bridge. 'If you win, you'd better get used to it,' Athers said.

The England bowling coach, Troy Cooley, a Tasmanian, is

putting the bowlers through their paces as he has done practically every morning for two years. He is one of the largely
hidden reasons for the team's success, forever patiently hon-
ing their techniques and refining their strategies. He has
formed a little clan with the quickmen, who find his knowledge and quiet counsel invaluable, and are less enamoured of
the more batting-orientated Duncan Fletcher. One of their
number apparently trashed his hotel room on tour, after a
minor disagreement.

Wednesday 7 September

The *Sun* previews the final Test with a piece entitled 'It's Not
All Over 'til the Fat Laddie Spins'. *The Times* has a special
Ashes pull-out with caricatures of the commentators, partly
because it's Benaud's (and terrestrial TV's) last Test. I look
like a rodent and am described as having 'the drawn look of
someone who has been cooped up indoors staring at a
screen'. Actually, I look like that because our Billy keeps getting up at five o'clock in the morning.

Radio 5 Live, the football channel, seem to have devoted
their entire morning airtime to the Ashes and the future of
cricket on TV. *Eureka!* Cricket's at last getting some real
recognition. In the *Telegraph* it has eclipsed the preview to
England's World Cup qualifier with Northern Ireland. Betfair
have a market on what Richie's final line of commentary will
be. 'That's the view from the Betfair Blimp' is 50 to 1.

Attend Vaughan's pre-match press conference, a
Wednesday-morning routine. He talks about the importance
of going out and enjoying the game. One of the journos
admits he was so nervous at Trent Bridge he could hardly
watch. 'Nervous, you?' says Vaughan uncomprehendingly.

'It's far worse watching than competing!' I say. 'You wait
till your daughter's six and she's competing in the school sack
race.' He nods in acknowledgement.

For the last time, the Sunset and Vine roadies are assembling the broadcast facilities out the back of the new stand. Plugging in wires, doing sound checks, camera checks (there are twenty-six in all), correlating Hawkeye, sorting out the set for the in-vision studio. The whole production is supervised by a Scot, Dougie, and though he looks frazzled, for once it's ahead of schedule. Everything's sorted and ready to go a day early rather than the usual two minutes before we go on air.

There are boxes of tapes strewn everywhere, vital for the various retrospectives that we're doing through the match. Jules, a VT editor, is cutting the series DVD with 'Geez', the highlights editor, in a small cubicle to one end of the main broadcast truck. They are both chuckling about a Channel 4 trailer for *Bremner, Bird and Fortune*, featuring Rory Bremner imitating 'the Analyst', with a split screen of the real Tony Blair and an impostor. 'Yozzer, you've finally made it!' says Jules.

Thursday 8 September

The first day of the final Test. Huge anticipation. England are poised to win the Ashes for the first time since 1987, it is the last sight of live cricket on terrestrial TV after more than fifty years of uninterrupted coverage, and it's Richie Benaud's final match commentating on British television.

England were humbled 1–0 by Northern Ireland last night and the *Sun* divides its front page in two. The top half proclaims, 'Ashes Heroes' and contains a pledge from Freddie that the team will leave no stone unturned. The bottom half is headlined, 'Taxi for Eriksson'. The rest of the papers are full of 'Ashes coming home' stuff, which must put the players under almost intolerable pressure to deliver.

I'm at the ground early (8 a.m.) to put together a pre-match piece looking back at key moments of the series and projecting ahead. I take extra time assembling the material – wickets, close-ups, graphics – not wanting to let the side down at our last match. I cut it too fine and end up garbling for a minute and a half.

Vaughan wins the toss and bats. It's a sign, and the country can breathe its first collective sigh of relief. I don't think many could take another dose of Warne bowling on a last-day pitch with the Ashes at stake. Paul Collingwood makes up the eleven and the England batsmen do just enough in the face of another virtuoso display by Warne, who winkles out the middle order with some clever top-spinners and changes of angle. Andrew Strauss remains unruffled to record his second century of the series, although Warne is still referring to him as 'Daryll' (after his favourite bunny, South African Daryll Cullinan). Flintoff contributes a forceful 72.

Go out for dinner with friends including Nasser Hussain, whose contribution at the outset of this England revival should not be forgotten. Mind you, I'm not going to tell him that, since he's in an argumentative mood and keeps his baseball cap on throughout the meal. He does encourage me to try my luck with Sky, though, pointing out that there are probably five times as many people watching their transmission of the series (100 million in India?) than in the rest of the world combined. It's been reported that one man's been following it on his laptop in the Malaysian jungle.

Friday 9 September

Extraordinary crowds outside The Oval. With the extra security, it takes an age to get them all in. People are hugely complimentary about Channel 4 as they pass, as if we've found a cure for ugliness or something. At lunch the commentators gather on the spectacular roof terrace of the new stand to present our 'moments' of the Channel 4 years. These range from Hussain's England being booed on the balcony at The Oval in 1999 (Atherton argued that it set in motion central contracts, the launch of the Cricket Academy and Fletcher's induction as coach) through England beating the West Indies at Lord's in 2000 (Benaud), Vaughan's emergence in 2002 (Nicholas), to Flintoff's coming of age with his 95 against South Africa at The Oval in 2003 (me).

On the field Langer and Hayden have replied to England's slightly disappointing 373 with their first century opening partnership of the series. Then they go off for bad light, declaring they are apprehensive of facing Flintoff in those conditions. It's a measure of his impact that he's turned ruthless champions into retreating also-rans. Dylan, the highlights editor, wants a little piece from me in the programme focusing on that. It leaves me about forty minutes to write my daily newspaper piece before the subs go ballistic. It's disconnected, cliché-ridden garbage. How do people like Simon Barnes and Paul Hayward produce such polished prose under similar pressure? Beats me.

Saturday 10 September

It's fancy dress day, and, walking from the truck to the middle, I'm hailed as 'the Analyst' by two men in the Botham and Lamb costumes from the Meat Marketing Board ads, and a bunch who've come as the Oompaloompas. Sneaking back round the boundary at the start of play someone in the front row beckons me over. It's the comedian Frank Skinner. 'Better get back inside or you might miss something!' he says. He's right, too: you can't take your eye off this duel for a second.

In fact, the match is constantly interrupted by rain and I'm on and off the pitch doing weather reports. During one of the breaks in play I manage to get a piece on air about the way players' footwear has evolved. It's just an excuse to highlight the holes in the soles of Atherton's shoes that I spied when he was walking away from the camera yesterday. They obviously don't have cobblers in his bit of Notting Hill.

There is a Benaud tribute at lunchtime, following him

about for the last week at book launches and the like. Essentially quite a private man, he was slightly uneasy about the idea of wearing a microphone as he wandered about meeting and greeting. As with his commentary, he is not one for idle chatter, or vague pronouncements, preferring to be in charge of what he says. He rarely offers an opinion in public. Television commentary – picking up his mike to deliver his words of wisdom, before replacing it on the desk – is his ideal controlled environment. The incessant babble of radio is not his cup of tea. He is a creature of habit, underlined by his revelation that he has seen the musical *Cats* twenty-six times.

My Jargonbusting slot is 'Benaudisms', revisiting his favourite words – including mullygrubber and gazunder (balls that keep low), leg-cutter, Dorothy (Dix – six), and she-mozzle. His greatest piece of commentary this summer was when England took that last wicket at Edgbaston. It was typically simple and to the point: 'Jones! ... Bowden! ... Kasprowicz – the man to go. Harmison has done it. Despair ... on the faces of the batsmen. Joy ... for every England player on the field.'

Australia end the day dangerously poised at 277 for 2.

Sunday 11 September

A sensational spell from Flintoff throughout the damp, gloomy morning, sustained, he says afterwards, by drinking Red Bull, cuts a swathe through Australia's batting. He really has the bit between his teeth and, ably supported by the unheralded yeoman Hoggard, his eighteen overs on the trot give England a slight, unexpected lead. Hayden even mouths 'Well bowled' to Flintoff as he walks off. These Aussies have gone soft. Now all England have to do is bat them out of the game.

They are aided by more inclement weather, resulting in an endless procession of people round the VT truck during the breaks wanting to see where it all happens. I feel like a museum exhibit. Gav, the tolerant VT director, has just about had enough when in walks my old classmate Hugh Grant, accompanied by a horde of kids (nephews, Jemima Khan's sons, etc.). It's a good fifteen years since we last met, and he seems fascinated by all the technology and the way that we can rustle up a wicket from a previous match in five seconds. I invite the lollipop-thin Jemima to pop in, but at the last minute she wisely declines, to the dismay of the VT lads.

I'm on the boundary at the end of play waiting to interview Hoggard. Michael Henderson stops by. 'Well done this summer,' he says. 'Channel 4's coverage has been absolutely wonderful. It's all come together.' The same applies to England, I guess. I spy Warne running across the ground to the commentary box. It emerges later that his sole purpose is to shake Richie's hand and wish him luck for the morrow. It's a poignant moment, emphasising the father-son nature of their relationship. From time to time, Warne will phone Richie just to get some reassurance or the odd bowling tip, which Richie is delighted to offer. They are like members of the Magic Circle, sharing leg spin secrets. For Richie, the emergence of Warne has given his work a new lease of life, reinventing his old leg spinning art, which, fifteen years ago, was in danger of extinction. 'When I first came here in the sixties, virtually every county had a leg spinner,' Richie says, lamenting their disappearance. The development – largely due to the advance of one-day cricket in the late sixties – he feels profoundly inhibited English cricket from there on.

In a new series of *Bremner, Bird and Fortune* that night, Rory Bremner mimics Benaud and Boycott commentating over aerial shots of the Houses of Parliament – 'Mmm, some signs there of reverse swing from the Labour Party' – then Benaud says, 'And now down to the Analyst Simon Hughes,' to find Bremner as me (bald wig, stripy shirt) in a darkened room surrounded by monitors looking at Tony Blair's changing 'stances'. He is depicted in a 1997 speech grandly rejecting the likelihood of war during his tenure; six years later (after several wars) he is seen almost glorifying the Iraq conflict. 'He has changed his stance over a variety of issues,' says Bremner-as-me, 'education, taxation, public health. Clearly his main objective is to stay in as long as possible.' Clever.

Monday 12 September

The most significant day in English sport for thirty-nine years. Can England (34 to 1 overnight) at last deliver? Will Benaud pronounce on their finest hour and say an emotional goodbye. Or will he do a John Arlott and finish with 'And now in the commentary box, Tony Greig and Michael Atherton'? Will Atherton remember to offer the mike to the winning captain at the presentation ceremony? Which captain will hold aloft the Ashes? (At 8.30 a.m. the answer to the last question was neither, since the only Ashes urn in the vicinity was the one I had bought at the outset to display in the truck. ECB representatives would later approach me asking to borrow it. 'Only if you put Test cricket back on terrestrial TV,' I said, trying to hide a smirk.)

I'm in the commentary box to greet Richie's arrival at 8.45. And, get this, he is – shock, horror! – wearing a blue jacket. Actually, come to think of it, the cream numbers seem to have been mostly absent of late. He sets himself up in a little corner at the back of the box, with his laptop and two battered leather cases (which come in handy when he emerges from the media centre at the end of a day, as, without a free hand to sign, he niftily manages to breeze through the regular scrum of autograph hunters). Fan letters are ferried to him in a cardboard box which is splitting at the seams. He painstakingly patches it together with tape.

'I just want to say thank you, Rich,' I mumble, just loud enough for him to hear. 'You were the inspiration behind what I do and you've remained so enthusiastic about it.'

'That's very kind,' he said, demurely, 'and it's been a

pleasure working with you. It's really good to work with someone who's always thinking.'

Slater, Greig and Atherton are around too, and we're all laughing about the notorious *Third Man* tapes, with funny spoofs of all the Channel 9 Australian commentators. The highlight for me has always been a take-off of Greig finishing his weather report with 'and the wund is coming from the north-east at fufteen knots and out of my arse at about thurty. Now back to you, Ruchie, in the central missionary position.' 'Central commentary position, you pigeon-toed pea-brain.'

There is a Channel 4 team photo in the stand before play, featuring the whole eighty-odd cast: producers, editors, sound and vision men, teckies and fixers as well as the commentators. Today signals the break-up of a large and very happy family. Back in the VT truck, all fifteen of us mill about taking commemorative pics.

At 10.25, after a rousing rendition of 'Jerusalem', Mark Nicholas hands to Richie in the commentary box for the last time. A camera is positioned alongside him to film those familiar words: 'Thanks, Mark. Morning, everyone … Stirring moments these …' The atmosphere is electric and England are off at a canter. Vaughan, particularly, seems to be in good touch.

Then McGrath changes everything. Who? Oh … McGrath … almost the forgotten man. He nips out Vaughan via a brilliant catch by Gilchrist, then a meek-looking Bell next ball. He's on a hat-trick and in comes Kev. Let's hope he hasn't had too much of that Red Bull. McGrath bowls a superb bouncer, it cannons off some part of Pietersen's anatomy and is caught by Ponting. The Aussies scream with elation, but Billy Bowden – a New Zealander, note – is unmoved. It turns out to be a brilliant decision as close-ups reveal it clattered off the batsman's shoulder.

The alarms are not over, though. Par for the course this summer. First Pietersen snicks Warne on to Gilchrist's leg and Hayden can't grasp the rebound. Then he edges a full Lee delivery straight into and out of Warne's hands at slip. I manage to illustrate with clips of past dismissals how Lee has consistently sought to get Pietersen out that way. What a wicked irony if it turned out to be Warne who'd dropped the Ashes.

At the other end, Trescothick is trapped by a big turner and a confident-looking Flintoff is caught and bowled by Warne. With ten wickets in the match already, he has turned in another virtuoso performance, brilliantly mixing top spinners and legbreaks. Pietersen just fends off a wicked lifter from Lee. It's 126 for 5. No one can eat much lunch. The nerves of Gary, our Thin Controller and passionate England fan, are frazzled and there is a misunderstanding over the timing of my last Jargonbusting slot. The idea, to illustrate how the innovations – Hawkeye, the Red Zone and the Snickometer – really worked, portraying their operators (Henry, Storming and Damo) as the real 'Analysts', bites the dust.

Pietersen seizes the initiative immediately after lunch, taking 37 off three Lee overs. There are audacious hooks into the crowd, flat-bat pulls and blazing drives. Paul Collingwood looks on in awe, sensibly propping up an end. A female streaker comes onto the pitch. 'Hope we had a big lens on her!' says Greig on the 'lazy' to Rob the director. 'We had about ten!' Rob replies. Doubtless one of them was Dave on Camera 7 (reverse slips), known to his colleagues as Rhino because 'he's always got the horn'.

Collingwood is finally out, followed soon afterwards by Geraint Jones. There are still 45 overs left and England (199 for 7) are not yet safe. 'We need anoother sixty-odd at least,' says Boycott. Giles receives a bouncer barrage and bravely withstands it. Pietersen continues to play outrageous shots and lashes a four to go to a maiden Test century. What a moment to do it. By the time he has swatted Warne for two sixes to give England an unassailable lead of 260, it has become an innings of near genius. Only Lara, among modern players, could have produced anything similar.

Benaud is beginning his valedictory speech. 'There's been some wonderful music played today,' he says, 'but one of my favourites is Sarah Brightman and Andrea Bocelli's "Time to Say Goodbye". And it's that time now. So I'd just like to say thank you for having me and it's been a privilege to be with you these last forty-two years. And, what's more important, it's been a great deal of fun' – at that point Pietersen is bowled by McGrath – 'but not for the batsman!' Then he goes on to describe the wicket.

It was the perfect end: the game, the thing he so reveres, proving exciting and surprising to the last, and he reacting to it with typical understatement. He handed over the mike with an Arlottesque 'and now the two new men in the com box are Mark Nicholas and Tony Greig' and retreated to the back of the box to a ripple of private applause. Forty-two years. Which means he began commentating here when I was three. That's part of my childhood gone.

It is getting towards 5 p.m., Giles has battled his way to 40, and England have a lead of over 300. I seize my chance. Voicing a little package on Giles's bravery and defiance, I reappear in vision at the end of the piece and, brandishing the little replica urn, pronounce, 'And I've waited eighteen years to be able to say this: England are about to reclaim the Ashes!' Actually, I lied: it's the realisation of a childhood dream.

An hour later, after the charade of the umpires deliberating about the light and theatrically removing the bails, I'm in the middle to see England's dream become a reality. Atherton does remember to offer the mike to Vaughan for his victorious interview, and there is an urn for him to collect (though I had mine in my pocket just in case). The sky is an explosion of ticker tape and the air is rent with cheering and whooping. Some time after Mark Nicholas has said goodbye on air and England's lap of honour is in full swing, I find myself standing next to Michael Atherton. Everyone is raucously accompanying 'Land of Hope and Glory', which is being broadcast over the PA, and dancing and throwing placards, newspapers, everything in the air. The atmosphere is so intensely euphoric, it brings a tear to my eye. The only experience equally moving is the birth of a child. 'Special moments these,' says Atherton emotioatly, and with some justification. He played in seven losing Ashes series.

We wander back across the ground to the media centre as dusk descends, with people clapping and calling out 'Thanks, Channel 4!' after us. What a way to go out.

My work is not finished. As well as writing my *Telegraph* piece, I have to record an insert analysing how England did it for the official DVD of the series. It's the result of team unity and cohesion – maintaining the same eleven for all but the last Test (no one has even mentioned Thorpe), fitness, a four-pronged pace attack almost the rival of the 1980s West Indies, Vaughan's drive and Fletcher's vision and England having two genuine match-winners (Flintoff and Pietersen) to Australia's one (Warne).

The truck, my mobile workspace for the last seven years, is being dismantled as I put my piece together. I voice my last line at 8.47 p.m., then immediately realise I've omitted to raise the Ashes urn to camera as had been requested. I press a button on my panel to speak to Dylan, the editor. At that precise moment the intercom has been unplugged. Everyone is desperate to get to the wrap party. Seconds later all the screens go black and the lights go out. It's over. The Analyst is dead.

Tuesday 13 September

I finally slump into bed at 5 a.m. after the party which ended up at a hotel with a motley collection of producers, cameramen, runners, and me singing along to Michael Slater's guitar. The room looked like a nuclear fallout zone.

Two hours' sleep, then back to reality, getting the kids breakfast then walking them to school (Tanya has had to fly to Milan on business). Luckily, my mother-in-law is on hand to help, and claims she now knows what an over is. There are Ashes celebration front pages and commemorative pull-outs in all the papers. The coverage is amazing. I get a congratulatory email from Sam Mendes saying he has been glued to the series from his attic room in New York, where he's editing his new film. Another from our production company boss Jeff Foulser says that trading on London's stock market was down by almost a third yesterday, and that various dealers had admitted that eight out of ten trading screens were tuned to the cricket. Wow.

The Analyst is alive again (barely), re-examining the series for a documentary Channel 4 are making on the Ashes. England's victory parade is on the telly and has just reached Trafalgar Square. I half wish I was there instead. What these players have achieved is incredible. After that, a twenty-four-hour drinking spree is not only justifiable, it's compulsory. They stagger to 10 Downing Street in mid-afternoon. Typical of the government to jump on the bandwagon, having done nothing whatsoever for cricket (or sport in general) these past two decades.

Wednesday 14 September

Back at The Oval. Day of filming with Fred, the new national hero, for the DVD, which has now been renamed *Freddie on Fire*. The papers are full of his puffy-eyed fizzog painting the town red yesterday, and I'm concerned, after his thirty-six hours on the razz, that it's going to be more like *Freddie Befuddled*. Not only does he turn up on time looking totally presentable, but he is clear-sighted and lucid as we look back on the series. His recollections are so enlightening I later write them up as a piece for the *Telegraph*.

I have not met a more professional, accessible, grounded sports star. And, like the rest of the England team, he's such a thoroughly decent bloke. Note there have been no revelations of nightclub fracas or 'roastings' after their big night out. The only three-in-a-bed situation you'll find Freddie in will feature him, his wife and their baby.

As it happens, both Mike Gatting and Mickey Stewart (the last English combination to win the Ashes) are at The Oval. Gatting salutes Vaughan's team and Stewart exudes praise. 'Well done, Freddie,' he beams, grasping his hand. 'I'm so pleased for you.' He asks what's to become of my truck now. It's been taken apart, I say, stripped bare. 'I suppose they'll slap "Pickford's" on the side and turn it into a removal van,' he says, smirking.

'Yep, that'll be me next year, humping furniture,' I reply.

Friday 16 September

Freddie is pictured on the front of the *Telegraph*, above which is a puff proclaiming, 'First interview with Flintoff – Sport 4&5', advertising my piece. Never before has anything I've done been mentioned on the front page (it must have been a slow news day). It's one of my father's 'Let's take a taxi down to Budgen's' moments.

I think back to a comment my mother once made. It was a few days after helping Middlesex win the 1990 County Championship, our fourth in ten years. 'You've had a wonderful time, haven't you?' she said. 'You'll be pretty lucky if you ever have so much fun in future.' Well, she's been right about most things, but she was wrong about that. It has not only been great fun but a huge privilege chronicling England as they gradually equipped themselves with the people, the crampons, the ice-picks and the direction they needed to scale their mountain. And what with that and the Rugby World Cup and London winning the Olympics, it's been a wonderful time to be an English sportswriter.

This is not the end. It is just the end of the beginning. Watch this space.